D0847828

To Arık

Black

TANKED!

Behind the Scenes with the
NFL's Biggest Stars by the
Game's Most Infamous
Super Agent

William H. "TANK" Black

CREATIVE PUBLISHING

Copyright © 2009 by William "Tank" Black.
All rights reserved.

*No part of this book may be reproduced in any form or by any electronic
or mechanical means including information storage and retrieval
systems without permission in writing from the publisher, except
by a reviewer who may quote brief passages in a review.*

Library of Congress Control Number: 2009926755

ISBN: 9780982473009

Design: Ron Dorfman *(www.RonaldDorfmanDesign.com)*
Front Cover Design: W. G. Cookman

Published by Creative Publishing

PRINTED IN THE U.S.A.

I Dedicate This Book to the eternal memory
of my grandmother Susie Barnes Black
and her children along with my mother,
a generation that has passed
but forever remembered.

James William Black

Stella Black Ripley

Edna Black

Elizabeth Black Jones

Charles Maurice Black

James Black Jr.

Janice Lou Black

Jeanette Black Blanton

William H. Black Sr.

Thelma Brown Black

*Your Spirit lives in all of us that carry the
Black family name into the future.*

*May the peace and grace of God
comfort you forever.*

"Some people think football is a matter of life and death.
I assure you, it's much more serious than that."

—Bill Shankly

CONTENTS

PART **III**: Penalties and Time-Outs 143

PART **IV**: End Game   *229*

About the
AUTHOR

WILLIAM H. BLACK Jr. became "Tank" the day he was born, March 11, 1957, when his father declared his nearly 11-pound baby "as big as a tank." Two years later his parents separated and Tank spent the rest of his childhood living with his fraternal grandmother, Susie Black, and an extended family of aunts, uncles, and cousins in a modest shotgun house on the black side of the tracks in Greeneville, Tennessee.

He excelled as an athlete from age six and by high school had become a four-sport all star, shining brightest in football. He was named an All-American and became Greeneville High School's first black quarterback.

He holds a Bachelors degree from Carson-Newman College in Jefferson City, Tennessee, where he is still the career receptions leader thirty years later. Tank was named a college football first team Kodak and NAIA All-American. He was selected offensive team MVP three years in a row; and named Player of the Year in the South in 1978. Tank's skills won him a contract with the Atlanta Falcons in 1979, as a wide receiver. Although nimble and able to out-maneuver most line and cornerbacks, he was short and the NFL was trending toward larger receivers, so he was cut during the pre-season.

He became an assistant football coach and head track coach at the University of Tennessee at Chattanooga for three seasons followed by six years as an assistant coach for the University of South Carolina Gamecocks. He worked with receivers and honed his recruiting skills spotting talented high school players from the Deep South and Florida. He quit after he was passed over for a promised promotion to offensive coordinator.

Soon after, he founded his Columbia, South Carolina-based sports agency, Professional Management Incorporated (PMI), with a hot first client, Gamecocks wide receiver Sterling Sharpe, a first-round pick by the Green Bay Packers in the 1988 draft.

By 1999, Tank Black had become one of the leading agents in the NFL, representing dozens of the most talented and promising black athletes from schools in the southeastern states, plus NBA basketball star Vince Carter. Tank had become a community leader and philanthropist in Columbia, with big plans for expanding his business.

But he had made enemies among competing agents and in the NFL Players Association, the players' union. He'd also taken on business partners with hidden criminal connections.

By mid-2000, everything he had was gone: his clients, the business, his career, his reputation, and his freedom. He had been accused of stealing from clients, money-laundering, securities fraud, and of illegally paying money to college players to win their business.

Vilified in the press, defrauded by business partners, exploited by zealous prosecutors, and the victim of his own poor judgment, he ended up spending almost eight years in prison. He was officially released from prison on May 16, 2008.

AUTHOR'S NOTE

I F YOU'VE NEVER been in trouble before, nothing prepares you for the experience of having your freedom suddenly snatched away. In my case, nothing was more frustrating than having my voice taken away as well.

The legal sacking that ended my career included court orders forbidding me from contacting my former player-clients, many of whom I considered true friends and a few who I regarded as family.

From the moment I found myself handcuffed in the back of a police car in July 2000 until the publication of this book in the fall of 2009, I had to wait to tell my side of what had been a widely-covered but sloppily-reported sports scandal. For nine years I couldn't apologize to those who deserved it, or explain what really happened to those whose trust in me had been shaken by the distorted versions served up by the media or cooked up by lawyers trying to win their cases.

I channeled my restlessness into studying the law and on my own, without the help of a single lawyer, I won an appeal in federal court that cleared my name of the worst of the allegations against me. But the appeal was done entirely by mail so the press never learned about it.

During those long years I periodically sat down and wrote on legal pads as much as I could recall of what I thought were the most important and interesting stories and players from my career. I wanted to write my own version of events, both to set the record straight and to lend my voice to those who sincerely want to reform the deeply flawed and hypocritical business of developing and recruiting professional athletes.

When I was released from prison in May 2008, I knew it would take a skilled writer to shape my raw material into a compelling and honest narrative. In the mysterious way that life sometimes sends you what you need when you need it, I was introduced to Foster Winans, a former *Wall Street Journal* columnist, author, and ghostwriter who had both the skills and the personal experience to bring my story to life.

Although we come from opposite sides of the track culturally, we had both lost our freedom because we had acted without thinking, ignoring the inner voice in all of us that always knows the difference between right and wrong.

Foster had experienced his fall from grace in 1984 when he co-wrote what was then the best-read stock market column in the world, "Heard on the Street." He was charged with insider trading and although he admitted and apologized for what he'd done, he fought his case to the United States Supreme Court arguing that what he did was not a criminal offense. The Supreme Court disagreed and he served nine months in federal low-security prisons much like the ones in which I served nearly ten times that many months.

Although my story is an inside look at the world of professional sports, Foster's similar experience with the criminal justice system made it easier for me to let my guard down during the many hours of interviews it took to flesh out all the details. It was sometimes painful to relive certain memories, but Foster insisted on turning over every rock in his search for the truth and his zeal to nail down the facts. "This is your chance to tell your side of things," he counseled, "and you need to do it with integrity, accuracy, balance, and an open heart, so readers will want to join you on your incredible journey."

The creation of this book has been part of that journey and I am grateful to have had Foster's wisdom, experience, and storytelling skills to bring it to life.

ACKNOWLEDGEMENTS

I T HAS TAKEN a great many people who have believed in this book to bring it to fruition. These people have given in many different ways yet have all been very instrumental in the making of my book. For their faith in me, their efforts, their support and their prayers I would like thank the following people in no particular order: Dorothy Black, Bill Isbell, Pete Lollar, Julian Bosworth, George Lesense, Nate Scott, Perry Palmer, Dr. Garry James, Sonny Marsh, Vincent Johnson, Ralph Freeman, Dorothy Freeman, Charlotte Freeman, Patricia Cumura Black, Larry Black, Garry James, Jenny Woolfolk, Joseph Swanson, Jennifer Woolfolk, Bernita Wilson, Michelle Decker and Jeremy Black.

Foster Winans was my ghost writer for this book. Foster is such an amazing writer. He can take the simplest of words and phrases and bring them to life and make them dance. Foster paid special attention to the details in this book and did a tremendous job of researching the facts and circumstances surrounding things that were going on at particular times in this book. For anyone looking for someone to write or co-write a book I would say look no further than Foster Winans. Thank you Foster for doing a masterful job of ghost writing. You are simply the best of the best!

Attorney Robert O. Bragdon and his wife Carol have been my friends since grade school in Greeneville, Tennessee. Robert wrote a letter to my criminal attorney offering me any assistance he could give me in my times of trials and tribulation. He is the main reason I won my Federal Civil Lawsuit against Vince Carter. He offered himself as my true friend. To Robert O. Bragdon and his wife Carol I say thank you for being my true friends when I needed true friendship. Thank you for all you have done for me. I will be forever grateful to your family.

To Judy Lamb I say thank you for always taking my phone calls and sending out packages for me on a regular basis. To Robert B. Bragdon I say thank you for taking the time to type my manuscripts in the early stages of my writing.

Attorney Dawes Cooke from Charleston, S.C and Attorney's Robert Gritton and Robert Bragdon from Murfressboro, TN represented me in my case against Vince Carter and they were more knowledgeable and more prepared than Vince's attorneys. They spent hours on hours preparing, researching and going over the facts of the case. To Dawes Cooke, Robert Gritton and Robert Bragdon, thank you for having faith in me and caring about my future.

Sylvester, Joyce, Shelli and Courtney Pue have been close friends of me and my family for years. I met Sylvester when I was coaching football for the University of South Carolina. He drove our team bus and was just a first class person with a great attitude. My daughter Shayla has always been a daddy's girl. When I went to prison it really turned her world upside down. She ended up in Columbia without any other family members and the Pue family took my daughter Shayla in and treated her like their own daughter. Thank you Sylvester, Joyce, Shelli and Courtney. I will forever be indebted to you for caring for my only daughter as a young teenager.

Attorney Jim Thomas in Detroit handled my criminal case. I could not have had a better attorney. He stayed with me long after I had paid him the last money I had to pay and he made sure I received the departures I was promised for doing the America's Most Wanted. I found that good honest hard working attorneys are very rare and I was blessed to have had Jim Thomas. I would also like to thank his executive assistant Bonnie Tessier. Everytime I called that office from prison she made sure to accept my call and I always heard a warm friendly voice on the other end. That means a lot to someone who is under the stress of incarceration. Thank you Bonnie.

Jack Gritton is an attorney in Murfreesboro, TN. He is the brother of Rob Gritton who worked on my lawsuit against Vince Carter. Sometimes God crosses your path with people that immediately make a positive difference. Jack has helped me with this book project because he believes in me and what I am doing. He has done things he didn't have to do and offered his assistance without me asking him to help. His has been a great professional advisor and friend. To Jack Gritton, his lovely wife Judy, his daughter Kallie and his son Evans, thank you for being friends to me and my family and assisting me with this project.

Linda Wilson and I had been friends and business partners for ten years when we caught our case. Linda could easily have avoided incarceration by giving false and misleading testimony against me. She was given several opportunities to say things about me that were not true in exchange for her freedom. She refused to tell outright lies against me as Brantley Evans, Jim Franklin and others had done. It ultimately cost her five years of incarceration. Many people had blamed Linda for my troubles and my incarceration. That was never true. She was the only person who stood on the truth in the face of severe punishment. It takes a person with great integrity to do what Linda did. That act of courage and integrity deserves special recognition. Linda was the first person who told me I should write a book. It was in 2002 while we were in prison. She did research and gave me invaluable leads and information that has help lead to the success of this book. I still consider Linda a friend. Thank You!

Terry Kelly has been my friend since the first day I attended the white school in Greeneville, TN as a fourth grader. True friends are rare in life. They are like precious stones. No matter what the circumstances Terry Kelly is always my friend. Thank you Terry for your life long support and friendship. You are the epitomy of what a real friend is.

Brandon Lollar is Pete and Penny Lollar's only son from Greeneville, TN. Brandon use to come and see me play high school football with his mom and dad. Brandon and his wife

Bridget have really been there for me. Sometimes you find people who believe in you and it does not matter what someone says or writes about you, they are not going to change the way they feel unless you do something wrong to them. Brandon and Bridget have placed so much faith in me and never cared about what anyone else said about me. Thank you for the faith and trust you have placed in me. Thank you for being my friend.

Bill Isbell has been like a father to me all of my life. He has always been the same with me no matter what the circumstance were. Mr. Isbell has helped time and time again with this book project and anything else I needed help with in my life. Thank you Mr. Isbell for always treating me like your son. People don't come any better than you.

Starting in early 2005 Carla Harris and her stepson Cameron began coming to visit me in prison. From early 2005 until my release in May of 2008. They averaged visiting me at least two times a month no matter where I was. Cameron was only seven years old at the time and they traveled all the way from Dallas, Texas to places in North Carolina, Tennessee, Virginia, Oklahoma and South Carolina. They sent me hundreds of cards and letters. They gave me love at a time when I needed it more than ever before. Everybody always thought they lived only a few miles away because they came to see me so often. Carla Harris is now my wife, Carla Harris Black and Cameron Pryor Harris is my stepson. To Carla and Cameron I give special thanks and appreciation for your love and support. Their will always be a special place in my heart for you.

The following business partners have been invaluable. I would like to thank the following in no particular order: Creative Publishing Consultants, Atlas Books, BookMasters, Ron Dorfman & Dorfman Design, Foster Winans and Walt Kuenstler of WK Publishing, Justin Loeber & Khuong Phan of Mouth Public Relations, Tom Antion & Associates, Dan Smith, Sandy Diaz & Chris Begelow of Smith Publicity, Hajni Blasko & Substance books.

— WILIAM "TANK" BLACK
June 20, 2009

PART I

The Grass Cutter from Greeneville

Me in my backyard cooking on the grill, Columbia South Carolina.

Members of the PMI staff at a North Dakota casino. Runningback Eric Bienemey far left, attorney Jim Franklin, far right, 1998.

Chapter 1

BEST MEETS WORST

THE WORST YEAR OF MY LIFE reached a climax on the morning of Wednesday July 5th, 2000, after the long Independence Day weekend when I found myself handcuffed, wedged into the back seat of a police car, sweat running into my eyes, wondering how so much could have gone so wrong so fast.

The year before, in the April 1999 National Football League draft—when all the professional teams sign the year's best and brightest of college football—I set a record for the most first-round picks represented by a single agent. The career total income for the players I represented in that draft alone would top $300 million, which would have earned me commissions of $9 million.

The money mattered, of course. It was a way of keeping score, and allowing me to be generous to family, friends, and favorite causes. But what mattered more was having earned a national reputation for spotting and recruiting the most talented black players. Few if any white players signed with black agents at the time, but the reverse was not true, so the competition was fierce. I had done it the hard way—on my own, without the backing of a big corporate agency, or a law degree, or any of the other advantages enjoyed by my competitors. I could spot a top athlete because I had been a top athlete and a top coach at a top college.

What most other agents lacked that I had in abundance was real empathy rooted in a shared cultural background and a shared athletic experience. My greatest satisfaction came from helping young athletes who had grown up as I had, in working-class families on the "black" side of the tracks. I understood their ambitions to get ahead, to make their families proud and financially secure, because that's what drove me.

I became a father figure in the lives of many players, a village elder of sorts, and as such I often talked with them about their potentials as black role models as well as in the game. I scolded players who ignored autograph seekers, and I protected players whose casual affairs with women threatened to blow up into major scandals.

My main job was to make sure they were well compensated for the skills and commitment they brought to a physically brutal business. But better than most agents, I knew from personal experience that professional careers are usually short, and injuries can shave years off an athlete's life expectancy. It's a great game, football, but it's a punishing way to make an easy living.

That 1999 draft had been the high point of my career, but from that point on, everything that could go wrong did. It began as a slow drip of missteps, bad breaks, and bungled responses to crises that accumulated into a flash flood. Now, just over a year after my draft triumph, under a hot South Carolina sun on a busy public highway in Columbia, a dam had burst and I was being swept away.

I sat in the caged back seat of a sheriff's cruiser, hands behind my husky torso, cuffs biting into my wrists, looking out grimy windows, stunned by what was happening. Minutes before I had been running an errand, minding my own business, staying under the speed limit, driving down Two Notch Road—U.S. Route 1.

An unmarked car with its magnetic roof light flashing had pulled me over. Moments later a half-dozen other police vehicles converged, boxing me in. Cops and detectives tumbled out, guns at the ready. Now that I had been cuffed and read my rights, a clutch of uniformed officers and shirt-sleeved detectives loitered around their Ford Crown Victoria's, smoking and gossiping.

I couldn't figure it out, this dramatic show of force. If the authorities wanted to talk to me, all they had to do was pick up the phone and call. By July 5th, 2000, so much had gone wrong that I was already under court supervision, out on bail. I had multiple legal troubles, but none involved violence, I owned no guns, had never used drugs, rarely had more than a glass of wine with dinner, and had obeyed all the rules.

I was already wearing an ankle bracelet when I was pulled over, part of my bail arrangement in a Florida fraud case. I couldn't go to the corner store for a candy bar after 10 o'clock at night without permission. The only explanation was that some prosecutor wanted to grab another headline.

I hunkered down in the seat to avoid the gawking stares as traffic crawled past. I was well known in town, a national figure in professional football, a noted black businessman, a leader in the community and in my church, and a large donor to local charities that served the kind of poor people I had grown up around. How the hell did I get here?

This short black kid from eastern Tennessee, born "as big as a tank," had come a long way in two decades: a starring high school and college wide receiver (All American); a stint with the Atlanta Falcons; a coach and leading recruiter for the University of South Carolina Gamecocks; a player agent for dozens of star athletes; one of America's most successful black businessmen.

In 1999 I became the hottest player agent in the National Football League. Five of the college players I had recruited that year were first-round picks, out of a possible thirty-one. It was a new record for an agent, and many would go on to make names for themselves: Jevon Kearse, Troy Edwards, Reggie McGrew, Antuan Edwards, and Al Wilson. All told, I represented more than 80 NFL players.

It had all started eleven years earlier with my first client, Sterling Sharpe, a first-round draft pick in 1988. I was proudest of Sterling because I'd been his football mentor his entire career, from the time I recruited him from high school in Glennville, Georgia, to coaching him at the University of South Carolina, and later when I left coaching and became his agent. His first two years with the Green Bay Packers he spent his off-seasons living with me in our home in Columbia. He was part of my family.

Sterling had lived up to his name. In his six years as a wide receiver with the Green Bay Packers—until a career-ending neck injury in 1994—he set records for the most receptions in a season, the most touchdown receptions, and he was both a Pro Bowl and All-Pro selection fives times each.

I already knew from playing and coaching that I had a sixth sense for spotting young athletes with that rare combination of athletic gift, attitude, and ambition. Because my player clients were all black, most from modest, fatherless homes like mine, we spoke the same cultural language.

As a result, they trusted me and I took that trust to heart. It was in part the empathy and obligation I felt for them that led to the worst year of my life. I made some bad calls, trusted some very bad people, ignored warning signs, and had acquired some determined foes.

My troubles began when I started having success recruiting player clients from the University of Florida Gators football team. The school is an athletic powerhouse, in basketball as well as football, and at the time it was the leader in the Southeastern Conference, the hottest conference in the country.

Gators' fans are fanatic, and sports—big business everywhere—is an economy unto itself in Gainesville, the home of the

University of Florida. That economy includes the alumni who put up the millions to support the teams and their recruiting efforts; the coaches who earn seven figures; the professional teams that pay millions to its athletes; and the agents who represent those athletes.

Who gets to participate in the flow of all this money is a matter of great interest in both the university community and the NFL Players Association, which, among other things, certifies agents.

Established agents with existing ties to the Gators started complaining to the NFL Players Association when I snagged some of the most talented players out from under their noses. They accused me of breaking a rule that was widely ignored: giving college players money before they were eligible. I had lent money to players, I knew it was against the rules, but I also knew that those same players were collecting money from other agents at the same time. The system was corrupt, and by all accounts still is today.

By comparison with most other agents, I was an upstart competing and improbably winning against the likes of IMG—a billion-dollar international sports agency. I was a David among Goliaths, and I was hitting my mark with consistency.

My success had the professional football world sitting up and taking notice. I was becoming almost as well known as my players, and some of my competitors were pouring poison into the ears of officials at the NFL Players Association. When I heard of this grumbling through the grapevine I dismissed it as jealousy. There was nothing I was doing that was different from the way the majority of agents operated. My business was booming, and I was expanding in several directions at once.

I had picked up as a client a hot new basketball player, Vince Carter, a first-round NBA draft pick by the Toronto Raptors. Carter became a near-instant super star, a consistent scorer who, in his first full season, led the Raptors to the 2000 NBA Playoffs. He was attracting lucrative endorsement offers from corporations.

Coming from my background, I was proud of having earned my way into the ranks of the country's most successful black entrepreneurs. My business had been valued at up to $100 million. I was involved in a promising hotel renovation venture in Detroit that would benefit from the legalization of gambling. I owned a business travel agency, an outgrowth of the sports agency. I was even in the talking stage of selling my sports agency business to Percy Miller, better known as Master P or P. Miller, the phenomenally successful rap star, music promoter, entrepreneur, and—briefly—professional basketball player.

Until the worst year of my life began, I had never been in trouble before. Now I sat in a police car on July 5, 2000, waiting to find out what new disaster lay ahead but wearily familiar with the drill of being fingerprinted, photographed, and locked in a metal holding cage.

I had been raised to live clean, work hard, and use my head. I knew plenty of young black men who had lost their way, but I wasn't one of them. But here I was, in much the same predicament from which I'd spent my career trying to protect my college players and professional clients.

I had bailed Vince Carter out of a jam with a girl he'd gotten pregnant, a scandal that would have scuttled millions in endorsement offers and stained his carefully cultivated All-American boy image.

I had been there for Rae Carruth, another one of my first-round picks and a Carolina Panthers wide receiver who was then on his way to a long prison stretch for his role in a conspiracy that resulted in the murder of his pregnant girlfriend.

I had loaned hundreds of thousands of dollars to players and their families: to tide them over the rough patches, meet a mortgage payment, get somebody a car, or pay for a wedding. I had helped many get back on their feet after they'd squandered their earnings and the flow of money had dried up.

Now I was being accused of things I didn't do, maneuvered into saying things that got me into deep trouble, and punished for following the same practices as everyone else in the business of professional sports. Some of my clients said publicly what many were thinking: somebody was out to get me. The unspoken element was race. I didn't want to believe it, but I was a realist: As one of the few sports super agents I had a big advantage in recruiting the best, and most sought after black players.

Although I had confronted my share of insults and acts of prejudice, I managed to take it in stride. As a child and young man growing up in socially segregated eastern Tennessee, and as a college football coach and recruiter for South Carolina Gamecocks, I got along with white and black equally well. Most of the influential men in my life have been white coaches.

I was beginning to wonder if the only thing harder than being a poor black man in America is being a rich black man in America. I've been both. Neither is easy. But when you're black and successful, the bar seems to be set a little bit higher, as we learned during President Barack Obama's election campaign.

I would have the next 108 months in prison to ponder the question, analyze my mistakes, acknowledge my "sins," and begin the process of clearing my name.

NFL players and camp coaches at Sterling Sharpe's Football Camp. (Left, rear) Brett Favre.

Me in the 4th grade Andrew Johnson Middle School.

(Below) My sister, Patricia Cumura Black.

Chapter 2

MY FIRST BIG PLAY

THE FIRST TIME I played football on a real field in a real uniform I was just six years old, the youngest and smallest boy on an all-black "grass cutter" team. We were the Rams, one of six little league football teams in Greeneville, Tennessee, and the only one that a black kid could join in 1963, when our schools were still segregated.

I had grown up playing football and other games with friends and neighbors in streets and vacant lots. I spent a lot of time as a tyke with my older cousin Bobby, and when he and his friends got together a pickup game in the street, they let me play, too. This annoyed my grandmother, who could be heard from some distance when she'd go out into the yard and call out, "TANK! TANK!", because I frequently tore the knees in my pants, or the collars of my t-shirts.

By my sixth birthday, I had learned to out run and out maneuver much older boys, and was developing my skills as a receiver. I was small, fast, and nimble, which made me hard to catch. I could stop, pivot, and turn without losing a beat. I became known as the little guy with the big head named "Tank" who could "stop on a dime, and give you nine cents change."

That summer—the summer Martin Luther King spoke to

the world from the steps of the Lincoln Memorial—I persuaded the coach of the Rams that although I hadn't yet reached the minimum age of seven for a grass cutter team, I was good enough to compete with the older boys. I begged, as children do, but Coach Williams was an easy sell. He was endlessly patient, kind, and encouraging. All the kids on the team liked and respected him.

He was also white, which must have caused him some grief during a time when racial strife was spreading like a killer virus across the South. That summer the Birmingham, Alabama, police loosed their dogs on unarmed civil rights demonstrators, blasted them with fire hoses, and beat them with batons. That summer the name of an otherwise obscure NAACP organizer, Medgar Evers, entered the history books when he was assassinated in cold blood outside his home in Mississippi. That September, the school year began with the news that somebody had blown up a black church in Birmingham during Sunday school, killing four little girls in their best go-to-meetin' dresses.

But all that bloodshed and mayhem seemed far away to us kids in Greeneville, a county seat of about 13,000 with a history of racial tolerance stretching back to well before the Civil War. The area had been settled by an influx of Quaker immigrants from Pennsylvania. Eastern Tennessee, a tobacco-growing region among the foothills of the Great Smoky Mountains, had been home to a strong abolitionist movement.

Named for the Revolutionary War hero General Nathanael Greene and the home and final resting place of Abraham Lincoln's vice president and successor, Andrew Johnson. Greeneville was said to be the only town in America that erected two Civil War monuments, one honoring veterans from each side. While violence marked the civil rights movement in the Deep South, we black kids in Greeneville grew up on the other side of the tracks, but without fear.

Coach Williams was a supervisor nearby at a Pet Milk Company plant where they canned condensed milk and made ice cream. As a coach, he had a dream team. If you were a black kid like me who loved to play football, you had one choice—the Rams. We had the best of the best black players, and the other five teams in town hated playing us because we dominated every game, year after year. The team's success was a matter of pride within Greeneville's small black community and it was an honor to be chosen to play, and a treat: after every game Coach rewarded us all with Pet Milk ice cream.

My debut on the gridiron came during the first play I was ever in, in the first game of my first season. We were ahead 42-0 with just minutes left on the clock.

Most of the other kids were at least three years older than I, just a squirt, one of the new kids. But I was too wound up and innocent to imagine that there'd be any reason I couldn't play. I knew I could keep up with the other boys, and as the game wound down toward our inevitable victory, I was practically jumping out of my skin for a chance to show what I was made of. I grew up around smart, ambitious relatives, and, like all successful athletes, I was born with a strong competitive spirit.

I watched the clock hand sweep away the seconds until there was only four minutes left and I couldn't stand it any longer. I ran over to the coach, tugged on his sleeve, and did what millions of boys had done before me in similar circumstances—I pleaded for a chance. "Coach, can I play? We're killin' 'em and the game's almost over. Please, Coach. Please!"

"Okay, Tank," he said. "In a minute."

The Rams had kicked off and then kept the opposition team pinned down, their backs up against their own end zone. Now it was fourth down on their ten-yard line, and they were preparing to punt when Coach Williams waved me on the field.

I had no idea where I was suppose to stand, so I raced over to the line of scrimmage and picked a spot at one end of the line of players. I adjusted my position so I was a little outside the end of their line. I knew from experience that I was quicker than most people guessed, and I might be able to sneak a flank attack on the kicker.

The boys facing us were huge, but they had that weary, dispirited look of players who have abandoned all hope near the end of a humiliating game. I must have looked to them like a bug of no consequence, which is exactly what I was used to. I had learned how to use preconceptions about my age and small size to my advantage.

At the snap it happened just as I'd expected. I darted around two defensive linemen who were preoccupied with defending the kicker from my bigger teammates. In the clear, I launched myself through an opening straight toward the punter, just as his leg began to swing. I leaped with my arms and small hands outstretched. The ball hit my palms and ricocheted backward into the end zone.

I jumped up and sprinted for the ball. I was just a couple of yards away when one of my friends, an older boy named Dale Arnett, darted in front of me and smothered it, scoring the touchdown. I flushed with adrenaline. Hey! I'm the one that knocked it down. That was MY ball. No fair!

My teammates, however, were jumping up and down, yelling my name, hitting my oversized helmet, and pounding me on the back. "Wow! That was some move, Tank!" But as I walked back to the bench, tears of frustration flooded my eyes.

Coach was grinning and clapping his hands. "Great play, Tank! First time out! They never saw you coming." But my downcast eyes and sniffles gave me away. He squatted and squeezed my arms and legs. "What's wrong, Tank? Are you hurt?"

I shook my head and stifled a sob. "I'm just m-mad 'cause D-Dale got my touchdown! I woulda had it if he'd let me."

Coach Williams burst out laughing. He took hold of my helmet and pulled me close. "Look at me, Tank. We got that touchdown because of YOU. That was one of the greatest plays I ever saw in all my life. And your first time out, too.

"We all work together. We're a football team. Blocking that punt was more important than anybody falling on it. So don't you worry yourself about not getting the touchdown. You're just the kind of player I want on our team."

His words calmed me some, but I was still feeling sorry for myself. Coach patted me on the shoulder. "Believe me, with your talent, you'll be in lots of games and you're going to score plenty of touchdowns."

He was right. For the next six years I played for the Rams, making dozens of touchdowns, learning the rules and the plays, and refining my skills as Coach Williams helped prepare me for a starring high school and college career. He became one of the most influential figures in my life, teaching me most of what I would need to know to be a successful young athlete.

At home it was my grandmother, "Miss Susie," who taught me what I needed to know about life.

Mike Armstrong, McDonald Story, Dee Reviere and me in Junior High.

Chapter **3**

MISS SUSIE AND ME

MY FIRST DISTINCT MEMORY is of standing in a gravel driveway one summer night watching our house burn to the ground. I was three years old but I can still remember how vulnerable I felt being outdoors in nothing but my underpants; the fierce, radiating heat; the smoke stinging my nostrils; the cries of my grandmother. Losing everything is bad enough, but it's a total disaster when you have almost nothing to start with, and if you live on the black side of the tracks in Greeneville, Tennessee, in 1960.

Like many people of my generation and culture, the engine and inspiration of our family and of my life was my grandmother. Her name was Susie Barnes Black but I called her Mama because she raised me from the age of eleven months. I was the first born of my mother and father. A beautiful Thelma Jean Brown was only seventeen when she married my father William Henry Black, a good-looking, smart twenty-one-year-old nicknamed "Doc."

When I look back on the opportunities I've enjoyed in life, it's hard to believe how different and difficult it must have been for my parents' generation, especially for my father whose opportunities for work in the hills of eastern Tennessee were mainly limited to laborer, custodian, cook, or worker in the tobacco fields and curing barns. A few lucky black people got production line jobs at the big Magnavox television factory nearby. Even if my father had been one of the lucky ones, he wouldn't have lasted. He and my mother were addicted to alcohol. On top of that my father was a rolling stone, and as the song says "wherever he laid his hat was his home".

My father's relatives were so concerned about my well-being when I was an infant that they intervened and brought me to live with them in my grandparents' house, the one that burned. My mother would have other children later, but neither she nor my father ever beat alcohol and both died of diseases associated with alcoholism in their forties.

My grandmother already had her hands full when I arrived. My grandfather was cruel and also a heavy drinker. He was especially tough on my father, after whom I'm named, and my Uncle James Jr. When my grandfather got drunk enough and mad enough at one of his sons over some infraction, he'd tie them up to a tree in the backyard and whip them with switches or ropes. He finally quit this brutality after Uncle James Jr. one day threatened to kill their father if he ever tried it again. By the time I was five years old, my grandfather was gone from the home and I never saw him again.

My grandmother's modest house was crowded—two aunts, an uncle, two cousins, and me. Two of my three aunts had boys' names. Aunt Jim, whose real name was Edna, Edna had two children, Bobby and Dorothy, ages eleven and seven when I was two. They became my beloved big brother and sister. Also living with my grandmother—called "Mama" by everyone—was Aunt Bill (Jeanette), and Uncle James Jr.

My stay with Mama and my aunts, uncle and cousins was supposed to be temporary, until my mother and father got their lives back together. But to me it quickly became the only home I knew. So I was stunned after several years living with my grandmother when she sat me down in the kitchen one day and announced that my parents had decided to take me to live with them in Johnson City, about 30 miles away.

I saw my parents infrequently although I many times wondered about them. Mama—my grandmother—was my mother, and better than a real one because I got the best of both generations: a mother's nurturing and a grandparent's indulgence. My grandmother taught me the basic lessons of life and behavior, but she did it with kindness and a little spoiling. She proved a unique role model who gave me the tools that led to my success and my ability to roll with the punches. Treat all people with respect and treat them like you would want them to treat you. You never know when you may need someone's compassion.

The idea of leaving my aunts, uncles, and cousins was overwhelming. I burst into tears.

"Child, don't you want to live with your mama and your daddy? They love you, baby."

"But YOU'RE my mama, now!" I wailed. "I want to stay here, with you and everybody. I can't leave!"

I wept to break my grandmother's heart and got my way. She and my parents agreed I would stay on with her. In retrospect, it was the right decision. My mother had two more children with my father, Patricia Ann Black and Larry Allen Black, then four with someone else, while slowly drinking herself to death. That would have been a steep hill to climb.

After the big fire, my grandmother moved us all into a small, abandoned shotgun house—a series of connected rooms so that to get from one end to the other you had to walk through every room. The place had been empty for five years and was in shabby condition, a glorified shack with no heat and floorboards so rotted in spots you could see through to the crawlspace. The bathroom was a listing outhouse in the yard.

We had a water pump in the kitchen, and had to heat water on the coal stove to wash dishes or take a bath in a battered tin tub. The first time I saw an indoor shower was in third grade, after the schools had been desegregated and we black kids got to see how the white kids lived. Someone had to explain to me how to use it!

With only a kerosene stove and nothing but clapboard and tarpaper between us and the weather, the house was bitter cold in winter. Five of us slept in the same bed—my cousins, their mother, Aunt Bill and me—with each other and some blankets to keep us warm. There were days when we didn't have enough kerosene for the heat and we did the best we could with the coal stove. But in those Smokey Mountain foothills, with nothing to beat the cold, one morning we woke to find our poor, old dog BoBo frozen to death in his sleeping spot.

In the early days, money for food was scarce and we ate a lot of fried bologna. I liked it, and because the adults didn't dwell on our poverty, I had no idea that we were as poor as we were. To my child's way of thinking, we were living the way other black people did in that neighborhood. But it was the poverty that led to one of the lessons I learned from my grandmother: the fabric of life is woven with ambiguity and contradiction.

On the one hand, Mama was a devout Christian, deeply involved in the local black church, the Jones Memorial African Methodist Episcopal (AME) Zion Church, right next to the George Clem school . The national AME Church played a major role in the life of black communities everywhere. It was founded in protest against slavery, under the motto, "God Our Father, Christ Our Redeemer, Holy Spirit Our Comforter, Human kind Our Family."

I grew up going to church with Mama and the rest of the family every week. I sang in the choir from an early age, and later sang solos. For most of my youth I spent all day Sunday at church and loved it. After Sunday school and services, many people would stay and put up a hot Sunday dinner for the congregation and people in the community. For years I was one of the younger kids expected to serve the meals.

After dinner, we'd have another service during which there was more singing, clapping, and spirited prayer. It was an old-fashioned black gospel experience. I loved singing at home, too. I often woke Mama up in the morning by singing to her, and always sang for her on her birthdays.

When I was a little older, my favorite song became Otis Redding's, "Sittin' On the Dock of the Bay." When the mood caught her, Mama would say, "Come on, Tank. I want you to sing a song," and most of the time it was "Dock of the Bay."

At one point we acquired an old record player and a few records that we would sing along with. Mama loved hymns and music easily moved her to tears of joy and longing. In fact, she cried easily when she was happy or sad. I grew up feeling safe about showing my own feelings.

As head of the household, Mama was the boss, but she ruled with gentleness and love. She had no patience with drama, and her first response to any sort of confrontation was to step in as the peacemaker. We all turned to her for guidance whenever an important decision had to be made. It was common for any of us to say, "Well, I'm gonna see what mama has to say about that," or "did you talk to Mama about this?"

Although Mama had dropped out of school in the ninth grade, she was instinctively wise in the ways of the world, and prepared to do what was necessary to keep her family together and surviving. My introduction to the moral ambiguity of life began after we moved into the shotgun house. Mama—the church lady whose husband had left her with a house full of mouths to be fed—sold moonshine liquor, known as Tennessee White Lightning, by the glass. Our kitchen was the neighborhood saloon.

From the time I was a child all the way up to my college days, Mama supported herself and us selling moonshine. She had some help from my Uncle James Jr. and from the sheriff. Uncle James Jr. was an auto mechanic and had rigged up a secret hiding place under the engine of his car where he would hide the big jars of liquor he'd buy from the distillers in the mountains nearby, between Tennessee and North Carolina.

When Uncle James came home with the jars, he'd pour the moonshine into a tank under the sink that was attached with a valve to the water spigot. When a customer arrived, Mama would reach under the sink and turn the valve so that instead of water coming out of the tap, it poured moonshine.

Ours was a busy little kitchen. Most of the people in our neighborhood drank, especially the men. We saw just about everyone at one time or another. People would be coming by to drink Mama's moonshine from early morning to late at night. They'd sit at the kitchen table and she'd serve it in small glasses with pictures of roosters on the side. There were four sizes depending on how big a drink you wanted or could afford: a quarter, a half dollar, seventy-five cents, or a dollar a drink. On a jug of moonshine that cost her $10, she could bring in more than $100.

Mama's moonshine business was more like a filling station than a saloon. No one stayed longer than it took to belt down their drink. The liquor tasted so awful that one of the regular sounds in the house was the hissing noise people made as it scorched their throats. I hated that sound. Mama always served the moonshine with a small glass of water as a chaser and some liked to taste salt after they had their drink. Then the customers would pay and leave.

One of her occasional customers was the local Sheriff, a white man who obliged her discretion by warning her when he knew there was going to be a raid by the authorities. Mama had a system for dismantling and hiding any evidence of the moonshine.

The local police officers would show up, look around, ask her a few questions, and leave. Afterward she'd cook up some fried chicken or other special dish and have James Jr. take it over to the sheriff's house as a thank you.

It was a common ritual in that place and time for a father

to bring his son to Mama's kitchen to mark his boy's eighteenth birthday with his first glass of moonshine. One day Mr. Combs, our next-door neighbor, knocked on the kitchen door with his oldest son William. I played with William's younger brother Kenneth all of the time.

"Susie," Mr. Combs said, "William is eighteen today and I want to give him a quarter shot."

They sat down and Mama handed William the quarter shot, which he drank in a gulp. He choked and reached for the water chaser. But before he could get the glass to his lips, the moonshine hit him like a sledgehammer. He pitched backwards. He and the water glass clattered to the floor. Ghostly gray, he was out.

Mama jumped up, eyes wide, wringing her hands. "Please, Mr. Combs do something! Oh, my Lord! Don't let him die!"

Mr. Combs filled up the water glass a couple of times and poured it on his son's face until William, glassy-eyed, could get back on his feet. His father patted him on the shoulder and they left, poor William hanging on his father's shoulder.

Perhaps because of scenes like this, I had never been tempted to drink the moonshine. Mama never touched the stuff either, even though she sold it the rest of her life. My parents were alcoholics and although Mama never used it as an excuse, her advise was "Don't you ever touch this stuff!" Seeing what it did to William that day was so disturbing that I had no trouble vowing I would never drink. I have kept that vow, with the exception of a glass of wine with dinner now and then.

As I got a little older I began to notice what the moonshine was doing to people in the neighborhood. There were men who, in warm weather, slept on the street at night so they wouldn't have far to go in the morning to get their first shot. Some of them wore the same clothes for months.

I grew to hate the parade of strangers coming through the kitchen, no matter how respectful or well-behaved many of them were. One day, after a particularly down-trodden regular had paid and left, I asked her, "Why do you do this? Why do you sell this stuff? There's got to be something else you can do to make money." She was always preaching to us youngsters about getting a good education and making something of ourselves.

"There are a lot of things you're too young to understand right now," she said, washing the glasses. "Later on you'll understand that sometimes people are thrust into doing things they'd rather not to take care of their families.

I accepted the notion that she was doing what she felt she had to in order to make ends meet.

Much later, when I would face the greatest adversities in my life I would draw strength from knowing that I was brought up to be a strong black man and with the love and grace of God I could overcome anything. The thought of my family members and all of the adversities they have faced gives me a strength I could never explain.

Me and my cousin Dorothy share an emotional moment at my surprise birthday party, March, 1993.

My Grandmother, Susie Barnes Black.

My Dad, William Henry Black Sr. "Doc".

My mother, Thelma Black.

Chapter 4

FRIED BOLOGNA
AND BIG DREAMS

THE ADULTS IN OUR HOUSE made it clear to us grandkids—Bobby, Dorothy, and me—that they expected us to work hard in school, get good grades, and go on to become the first generation in our family to earn college degrees. Graduating from high school was never even discussed, it was college that was the important goal. Mama had left school after the ninth grade. Three of my aunts cooked for a living, in private homes, restaurants and hospitals. Aunt Jim also did hairdressing on the side. Uncle James Jr. worked as a car mechanic and would later be the first black person in Greeneville to own his own gas station.

If any of us kids groused about our schoolwork, any aunt within hearing distance was likely to give us the standard lecture. "You wanna be workin' all day long, cookin' and cleanin' for no kinda money? Then you're gonna get an education and be a doctor or a lawyer or somethin' else where you get to be your own boss." The message was clear and persistent. There was no doubt in my mind that I would succeed and make them all proud.

Dorothy was in sixth grade and Bobby was in eleventh when I was old enough to start attending the only school for black children in Greeneville, the George Clem School. In September, 1963, when I entered first grade, President Kennedy was still alive, and the Civil Rights Act outlawing Jim Crow segregation would not become law until the following summer. There were still businesses in town where a black person wouldn't think of entering the front door, or sitting at a lunch counter. If you wanted a hamburger from the cafe, you placed your order at the back door and waited for it outside.

Children from the far reaches of the county, from the smallest hamlets, rode the bus past two whites-only county schools to reach George Clem. In dry, hot weather, they arrived covered with a thin layer of dust on their clothes and hair.

Perhaps a legacy of the abolitionist sentiment dating to before the Civil War, Greeneville boasted one of the best black public schools. The George Clem School had a long history, built on a plot of land bought in 1886 by a black minister who helped start and build a number of black schools and churches in the region between Knoxville, Tennessee and Asheville, North Carolina. The one-story, plain brick building nestled on the ridge of a low hill at the edge of town, on the black side of the tracks.

George Clem had been one of the school's founders back in the late 1800s, and his son, also named George Clem, had been the principal. Originally named the Greeneville College High School, the school's name changed in 1939 in the Clem family's honor. In 1950 the board of education built a modern new brick school, and the program evolved to offer all twelve grades.

There were about 200 students by 1963, and the school had become a source of great pride in the black community as more and more graduates went on to college, or came home on leave in their freshly-pressed class A military uniforms. Before I started first grade I already knew the school song because Bobby and Dorothy had sung it for us so many times at home.

> *Hail to old George Clem High School that we so love,*
> *and there shall be no other to surpass her love....*

My first September, I was torn between my eagerness to join

Dorothy and Bobby at school, and dread at leaving my grand-mother's side. I had spent virtually every moment with her from age one to six. I was rarely out of her sight for more than an hour at a time. She was my guardian angel twenty-four hours a day.

Mama walked me the half mile to George Clem the first morning, made the necessary introductions in the office, filled out the necessary forms, and then left me in the care of my first-grade teacher. She gave me a hug and a kiss. "Don't cry, Tank. You already know some of these boys from football. You'll have a fine time. Nothin' here to cry about. And I'll see you right after school."

I sat at my desk crying as silently as I could, feeling sorry for myself until the misery became too much to bear and I bolted. I ran home, burst into the kitchen, hugged Mama with all my might, and sobbed my heart out into her apron.

"Child, you can't be runnin' away from school like this!" She untied her apron, pinned on her hat, and took me by the hand. "Come along now. You're goin' back to school."

This time she stayed awhile hoping it would help me feel a little more at home. But as soon as I realized she had left, I ran home bawling. The first few days the other kids made fun of my old clothes and battered shoes, which only added to my unhappiness. This went on for a few days until I got smart and instead of going home, I'd go hide somewhere else.

By the time Mama caught me playing hooky, I had missed a week or so of school and earned myself a rare whipping. She used a belt on my behind, but always with my pants on. It hurt some but caused no harm. The humiliation was worse. Once I got over my initial jitters, I discovered how much I enjoyed school, and how much I'd learned living with Mama.

I already had a working knowledge of math. I'd spent hours at the kitchen table counting up the quarters, nickels, and dimes Mama collected each day from her customers. When our teacher Ms. Grace Bradley brought out some coins to introduce us to math, I made a big impression on my classmates with how smart I was.

All twelve grades were in the same school building and George Clem was run in some ways like an overgrown one-room schoolhouse. During breaks the hallways would fill with children as tiny as me, and towering, senior boys who were fully grown men. It was a community unto itself, and the staff encouraged older students to help the younger ones who were struggling with their lessons.

If Mama was my guardian angel, Dorothy was my life tutor. My grandmother taught me a lot when I was young, but she unofficially appointed Dorothy to teach me the basics.

Standing at the stove, head back from the spattering grease, she'd say, "Dorothy, show Tank how to cook this bacon. Make sure he knows how to tell when it's just about to burn."

Mama was on a mission with her grandkids. To me she'd often say, "You want to learn how to do everything, Tank. You don't want no one else to do this for you. Don't think a woman is going to do everything for you, because women don't always stay with men forever.

"You're gonna find yourself out there in the world and you might be by yourself. When you go off to college, you're gonna need to know how to take care of yourself."

Dorothy was younger and a girl, expected to stay close to home. We had more of a chance to bond. My cousin Bobby was just as nurturing but he was much older and already busy with school, social life, and sports. He was a quarterback on the George Clem High football team and now and then he would take time to teach me the proper way to catch a football or throw a pass.

Both were my role models in life, and both ended up fulfilling Mama's dream. Bobby attended Howard University in Washington, D.C., on an academic scholarship were he studied psychology. He went on to become Greeneville's first black police officer. Dorothy would go on to earn a bachelor's degree in Psychology from nearby Tusculum College.

Dorothy was the first to start teaching me reading and writing, and when I started school she helped me keep up with my homework. She taught me how to cook breakfast, eggs over easy, biscuits and bacon, which I sometimes made for Mama on special occasions.

She taught me how to brush my teeth, keep a tidy house, and wash and iron my clothes, which was important because I owned only three outfits. I had two pair of pants and shirts for school, and a suit for church. I wore these same clothes to school five days a week, except for a change of underwear and socks.

Those lessons were so profound that years later when I could afford to send my ironing out, I would often do it myself, to the astonishment of friends and family. It's a habit that both honors and reminds me of my grandmother, and my heritage. It reminds me that even though we had nothing to speak of, we had the thing that mattered most—self-reliance and self-respect.

I worshipped Dorothy and we spent so much time together that when boys started showing an interest in her, I became a jealous, protective pest. By this time we had moved out of the run-down shotgun house into a new, tiny cinderblock house with a tin roof that the people in the community and Mama's church chipped in to buy for us.

There wasn't much to it, six very small rooms, but, to us it was as good as a mansion, with a brand new kitchen, running hot water, and an indoor toilet. It was all paid for by the people from the neighborhood, many of whom bought liquor from Mama, contributions from the church, and even from the sheriff.

Dorothy had a particular boyfriend I didn't like who'd come around in the early evening and sit with her on the cinderblock steps. I'd usually mouth off when he showed up. "What're you doing here?" Then I'd loiter while Dorothy would sigh loudly and roll her eyes at me. "Don't you have something you need to do, Tank?"

I'd just shrug and plop myself down next to her on the step. "No, I got nothing I need to do. What are you-all gonna do? Want me to pop you some popcorn?"

I drove poor Dorothy crazy and made it very difficult for her to have boyfriends. My grandmother and our aunts were strict: girls didn't just wander off on their own with boys in our house. Dorothy's romantic life finally improved when I got a little older and started becoming interested in girls, and busy with sports.

My motive was more than jealousy. I'd seen how some men mistreated women in our community, and I'd heard plenty of gossip about domestic abuse in Mama's kitchen. I wanted nothing bad to happen to my cousin, and I vowed I would never become the type of man who drank or abused women.

My cousin Bobby at the house at 333 Railroad Street, Greeneville, TN.

Chapter 5

THE FIELDS OF
FRIENDLY STRIFE

MY LIFE, ALONG WITH the life of Greeneville and the rest of the country, changed dramatically after passage of the Civil Rights Act of 1964. It required that all the public schools in the south become desegregated. The graduating class of June 1965 was George Clem High School's last. The building was converted that summer into school district administration offices. The Clem students were re-assigned, scattered among the formerly all-white schools.

The George Clem School family, and the black community in general, was on edge that summer. The year before, three young civil-rights workers had been murdered by Klansmen in Mississippi. There had been riots in Harlem, New York. In February of 1965, Malcolm X was assassinated. In March the Alabama State Police unleashed its infamous "Bloody Sunday" attack at the Edmund Pettus Bridge, clubbing civil rights marchers on their way to Selma and putting 50 of them in the hospital. In August, just before school started, there were riots by thousands of black people frustrated by police brutality in the impoverished Watts area of Los Angeles. It took six days to restore order. More than a thousand were injured and 34 killed as people looted stores and torched their own neighborhoods, chanting a chilling new slogan: "Burn, baby, burn!" The adults in my life watched this news with a mixture of fear and hope, expressing the opinion that as bad as things looked, the movement was necessary to bring about real change for black people.

All this was taking place far away from sleepy, peaceful Greeneville, but the mood of the country was foremost in our minds and our conversations as the day approached when we school-age kids would have to report to our new schools. I was nine years old, starting third grade.

Although there was minor tension the first few days—a dark look here, a deliberately bumped shoulder there—I don't recall any open hostility. The transition was a little easier for me than some others because I had spent many hours on the football field playing against all-white teams and getting to know them. I had earned some credibility on the gridiron as an outstanding player on the team that always won. I also had experience with white adults because of Coach Williams of the Rams, who I loved and respected and who treated us black kids with respect and affection.

One of the unexpected things we George Clem kids discovered about our new schools was how much unruly behavior the teachers in the white schools tolerated. Discipline had been strict at George Clem. Students had to walk quietly to and from the cafeteria, and if we raised our voices at lunch we got a good scolding.

When Dorothy came home from her first day in high school, she told Mama, "You should see the way the white kids run in the hallway, and carry on in the cafeteria. And nobody says anything to them!"

I enjoyed school, earned good marks, and made friends among the white boys with whom I played on various team sports. By the time I became a sophomore, I had started to get serious about training and practice in four sports: football, basketball, baseball, and track.

My first black football coach was John Jones, a teacher and

head coach at George Clem when it closed. Coach Jones ended up as assistant football coach at the same white high school with me, under Coach Roy Gregory, who became one of the most important people in my life and my career.

In 1972, when I was 15 years old and started playing for the Greeneville High School team, Assistant Coach Jones pulled me aside one day during practice.

"You know, Tank, over at Clem and now here, I don't think I've seen a better athlete than you." No sweeter words had I ever heard, but then he delivered a verbal blow I never forgot.

"It's a shame that with all your talent, you're not going to go to college. You're slacking off in school. You used to get A's and B's, and now you're getting Cs and Ds. When the college recruiters come around, they'll be impressed with your abilities, but those are not the grades they're looking for. Yes sir, it's a real shame you're not going to get to go to college. Unless…"

My whole body blazed with shame. I spent most of my youth around adults, and Coach Jones was one who I respected above most. In many ways, he was the grandfather I never had. I often went to his house, which was near ours, and Mrs. Jones would cook us a meal and we would spend an evening talking out on his porch in good weather, and over the dinner table during the winter. He loved to tell stories about the good and bad old days, and I loved hearing them.

My friends made fun of me spending time with coach and Mrs. Jones but I didn't care. "They'd been good to me and I found their wisdom inspiring.

So I was stunned and embarrassed when he scolded me for letting my grades slip. It felt as though I had personally let him down. I immediately battened the hatches, and kept my grades up the rest of my school career, right through college.

My favorite school teacher was a white lady named Joan Parrish. Her husband Ben Parrish was the local eye doctor in Greeneville and they were always very good to me. She took a special interest in me and always had words of encouragement. She made me realize that excellent students are made from hard work and dedication, they are not born.

One of the skills I learned from a very early age was public speaking. When I was nine years old, one of my teachers told me one day that I had a knack for speaking. I was good on my feet in class answering questions. "You ought to participate in our school oratory program. I think you'll do really well," she said.

She taught me how to begin a speech, set up the point of it, flesh out the details, and pace myself not to finish early or go over the time allotted. In short order I won a couple of speech contests and was chosen among a group of students to compete in a big speaking contest in Johnson City, in a conference room at a hotel. I was the youngest contestant, about ten years old among kids who were thirteen and fourteen.

My teacher told me there would be about sixty people in the audience, but when it was my turn and I walked onto the stage and up to the podium, I looked out on a sea of hundreds of faces. My hands began to shake and I could feel the sweat running down my sides.

My talk was going to be about what I had learned from my family about the importance of respecting other people. I grabbed the edges of the podium but my hands were trembling so that I let go and just let my arms hang at my side. My legs were shaking and I could hardly breathe. I took a deep breath, cleared my throat, and then I was off to the races.

I ended up winning third place and a trophy. My teacher was beaming. "Oh my goodness, Tank, you did so well! Congratulations!"

I was hooked after that and took every opportunity to give a speech. Once I talked about what it was like being a black kid in a white school, about how I didn't know what to expect or think. I told how before I went to a white school with a gym and locker room that I had never seen a shower before and didn't even know how to turn it on.

My message was that we were all the same under the skin, that the things we do different are what make us different, not our color. That speech was a big hit and I often used it in the years ahead because I enjoyed playing a role in bridging the racial divide.

As an athlete, one of the lessons I learned from the examples of Coaches Jones and Gregory, and my own experience later, was that a good coach loves being around young people and being a positive influence on their lives. A coach's principal job is to bring out the best in a person's athletic ability, but what gives you the greatest satisfaction is teaching players about life, hard work, dedication, and bouncing back when you're knocked down.

"Everything's not going to go your way all the time," Coach Jones would say. "Remember, it's not always the best player that wins, or the best team."

He taught me a quote by General Douglas MacArthur that was carved in stone above a gate at West Point: "Upon the fields of friendly strife are sown the seeds that upon other fields, on other days will bear the fruits of victory." MacArthur said it in a speech he made when he left his post as commandant of West Point, on his way to what would prove to be a date with destiny as commander of US forces in the Philippines, before the Japanese invasion. MacArthur had been the Army football team's student manager, and was a huge fan of the game.

The first time Coach Jones quoted it to me he asked me what I thought it meant. I pondered for a moment. "If you work hard you'll have success?"

Coach Jones nodded his head, but I sensed there was more to it. I wrote the quote down, memorized it, and as the years passed, turned it over and over in my mind, trying to extract the deeper meaning. In my history lessons, I came to understand what it meant in a military context, that lessons learned in sports competition—team work, strategy, practice, and so on—would prove valuable in combat.

I repeated it in my own coaching experiences to inspire younger players and, in time, I came to interpret it as meaning that if you can learn to maintain good relationships with people during sports competitions, that lesson could take you far in life, which is often a form of combat.

Coach Gregory, the head coach of the Greeneville High School team from 1972 to 1976, was equally inspiring. He had just been hired from a school in Greenwood, Mississippi, a small town in the middle of cotton country. He was down to earth, deeply religious, and had his own favorite sayings. "Just remember," he often said. "Without God, there's nothing."

The other saying that always stuck with me and helped sustain me through some of the hardest moments of my life was, "Tough times never last, but tough people do." This saying has become a cliché since it was used as a book title in the early 1980s. But like the Golden Rule, it conveys an eternal truth for life as well as football, and my young ears latched on to it with fervor.

In my senior year of high school I was presented with an opportunity I didn't seek. Our star quarterback Mike Armstrong had suffered a season ending knee injury and our backup Toby Boozer had moved away. Coach Gregory wanted me to be our starting quarterback for the season opener.

I had never received a snap under center even in practice before, but Coach said that if I played wide receiver, there'd be no one to throw the ball to me. I couldn't say no, so I spent the summer of 1974 training and doubling as a grounds man around the field house. Half of every day I did chores, earning some extra money mowing or chalking lines or painting stands. The other half was practice.

All this was in preparation for the opening game of the season against a powerhouse team, Tennessee High School from Bristol. Tennessee High had won three straight championships, and the year before a national title. My first year on our team Tennessee High clobbered us, 42-14. The second year, was a close, hard-fought match—they beat us by only 7-0. This year it would be the season opening home game. If we could beat the team that had just won a national title, the town would go crazy.

It was also an important game for my future. A number of colleges had begun to show interest in me in my junior year, for their football or track teams. My hope was to go to the University of Tennessee. It was just 60 miles away from home, in Knoxville, so it would be easy to come home and visit. The school had a huge, enthusiastic army of football fans. Ninety thousand of them would pack into Neyland stadium every home game, creating a sea of orange and an atmosphere of excitement and pageantry that would rival any college in the country.

The head coach of Tennessee, Bill Battle, had written to me during my junior year to say that I was considered the most gifted high school wide receiver in the state, and one of the top five all around athletes. When Coach Gregory put me in the new position of quarterback, I was worried about how it might be perceived. "Will this hurt my chances of getting a football scholarship, since I'm known as a wide receiver?"

He assured me that putting me at quarterback would signal that he had complete confidence in my flexibility and leadership. "It'll improve your chances, Tank. Don't you worry about it. You'll do just fine. Besides, the experience will be good for you later on." Coach Gregory was a great salesman in his own right and I had no choice but to buy what he was selling but he was also someone I knew I could trust and who always had my best interest at heart. I was our team captain and I was always willing to just do whatever the coaches ask me to do. If coach Gregory wanted me to play quarterback then I would play quarterback.

The night of the big game was a warm, humid mid-September Friday night, with rain showers on and off during the day I had worked as hard as I ever had all summer to be ready. I watched film of my practices and of games. Coach Gregory had brought in a star quarterback from East Tennessee State, Alan Chadwick to work with me on my footwork and passing skills. He really helped me improve my footwork and my delivery.

My coaches also schooled me about the leadership role of a quarterback. Instead of running the plays called by someone else, and making sure I was where I was supposed to be, I had to think like a general.

We had one of the most talented teams Greeneville had fielded in years and the fans were pumped for a huge opening season upset. The stadium crackled with electricity. The stakes were high for both sides—the defending champs versus the hungry challengers.

I set our offense up in the positions the coaches wanted me to, but during the game I changed the play at the line of scrimmage some two dozen times. For a quarterback starting his first game it's unusual to change the play so many times at the line of scrimmage, but I was well prepared and confident .

We managed to prevent Tennessee from scoring when they had the ball, and the atmosphere grew especially tense as both sides fought hard to score first. We had the ball on a third down and Coach Gregory called for a 28-sweep play—the quarterback takes the snap, turns, and tosses the ball to the tailback as he starts his run. Our tailback was McDonald Story, a very close friend who lived in my neighborhood. O. J. Simpson and the Southern California Trojans made the sweep play a signature play in the early 70's. They called the play student body left and student body right.

We were only a few yards from a first down, and after the coach called the 28-sweep, I decided to change the play to an inside trap. This called for McDonald to punch through a hole in the line of scrimmage created by what's known as a trap block. It was a little more conservative than the sweep because we would have more players to help push McDonald through to a first down.

At the snap, everyone executed his role in the trap play, except McDonald. When I turned to hand him the ball for the trap, he was running the sweep and I got tackled behind the line of scrimmage.

I was annoyed, doubly so because I trusted McDonald to pay attention. I needed to give him a good cuff, friend or not. In the huddle, in front of everyone, I growled, "What the hell were you thinking about? Get your head in the game, Mac ".

McDonald always sat by me on the bench, and ran on and off the field beside me. But this time he came off the field behind the rest of the team, avoided eye contact, and sat on the bench next to someone else, staring down at his cleats.

The tension between us continued through our next possession. We made some errors and had to surrender the ball. We held Tennessee High off, and got the ball back. We were in midfield when I decided to try the trap play again. This time McDonald was right where he should have been, plunged through the gap, and ran the ball more than 30 yards before he was caught, within the 10-yard line.

The crowd exploded. We were at least close enough for a field goal. In the next huddle, I looked McDonald in the eye and said loudly, "Great play, Mac."

"Thanks, Tank." He flashed a sheepish grin that said, 'I understand you're the quarterback. You have to do this and I need to focus.' Who would have thought that three years later my friend McDonald Story would be killed in a car wreck. I would miss him for the rest of my life.

On the next play my friend and our fullback Terry Kelly scored on an inside dive. The crowd went berserk. By the time the clock ran out, we had won, and kept Tennessee High from scoring a single point: 13-0. We had beaten a National Championship

Team, and Coach Gregory had told me before hand that there would be more than the usual number of college recruiters attending the game.

That night I returned home feeling proud, with a new level of confidence that I would be able to meet my family's expectations by getting the athletic scholarship I would need to go to college. It was looking like I would not need my backup plan to join the Marines to pay for my college education. A degree would help me toward my goal of going into business someday. Our stunning victory advanced my other goal—to one day play professional football. I had no doubt I was on my way to realizing all my dreams.

Coach Roy Gregory, my high school coach and friend. A true disciple of God.

Coach and Mrs. John Jones in Greeneville, Tennessee.

Chapter 6

LEAVING THE NEST

COACHES HAVE PLAYED a central role in shaping my life, teaching by example a lesson I would find useful when I became a coach myself, and later an agent: "Kiss them in their ear before you kick them in the ass." A good coach shows his players that he's there for them, that he genuinely cares about them, so that when he has to get tough or seem mean, they'll understand that it's medicine instead of poison.

Others from outside of sports also played important roles. Chief among them was a white businessman in Greeneville whose path crossed mine when I was in sixth grade and a star player on the city basketball-league team. We won the tournament that year, thanks to my consistent high scoring, averaging 24 points per game. The same agility that gave me an advantage on the football field, and the same speed that made me a track star, also gave me an advantage on the basketball court. In the deciding game, I scored 31 of our team's 55 points.

A ceremony afterward included handing out the usual forest of gleaming trophies. The one I had my eye on was the most prestigious—*Most Valuable Player.* I had the best personal record, so everyone assumed I'd get it. As the announcer prepared to name the MVP winner, a chorus of voices called out my name: "Tank! Tank! Tank!"

When the announcer spoke the name of another player whose record couldn't touch mine but whose father had put up the money for the tournament there was a moment of stunned silence, a muffled gasp, and then polite applause. I'd never been in a more awkward situation. A roomful of eyes studied my reaction. I struggled to keep a straight face but a lump formed in my throat and I had to blink away some tears.

The ceremonies ended and as everyone began milling around and talking, the lump and the tears were gone. But I was feeling very short-changed and disappointed when a white grownup I'd never met approached and gave me a hug.

"Here, son," he said, pressing some folded money in my hand. "You sure got robbed tonight. Here's your MVP trophy." I was so caught off guard that I forgot my manners and failed to thank him as I shoved the money in my pocket. He smiled and then was gone.

Distracted by friends and celebration, I forgot about it until I got home later and showed Mama my all-star trophy, the same one the top five tournament players received. Then I reached into my pocket for the money. I always gave Mama any money I earned. It was understood that we all had to pitch in to keep food on the table. She would give me change for spending money that I kept in a ceramic bowl in the bedroom.

I unfolded the money and discovered two twenties and a ten, more money than I'd ever had in my pocket at any one time. To a twelve-year-old in 1969, earning 50 cents an hour cleaning offices, picking tobacco, and mowing lawns, it was a big windfall. Fifty dollars would feed our entire family for a couple of weeks. Mama's jaw dropped. I instantly regretted I hadn't been more polite to the man who gave it to me.

I tried to explain to Mama the unexplainable.

"Everybody said I should have won most valuable player, but they gave it to another boy whose father was a sponsor. Then this white man came and just gave the money to me. He said it was because I got robbed of the MVP."

Her eyes narrowed. "A white man gave you fifty dollars? What white man? What's his name?"

"I don't know. He didn't say. I forgot to ask. He just gave me a hug, handed me the money, and said it was my trophy for being the best player even though I didn't win the trophy."

Mama shook her head as she smoothed the creases out of the bills on the kitchen table. "Now why would a white stranger just walk up and give you fifty dollars? What did you do that's worth fifty dollars is what I wanna know." "All I did was score the most points. I guess he was just being nice." I shrugged. "He seemed like a good man, and everybody thought I should've been MVP." I hoped she wouldn't make me give it back. It made me feel grownup to be able to contribute so much to the household expenses.

Mama's interrogation continued, my I-don't-knows piled up, and so did her skepticism. "I want to know who this man is that just goes around handing out wads of money to children. You tell that coach I want some answers."

The next day I told my coach, Bill Gudger, about the money and that my grandmother wanted to know who gave it to me. He already knew about it and came to the house to explain that Bill Isbell, my benefactor, owned a local insurance agency and supported the basketball program.

Coach Gudger assured Mama that Mr. Isbell was a good man who was just upset that I had been passed over for the MVP and thought this was a way to make up for it. Only then did Mama accept that the fifty dollars was legitimate.

That launched a lifelong friendship. Bill Isbell became an enduring father figure to whom I still often turn to talk honestly about my dreams, frustration, joys, and sorrows. He talked to me about business and nurtured the seed of my dream to own my own business someday. He was there for me in big ways, and in a hundred small ways. When the senior prom came and I had no car, he let me borrow his. Later, when I went off to college, he promised that if I broke any football records, he would buy me a car. I broke a whole string of records, and he kept his promise. Mr. Isbell always treated me like I was his son. He will always be family to me.

In my senior year of high school, college coaches came to Greeneville to talk about my future. I would later learn as a recruiter and coach that the people who really count are the parents. In my case, my grandmother was the person they had to convince.

They came to our little house to sit down with Mama and me and, if they were around, Dorothy and Bobby. They told Mama how I'd get my education paid for with an athletic scholarship, and why my attending their school was better than the others.

Mama had her own agenda. "What I want to know is who's gonna be lookin' after Tank?" She had gotten over her earlier worry about me getting hurt. She just wanted to make sure that if I had any problems or got homesick or anything bad happened, I'd have someone I could trust to go and talk to.

Sitting at our kitchen table where she had served thousands of shots of moonshine to people who may never have had anyone watching out for them, she said, "Tank has never been places. This is a small town and if he ever needs something, he's got a hundred people to ask. He's never been away from home. There are a lot of things he's gonna see that he's never been around. He's never even been around a lot of girls."

It was true. Mama kept her brood on a short leash. In part because of her, I never touched alcohol or smoked cigarettes.

Mama was right, I had all kinds of people in the neighborhood who cared about me. I spent most of my time with older men in the community. I always seemed to be more grown up than my age. I spent a lot of time with Pete Lollar. He always had an encouraging word for me and many times would give me a few dollars and say here go get you something and stay out of trouble. Pete had a beautiful wife named Penny and she was the nicest lady. They were very well respected in our community. They would make it a weekly ritual to come and see me play high school football on Friday nights and then take their young son Brandon, to get pizza at Pizza Hut. Brandon would later tell me that their family wasn't going to see Greeneville High School play so much as they were going to see Tank play.

I spent time with Wayne Horton and his family. His mother Ms. Willie Lee Horton was the best cook in town along with my aunt Stella. She also had a heart of gold and was an angel in disguise. I could go to their house anytime and get a meal. I would play cards with Wayne and Larry Anderson and Jimmy Whiteside. Jimmy's wife Francis would cook for us and play some cards with us also. We would stay up all night on the weekends playing bid whiz.

Joy and Bill Gudger treated me like a son and we played cards and went fishing and Bill coached me in basketball. I ate meals at their house and baby sat their children Bill Jr. and Twila.

Donald and Nancy Hamilton and their family treated me like family and I spent all kinds of time with them and their children Donnie Jr. and Robin. We did not have a phone until I was in high school and Bob and Margaret Hackett would let us use their phone.

I would walk 5 miles across town to the white side of town to get to my friend Terry Kelly's house. His mom and dad treated me like I was one of their sons. They never had a prejudice bone in their body. I was a big Tennessee Vol's fan and Terry was a big Alabama Crimson Tide fan and we always got along. That is true friendship.

I was Ms Susie's grandson. Yes, everyone in the community had a hand in my development. There are so many others that looked out for me in our community. I developed a sense of responsibility because I never wanted to let any of these people down.

Mama always spoke plainly, and she was especially determined to get her point across. "If Tank goes to your school, I want you all to keep a strong hand on him. I want to know that you're gonna be personally responsible for making sure he stays out of trouble. And if you don't, you're gonna have me to deal with!"

It was the same conversation I would later have with dozens of players' parents and grandparents in equally modest homes all across the southeastern states. Going through it with Mama was great training for what lay ahead.

I'd grown up a University of Tennessee Volunteers fan so that was my first choice. But when it was time for invitations to be made, Tennessee offered only a half scholarship. The school had a rich athletic budget, and 90,000 ticket-buying fans. I couldn't figure out why they didn't have the money for a full scholarship, and concluded that Tennessee didn't want me.

Later, when I became part of the system, I understood that the school knew they could save some money and get me on their team by tapping into the federal Pell Grant program, designed for kids like myself from poor backgrounds. But I also think my short stature tempered their enthusiasm. My size, which had been an advantage when I was younger, was shaping up to be a disadvantage as an adult athlete.

On the other hand, Carson-Newman College, a Baptist liberal arts school in Jefferson City, Tennessee, offered a full scholarship, plus they would help me with a Pell grant so I'd have cash money for clothes and other necessities.

The coaches' pitch was, "You can go to a place like Tennessee and be a small fish in a big bowl, or you can come to a place like this and be a big fish in a small bowl. With this skill you've got, from the day you walk on campus, people are going to be writing and talking about you all the time. That will also improve your chances of going pro."

All of this made sense, and there was one other big advantage. I hated the idea of being far from Mama. Like the Pa and Opie characters in The Andy Griffith Show, my favorite, Mama was the center of my world, and I was her sidekick. She knew me better than anyone. She was my guiding conscience and my fierce advocate. I needed to know she was nearby. Carson-Newman was about an hour's drive from Greeneville, so it would be less difficult for me to come home and easier for her to come and see me play.

I signed with Carson-Newman, and spent the time between May and the start of football practice in July getting myself physically prepared. I trained in army boots, running around the track on the grounds of the old George Clem School. I would go out in the heat of the summer days and run five miles in those heavy, clunky boots.

I had already established myself as an exceptional sprinter, breaking ten seconds in the hundred yard dash. But I wanted to test myself to the limits so when I got to school, I'd be ready for anything. The neighbors would watch from their chairs in the shade as I paced myself around the track. They'd shake their heads, but then tell each other, "That's Tank. He's training to go off to college!"

On one of those hot days in July, My aunt Ebbie drove Mama and me to school with all my belongings in the back seat, in trash bags. We couldn't afford luggage, and I'd never had to go anywhere before on my own. When aunt Ebbie coasted to a stop in front of my dorm, Mama's lower lip quivered as she fought back tears. Mine did, too. I unloaded my things and gave her a kiss.

"I'll call you some time, Mama. Don't worry about me. I'll be fine." I waved as she drove away, stifling a sob. For the first time in my life, I was on my own.

My second father, Mr. Bill Isbell and family.

My lifelong friend, Terry Kelly, Greeneville High School, 1973.

Aunt Edna, nicknamed "Jim".

Aunts Ebbie and Stella with Uncle James Jr.

Family men at Aunt Ebbies funeral. It broke my heart not to be there.

My Carson Newman College All-American photo.
I bleed Carson Newman Eagle orange and blue!

Chapter 7

A WHOLE LOTTA MOONSHINE!

THE MOMENT I put my belongings down in my dorm room at Carson-Newman College, my heart began to ache with homesickness. Because classes hadn't started my roommate hadn't arrived yet, so I was living by myself for the first time. It took some adjustment, but between team meetings, practice, and eating meals with my teammates in the dining hall, I soon overcame my insecurities.

For the first time I became aware of just how poor I grew up. At college I ate better than I ever had before. My favorite meal was pot roast because it was big pieces of meat, a rarity at home. Our luxury meal was fried chicken. In between, there was plenty of fried bologna on Wonder bread.

As the pre-season days dwindled toward the start of the school year, I pushed myself hard at every drill and scrimmage, and I studied films of past games memorizing great plays and colossal foul-ups. I knew I was as good a receiver as the upper classmen on the team, but I also knew it would be unusual for me to land a spot on the starting lineup.

But on the Monday before the first game when the coaches posted the starters for the opener, there was my name —BLACK— as the starting wide receiver. I was the only freshman starter. The recruiters had been right. I was a big fish in a little pond.

Our first game was against Middle Tennessee State in Murfreesboro, September 1975. They were favored to win by 28 points but we lost by just one point: 22-21. I caught the first pass thrown to me and ran fifty-five yards to the five-yard line. I failed to score a touchdown that first game, but I caught seven passes and made plays that put us in scoring position. I started every game during the next four years, forty-four straight, leading the team in receiving, every year and being named the offensive MVP three years in a row. I would go on to break most of the school's receiving records, some of which still stand today. I was named first team Kodak and NAIA All-American. There are less than forty receivers in all of college football history who have caught over 200 passes in there careers. I am one of them with 209 receptions.

Carson Newman College was the absolute best place for me to go to school, get my education and play college football. The people at Carson Newman genuinely care about its students and truly want to prepare them for a demanding and ever changing future that awaits them. Carson Newman became my family away from home. I will always be a Carson Newman Fighting Eagle at heart.

Coach Ken Sparks who was coaching there when I was there is the head football coach and he is one of the top winning coaches in the nation and David Barger is an athletic director that has been affiliated with Carson Newman for over 30 years. I would recommend any young person to consider Carson Newman College for your higher education and athletic opportunities.

Carson-Newman had an enrollment of about 2,000 students, but it had such a strong football program that some of the guys I played with went on to become top coaches. If I did not make it into the NFL I thought coaching would be a good career for me.

Sparky Woods was our free safety and he later became head football coach at the University of South Carolina. Sparky and I stayed in touch over the years. Sparky started his head coaching career at Appalachian State University and was very successful. Carl Torbush, a linebacker who was a couple of years ahead of me, became head football coach at Louisiana Tech University and the University of North Carolina. I have always had a great deal of respect for Carl Torbush as a top quality person and coach.

My favorite former player at Carson Newman College was Ken Rucker. Ken grew up in Morristown, Tennessee about 25 miles from where I grew up in Greeneville. Ken was a senior at Carson Newman when I was a freshman. He really took me under his wing and was a very positive influence on me coming in the door to college life. He was a great leader and a Christian who led by example. Ken has been a very successful college football coach for many years. He finally got himself a deserving national championship ring when Texas won the 2005 season National Championship. Ken has positively impacted the lives of so many young people including myself as a young freshman at Carson Newman.

College life for me was mostly about getting good grades and staying on top of my game, preparing for a spot on an NFL team. I had an advantage over a lot of other men in that I had no interest in liquor and never smoked or took illegal drugs. My personal habits would never slow me down. It wasn't a struggle. None of that behavior appealed to me. I had seen plenty of evidence in our kitchen of what happened to those who got hooked, including my parents.

What I missed in the area of substance abuse I made up for in my social life, beginning my senior year in high school when I experienced the heady sensation of being the football star and having girls come at you right and left. Like many of the player clients I would later represent, young men who were stars in their worlds, I found this aphrodisiac powerful and perilous. A girl I was dating became pregnant when I was 19. I was embarrassed and not sure what to do. Time to consult Mama.

"You need to make sure she knows you're gonna help support that child," she said. "You're gonna give her money and be a father, and do the things you're supposed to do. You tell her that this isn't something she should have to go through by herself."

When I did as she suggested, the girl swore it wasn't my child. But there was doubt in my mind that never went away, and was fanned in later years when people said her boy looked just like me. More than two decades would pass before I learned that the boy was, in fact, mine. It broke my heart. I had been fully prepared to accept my responsibility but her lie denied this child the love of his biological father, just as I had been denied mine. It was in 1999, this young man, my son Michael Oshea Brobeck took it upon himself to confirm with his mother that I was indeed his father and he searched and found me. It was bittersweet because at the time I was in the heat of all of my legal problems. We had missed out on so much time. It was all so unfair. I found Michael to be a very smart young man with a big heart. I thought of how I could have been such a positive influence on his life growing up if I had been afforded that opportunity. I will go to my grave regretting that Michael spent his entire childhood not knowing his father.

He had spent the first 22 years of his life not knowing for sure who his father was. I went to Greeneville and bought him a new SUV, some clothes, paid his rent up for a year and gave him some money. It was a small token of what I would have and should have been able to do for him over those past 22 years.

My senior year in college ended in June, 1979, with Mama in attendance at my graduation. There was a lot to celebrate. All three of her grandkids had made it through college. And I had been wooed by the Cincinnati Bengals, the Washington Redskins, the Miami Dolphins, the Cleveland Browns, and the Atlanta Falcons. I signed with the Falcons as a free agent, the status of players who are not drafted.

I chose the Falcons because Atlanta was closest to home. They offered me $5,000 to sign, and my salary was $55,000 plus bonuses. I was in Heaven.

I didn't tell Mama about any of this because I wanted to surprise her. When I got the check, I cashed it at a bank and just for the thrill of it, walked around Carson-Newman with that $5,000 cash in my pocket. Then I went home to break the good news to Mama over the kitchen table.

"Mama, I'm on the Atlanta Falcons." She gave me a big hug and a kiss. Then I reached into my jacket, pulled out a stack of forty hundred dollar bills, and fanned the bills out on the table. "My Lord, Tank!" she cried.

I grinned with pleasure. "They paid me $5,000 to sign with them, Mama. It's money I get to keep. This $4,000 is for you. I'm going to keep a thousand for myself, to get settled in Atlanta."

My grandmother's face lit up. "That's a whole lotta moonshine, ain't it?"

I glowed with love and gratitude. It made me happy to see Mama happy. Mama loved her family, but she loved having money almost as much. She never let on that she ever had a cent, and my cousins and aunts and uncles would later discover that we were all slipping her five dollars here and ten dollars there. But if anyone asked if she had any money, she'd always say, "No, I ain't got no money." If they asked if she needed any, she'd say coyly, "Oh, I suppose I could use some."

She gathered up the hundreds, folded them into a wad, and stuffed it into her apron. "Now don't you be tellin' nobody you gave me this money. You know how folks are."

In July I reported to Atlanta for training camp and discovered what money can buy when you have an almost unlimited supply. The fields we practiced on were immaculately manicured. The equipment was brand new or in perfect condition. The dressing rooms were like five-star hotels. The dining hall offered the best of everything. This was big time.

Although I was at the bottom of the pay scale, the top wasn't nearly as far away as the spread is today. Walter Payton had just signed the richest contract ever negotiated in NFL history with the Chicago Bears: $450,000 a year. It was the talk of the sports world. Today, in 2009 a player with ten years in the NFL must receive a minimum of $845,000 and a player with just two credited seasons would receive $460,000. There is no recession in the NFL.

Training was hard and the competition was tough. The other players all had a size advantage. Once again, I was the smallest guy on the field. In the pre-season the NFL teams put their recruits through a rigorous winnowing process. They sign more players than the NFL rules permit during the season, and gradually cut those who aren't measuring up.

The Falcons started out that preseason with more than 100 players, but by the time the regular season started, they could have no more than 53 on the active roster. The cuts are made after each of the preseason games. I made the first cut, but it was becoming clear that it would be a close call whether I would make it through this entire process.

I worked hard to make up for my shortness. I attended every meeting, studied the films they gave us, and made some great plays that showed off my skills. But in the end, my NFL career ended before it had a chance to begin. I was cut after the third pre-season game.

If I were in that same position today, chances are I would have had a good ten-year run. In 1979 there were fewer play formations and unlike today players were not going in and coming out during the game to take advantage of a specific skill for a specific situation. For the most part the same players were in for the whole game.

The game has changed since then and smaller players have a role, especially in third-down situations where speed and agility are most needed. I arrived on the NFL scene at the wrong time on a team that already had a full roster of good receivers. I considered my options: I could try to win a slot on a Canadian team and maybe move back to an NFL team in the States later. The

Toronto Argonauts wanted me to come to Canada the same day I was released.

It was a big let down, but I decided to move back to Greeneville because Mama was having health problems and I thought I could be helpful. Just like her finances, Mama made sure no one knew her true age. It was a detail she carefully guarded from all of us, but we guessed she was somewhere around sixty-five. However old she was, her body was beginning to betray her. She'd hurt her hip, her back ached, and she had glaucoma, which was interfering with her vision.

While I helped Dorothy look after Mama, I landed a good management job at the Magnavox television factory. Everyone there knew me from my football career, so I felt right at home. I kept my hand in the game by helping out with the Greeneville High School team as a coach.

Mama's doctor had wanted her to go to the hospital to have some tests to see if she ought to have an operation for the glaucoma. But she'd been balking. She mistrusted hospitals her whole life. "People die in hospitals," she said. "I seen plenty of folks go in healthy as a horse and come out in a box." We wrote it off as superstition, and her generation's experience in the bad old days of Jim Crow when hospitals refused to treat black folks.

In early December, the doctor, Dorothy, and I finally talked her into it. The doctor assured us that any procedure would be low-risk, there was nothing life-threatening to worry about, and she stood a good chance of getting back some of her eyesight. Other than aches and pains, Mama seemed fine.

I visited her in the hospital every day after work. Christmas Eve, which was her birthday, we celebrated at her bed side. A few days later I was at work when I was summoned to the phone. It was Dorothy, crying and frantic. "Mama's awful sick, Tank. You've got to come over here right away."

I drove as fast as I could, heart in my throat, bargaining with the Lord. Dorothy met me outside Mama's room and fell into my arms sobbing. She couldn't speak but she didn't need to. I knew that my grandmother's worst fear had come true. She had died in the hospital, and we had talked her into it. How could doing the right thing turn out so wrong?

The worst of it was having been robbed of the chance to say goodbye and to be a comfort in her final hours. Nothing had prepared me for the swift and merciless hand of death. Lost and numb, I was too broken up to speak at her funeral, and I couldn't bear to attend the burial service.

The beacon that had guided me my entire life had suddenly and cruelly been extinguished.

Me (front, left) and Carson Newman dorm residents having fun.
Wide receiver Ralph Rogers, (center, back row), was one of my
best friends.

My son, Matthew, and his dog, Rocky, in the back yard.

My oldest son, Michael O'Shea Brobeck.

PART II

From Player to Coach

Chapter **8**

STERLING SHARPE'S STAR is BORN

S TERLING SHARPE had ticked me off and I needed to teach him a lesson. My young starring wide receiver had just ad-libbed a play in an away game against the University of Pittsburgh Panthers. From my coaching position high up in the press box, I looked glumly down on the field as we completed another in a series of drives marred by turnovers, interceptions, and fumbles. We seemed determined to lose the game.

'You may be the star of the show, Sterling,' I thought, 'but you're still playing on a team, and you're about to get a reminder.'

It was 1985, Sterling's third year with the University of South Carolina Gamecocks. Sterling came to South Carolina in 1983. He played some on special teams as a freshmen in 1983 and in 1984 we red-shirted Sterling because of the depth of our receivers. Of several wide receivers I was responsible for coaching, Sterling had phenomenal potential that I was coaching him to fulfill. In fact, he was on his way to becoming one of the school's all-time top receivers, a Heisman Trophy candidate, a pro-football legend, and a television sports commentator.

My sometimes bumpy journey with Sterling began when I found him running track and playing high school football in sleepy Glennville, Georgia, a farm town of about 3,000 in the state's southeastern coastal plain. A tape of some of his games had come to the attention of the Gamecocks' coaching staff. Coach Billy Michaels was the main recruiter in South Georgia. We watched some film on Sterling and he looked good on film. I was dispatched to Glennville, Georgia to find out more about Sterling Sharpe. I first saw him at the school. I was impressed with his clean cut appearance. His coach, William Hall was very high on Sterling's future potential.

Sterling and I had such similar childhoods we bonded from the start. Sterling and his siblings, including future pro-player and younger brother Shannon, were being raised on a small, subsistence farm by their grandmother.

Like me, his parents had been out of the picture. Their father hadn't been around for years and their mother lived in Chicago, where Sterling was born. Like me at some point the Sharpe youngsters had been sent to live with their grandmother. They grew up about as poor as I had and like myself Sterling had worked from an early age, in his case as a farm field hand, which I had been as well, picking tobacco.

He and I shared a love of athletics. He ran track and played basketball in addition to football, as had I. He was smart, gregarious, and like myself saw sports as a path to a good education, self-respect, and the potential to earn a good living so he could take care of his family.

Sterling had been one of my first recruits to South Carolina after I'd come on board as an assistant coach in December of 1982. For the three years before that, ever since Mama died, I was on the football staff at the University of Chattanooga (now known as the University of Tennessee at Chattanooga) under Bill Oliver. It felt like home because my old high school mentor coach Roy Gregory was the offensive line coach. Mike Dubose was the defensive ends coach on that staff and he would later become the head football coach at the University of Alabama. I didn't know it then but I was rubbing shoulders with many future football legends.

The pay was less than half what I could have earned staying with Magnavox, but I couldn't resist the chance to work with players, work with Coach Gregory, and be part of a team. I was the head track coach at Chattanooga and the head "B" team football coach along with my primary responsibility of coaching the wide receivers and tight ends.

Joe Morrison had been very successful at New Mexico and gotten hired at South Carolina. He called me and offered me the job and a week later I was in South Carolina coaching. When I took the job at South Carolina it was to coach the wide receivers only. I did not have all of the other responsibilities I had at Chattanooga.

The Gamecocks had fired Jim Carlen after the 1981 season. Hired and fired Richard Bell in the 1982 season and now hired Morrison. In the span of one year they had three head football coaches. The players on the squad at that time were hard workers and hungry to win. Morrison assembled one of the top coaching staffs in the college game and we began to teach the Gamecock players our system and the levels of dedication required to compete and win. The players bought in and the first year we won five games and lost six. We had one really big win at home over Southern California 38-14. I remember it was so loud that night in Williams Brice Stadium that Southern California head coach Ted Tollner had to put his face in the ear of his quarterback on the sideline because they could not hear each other.

The following season in 1984 we returned 18 starters and our players had learned our system inside and out. We opened the season against the Citadel and they almost beat us. We won the game late 31-24. There was concern that we may be in for a long year after struggling to beat the Citadel. We had eight starters not play in that game so our full squad was not on the field.

The next game we played Duke and we beat Duke 21-0 in an uneventful game. The strangest thing however happened in that game. We were redshirting Sterling for the 1984 season. That means he cannot play in any games. The staff did not know it but coach Morrison was practicing Sterling and a few other players on some special plays. At the end of the Duke game coach Morrison sent this group of players into the game and I was in the press box. I looked out on the field and saw #2 Sterling Sharpe on the field. I screamed into the headset "Coach Morrison Sterling Sharpe cannot be on the field of play, we are redshirting him". Coach Morrison said, "okay Coach Black." Sterling had one carry for seven yards. He played three plays. Once you play him in a real game he loses his redshirt for that year. After the game I went into Coach Morrison's office. I told him we had just lost Sterling's redshirt year on three plays. Coach Morrison got with the statistics people and changed the carry Sterling had to another player and took Sterling off the stat sheet. No one ever mentioned it again and we redshirted Sterling for the 1984 Season.

The following week we would play the Georgia Bulldogs at Williams Brice Stadium. It was the game all of our fans were waiting on. The atmosphere was electrifying. This was our players time. This was there time to become winners. We battled Georgia in a hard fought game and finally in the second half our defense held Georgia on a 4th and 1 on the goal line. Then Mike Hold came in and threw a sixty five yard pass to Ira Hillary down inside the five yard line. The score was tied 10-10 and we scored and went up 17-10 to win the ballgame. That catch by Ira Hillary may have been the biggest play in our season.

Ira Hillary was my favorite player to coach while I was at South Carolina because he went full speed in practice and he tried to do everything the way I coached it with no excuses. The Gamecocks were 3-0 on the season for the first time since 1976.

We would run off nine straight victories beating Notre Dame at Notre Dame and Pittsburgh, Kansas State and North Carolina State in Raleigh. We would be ranked #2 in the country when we went to play Navy in the freezing rain in Annapolis. The game had dangerous written all over it. We had just beaten

Florida State on National Television 38-26 and we had arch rival Clemson after the Navy game. With the national championship and the Orange Bowl on the line we lost to Navy 38-21. It was one of the sickest feelings I'd ever experienced. We were originally suppose to play Navy at home but our Athletic director Bob Marcum switched that game to an away game to give us another road game.

Our only salvation left for the season was to go to Clemson and beat them on their field. We had great practices that week and our players felt sorrow for themselves but really wanted to make the feeling go away by beating Clemson. Clemson had the best eleven defensive players I had ever seen on one defensive team. I thought Clyde Wrenn was the best recruiting coordinator in the game. Clemson had won 22 straight home games and had never lost a game in their all orange uniforms.

On game day the tigers came out in white shirts and orange pants but after warm ups they came down the hill in their all orange uniforms. It was definitely a hard fought game and we won it in the end 22-21. It was the sweet taste of victory to end the best season in South Carolina Gamecock history. 10-1 was our record and our only lost came to a very unlikely Navy team.

In 1985 Coach Morrison brought on a volunteer coach named Charlie Weis. Coach Morrison hired Charlie to assist with the offensive line but he wanted to learn the passing game. He wanted me to speak to coach Morrison for him and see if Coach Morrison would allow Charlie to be my assistant working under me. Morrison agreed to allow Charlie Weis to work as my assistant. From that day forward I would teach Charlie Weis everything that had been taught to me about the passing game, play action, bootlegs, pick plays, shotgun and the whole nine yards. Charlie was as eager to learn as anyone I had ever worked with. He was also very intelligent with a fantastic memory. Charlie did not fit the prototype build of a receiver coach because he was very heavy set but he wanted to learn about everything nonetheless.

He would leave South Carolina and go on to win a state championship as a high school head coach in New Jersey and end up as film assistant with Bill Parcells New York Giants at Coach Morrison's recommendation. Charlie is of course the head football coach for the University of Notre Dame. Charlie has super bowl rings and is a major college head coach because he consistently coached his heart out one day at a time. He would never let anyone tell him he couldn't do something and taught the players the same. He wanted to learn everything from everybody.

Charlie Weis started his transformation as a passing game and play calling expert with me on the practice fields of the University of South Carolina. That is a fact. I am not saying that I am in some way responsible for the success of Charlie Weis because that is not true. I am saying that Charlie started his learning curve with me and I took the time with him day and night because he wanted to be the best coach in the business just like I wanted to be the best. Charlie would learn from me and go on and learn from others. I admire Charlie Weis and his accomplishments because I was there when he started at the bottom and worked his way to the top. It is because of that hard work and dedication that Charlie has been successful. I am proud of Charlie and will always be one of his biggest fans.

In addition to our similar childhood experiences, Sterling, like myself, had played both sides of the football—offense and defense. He was also a quarterback, which required leadership and strategy skills. But I saw potential in him to become a successful wide receiver, and that's how he got to South Carolina, on my recommendation.

In the beginning, Sterling proved to be a good listener and a fast learner. I enjoyed coaching him and watching him grow as a person and as an athlete. But like some handsome, young, rising stars, the limelight blinded him now and then and he fell into the trap of acting like he was bigger than the game. It was an aspect of his character that has dogged him his whole career.

In the play that set me off, Sterling was to run a hitch route. The designated pass receiver fakes running a long, downfield pattern. But he stops short a few yards beyond the line of scrimmage and turns to receive a bullet pass before the defenders have a chance to react. In this instance, the play called for Sterling to stop and turn toward the outside. Instead, he had turned inside.

There are times in some players' careers when they become so experienced and accomplished that a coach can trust them to know when it's okay to improvise. But as promising as Sterling was (he would later be dubbed "a freight train with stickum"), he was only twenty, in his third college season, and still honing his skills. He was a work-in-progress and had a ways to go before he'd earned the right to improvise.

My "desk" during games was up in the press box where I sat behind a window wearing a headset that had an open line to the offensive coaches and head coach on the field down below. I was the game's eye-in-the-sky, shielded from the noise and confusion. Like a field commander, I stood far enough back to be able to see the big picture as the battle unfolded.

When Sterling hitched the wrong way, I told the assistant coach Ricky Diggs at the other end down below to hand his headset to Sterling as soon as he came off the field. As he jogged to the bench coach Diggs tapped him on the shoulder. Sterling glanced up at the press box, pulled off his helmet, and held the headset to his ear.

"Yeah, Coach. What's up?"

"Listen to me, Sterling." I made sure my displeasure was clear from my tone of voice. "You were supposed to turn outside on that hitch. What gives?"

"Coach, the coverage was outside. He'd have been right on top of me. The opening was inside. What was I supposed to do?" He waved an arm in a gesture of frustration, staring at the ground.

"That's all well and good, Sterling, and we'll run some other plays to draw the defense away next time. We'll set 'em up so they won't expect it. But when the play's called as an outside hitch, I need you to go outside. You got that?"

There was a beat of silence followed by a rattling sound and a muffled curse as Sterling flung the headset to the ground and stalked away, shaking his head, hands on his hips. "You're lucky I ain't down there with you," I muttered. Coach Diggs retrieved the headset.

"Get Eric on the line," I snapped. Eric Poole was another of our wide receivers, a solid soldier whose steady demeanor would later that year earn him a Best Attitude Award. "Eric, go tell Sterling you're goin' in for him, and then put him on the headset." Sterling's head jerked as Eric delivered the news. He shot a dark look up at the press box and got on the horn.

"Yeah?" His tone was surly.

I put some steel in my voice. "Sterling, you go have a seat on the bench and let me know when you wanna go back in. You let me know when you wanna listen to me, okay? I'll be sittin' right up here. Now go on and sit down."

He slouched to the bench where the other players greeted him with wagging heads, no doubt a response to something rude he'd said about me. He sulked through the rest of that quarter, but as soon as it ended he was on the headset, doing his best to sound chastened. "Uh, Coach, I'm ready, Coach. I'm ready to listen. Honest. I'm ready to go back in. Okay?"

One of the benefits of having been a player before becoming a coach is that I often knew what my players were feeling before they did. I had been in Sterling's shoes many times since I was a fidgety six-year-old on the bench in Greeneville, chomping at the bit. I figured Sterling had suffered enough humiliation that he wouldn't make the same mistake again.

"Okay, Sterling. I'm ready, too. Tell Eric."

This would prove to be one of many awkward moments in

an athletic partnership and a friendship that would last more than a decade. When it was good, we were as close as family. When it was bad, I took solace in knowing that without my advocacy and coaching, Sterling's career may well have ended before it began, or at least been a lot less successful.

In the same way that a sculptor turns a piece of marble into a work of art, I created a great player out of a good one. It can also be said that in doing so, Sterling recreated me. But in the beginning, it took all my empathy and coaching skills to keep him from losing his focus.

His first season on the Gamecocks, he had trouble catching the ball. Because he was big, the coaches thought he might be better on defense. I still saw his potential as a receiver and lobbied the offensive coordinator (my boss) and Gamecocks' head coach Joe Morrison to give Sterling a chance to bloom.

Morrison had been hired the same year I was, with a mandate to pull the team out of a slump. He had been coaching college teams for many years after a thirteen-year stretch as a running back and wide receiver with the New York Giants. He held the team's record for receptions.

He'd been known during his Giants' years as "Old Dependable" because he was always willing and able to play any position. At South Carolina, he was proving to be just as versatile and an innovative strategist to boot. His second season, 1984, he was named the National Collegiate Athletic Association (NCAA) Coach of the Year—first among 117 college and university head coaches.

"Just leave Sterling with me for the rest of this year," I suggested. "If it doesn't pan out, we'll red-shirt him (sideline him) or move him to defensive back. But I still think it's gonna pan out and he's gonna be a great receiver. I think I can coach it out of him. Right now he's thinking too much about the play and then, all of a sudden, here comes the ball."

Coach Morrison agreed to give me time to help Sterling find his game. It was an act of trust I took as a commitment to make it happen. I started by telling Sterling the truth.

"It's time for you to fish or cut bait. Do you want me to keep coaching you to be a receiver, or do you wanna go play defensive back? I'm asking because if you don't start catchin' the ball, that's what's gonna happen."

"Coach, man, I'm really—"

I held up my hand. "Just hold on. Hear me out. I want you to stay with me. I think you're gonna be a fantastic player at this position. But you gotta help me out. You gotta quit thinkin' so much and just catch the ball."

Having been a wide receiver, I know how complex a role it is, second only to quarterback. A good receiver is to football much like a catcher is to major league baseball. A good receiver has the hand –eye instincts of a good catcher who can snag a blistering pitch and instinctively fire the ball right where it needs to be to put out a runner trying to steal second base.

A receiver has to memorize and be able to run all the possible routes in the playbook on a moment's notice, needs the eye to know where the ball's going, the speed and control to get there at the same time as the ball, and the coordination to be able to hold on to the ball when it gets there while his opponents do everything in their power to make him miss or drop it. A good receiver does it all as naturally as breathing.

A good coach knows how to bring that instinct out. In a college setting, where the players are all young and still learning life's ropes, there is an aspect of coaching that has nothing to do with training for speed and coordination. In school it's also dealing with a student-player's academic, personal, and emotional lives— helping them cope with family stress, excess partying, and sagging grades, which Sterling needed to improve. Some coaches let their players get by with the minimum. Coming from my background, the chance to earn a college degree was a big deal, not to be wasted coasting toward a dream of the good life as an NFL player. I reminded him of the big picture.

"You're getting your education paid for because you're out here working hard as a player. Nobody's givin' it to you. Now it's up to you to take advantage of it. If it works out, you might play pro for four or five years, which is about the average. What are you gonna do after that?"

Sterling rose to the occasion. Over the next year he buckled down in his school work, getting himself on track to earn his BA early majoring in interdisciplinary studies and then take courses for a second degree in retailing.

His game improved so much that by the following season, pro scouts were starting to look at him as a draft prospect. In the 1986 season, as a junior, he made several big plays against the University of Georgia, a powerhouse, and against our arch rival Clemson University. He ran some long touchdowns by outrunning tacklers. He was making himself indispensable—a receiver who can catch the ball and score with it from anywhere on the field. As our star quarterback, Todd Ellis, put it, "Sterling is like a 10-speed bike. He's got a different gear for every situation."

Between seasons, during the summer of 1987, I received an offer from Mississippi State coach Rockey Felker to become his offensive coordinator. If I took the job I would become the first black offensive coordinator in the Southeastern Conference. That was really something in a region of the country where a black college coach had to work harder than a white coach to prove himself worthy of promotions. No one came out and said it, but it was common knowledge, especially among black coaches who'd seen plenty of less-accomplished white coaches promoted ahead of them.

I had previously been offered the offensive coordinators job by Carl Torbush when he was the head coach of Louisiana Tech. I decided to stay at South Carolina. But this offer at Mississippi State was intriguing and I was actively considering it.

Because Sterling and I had become so close, I thought I ought to let him hear about it from me first, so he wouldn't feel betrayed. Over dinner in my home one night, I told him and explained why I might accept. "If I do a good job down there, I'll have a chance to do what I really want—be a head coach at a major university."

Sterling's eyes popped open. "Jeez, Coach. I've got one more year and I'm outta here. Is there any way you could just stay for this year, and do somethin' next year? I really, really want you to stay with me and help me get on through."

I'd been the only college coach Sterling had ever had. I promised to think it over, and I did. It weighed on me, the prospect of leaving him with a new coach for the crucial senior year when his every move would be watched so closely and his performance would be so vital to his chances in the NFL draft.

When I told Coach Morrison about the offer, he hinted that my boss, Frank Sadler was actively searching for a head coaching job and would likely leave the Gamecock program soon. He said I was the logical person to step in as the Gamecocks' next offensive coordinator since I had already been promoted to passing game coordinator and I also coached the quarterbacks in the passing game.

There seemed to be no doubt I'd proven my mettle. As one sports reporter would write a few months later, I was considered one of college footballs "most successful recruiters and sharpest offensive minds."

Morrison made it clear he wanted me to stay. "Be patient Tank. When this job comes open, I'll give it to you. And you know Sterling would have a fit if you left."

I told him I wanted to sleep on it, but the scales were heavily weighted toward staying. A promotion like that, a vote of confidence from a well-respected head coach at a major university, was a powerful incentive. Morrison was only 50 years old and the way things were going, it couldn't hurt to have my wagon hitched to his star.

Also, I had become a minor celebrity in Columbia and I would have hated to give that up. From the time I went to work at Chattanooga, I often spoke to high school kids and community groups about sports in general and football in particular. My talks were about motivation and hard work and dedication to the game, and how football is a metaphor for life and business. I felt right at home in the Columbia community, and I was reluctant to uproot my wife and put my kids through the stress of changing schools. It made sense to sit tight.

The next day I returned to Morrison's office to give him my answer: I would stay at South Carolina. He reiterated that he intended to hire me as offensive coordinator when Frank Sadler, the current coordinator, left the team.

When I called Felker at Mississippi State to thank him for the offer and explain why I decided to turn it down, he made one last pitch. "If Morrison's promising he'll promote you down the road, I don't believe he'll do it. He wants to keep you because you're so damn good. He may or may not hire you when that job comes open.

"Tank, if the promise is the only reason you want to stay, you can come work with us and he can always hire you back." The promise was important, but it wasn't the only reason, so I thanked Felker for the offer and hung up the phone. His comments were vaguely unsettling, but I couldn't imagine Morrison breaking his word.

Me and Sterling on
the sideline at a
Gamecocks scrimmage.

Coach Charlie Weiss
as a volunteer coach
at South Carolina.

Chapter 9

BLINDSIDED

OUR 1987 SEASON was a success. The team won eight and lost three during the regular season, and got to the Gator Bowl where we lost to Louisiana State. Sterling, finishing his last year, broke several records and became only the fourth player in the team's history to have his number—2—retired, and the first to have it retired while he was still a student.

Meanwhile, our offensive coordinator Frank Sadler was cruising toward disaster, only he didn't know it yet. That fall, he was sent to recruit players in the Greenville-Spartanburg area, but the university's athletic director happened to be 200 miles away in Charleston and spotted Sadler at a resort, relaxing with his wife at poolside.

When he returned to the office, Sadler's expense reimbursement request listed hotel charges for a Greenville-Spartanburg visit, not Charleston. Morrison kept his powder dry until the end of the season. Then he fired Sadler without warning, on January 9, 1988. The state's principal daily newspaper, *The State*, reported the story prominently, under a career-killer of a headline: "Problems adapting to run and shoot cost Sadler his job."

Sadler, the paper reported, was being held to account for a late-season slump by quarterback Todd Ellis that cost us several games and knocked down the Gamecocks' national ranking from eighth to fifteenth. It was an unhappy ending to a season that had been going so well. We were 7-2 before losing two of the last three games.

Sadler was said to be a mismatch with Morrison's offensive strategy, which was somewhat unorthodox and aggressive. I felt bad for Sadler, especially because he had come to South Carolina with Morrison. He had been extremely successful as an offensive coordinator over the years with Morrison from Chattanooga to New Mexico and even at South Carolina. They had a history together and Sadler no doubt thought he was a member of the family. But according to press reports, Morrison demanded Sadler's resignation, Sadler balked, and Morrison let his contract expire, in effect firing him. Sadler told *The State*, "It was a surprise to me. I don't understand it."

Bob Gillespie, one of *The State* reporters who covered the Gamecocks, interviewed me for a follow-up story that ran a week after Sadler's firing, under the headline "One Man's Disappointment, Another's Dream Fulfilled." Although I stressed to Gillespie that my replacing Sadler was a "possibility" and not yet a fact, he wrote that I was "just days away from his eagerly expected elevation to the job Sadler leaves with sadness."

Gillespie's enthusiast language made me a little nervous, but it was exciting and gratifying to be so publicly recognized for the work I loved doing. How I wished Mama had still been alive to share the experience.

Sadler put as good a public face on it as he could muster, but the press coverage was brutal. Details that emerged included the fact that Morrison had dropped the bomb on Sadler practically as the head coach was walking out the door for a flight to Hawaii, for the Hula Bowl. Reporters couldn't reach him in those pre-cell phone days, so he neatly avoided having to answer any messy questions.

Following Gillespie's article about my rosy future, Sadler retaliated by spreading a rumor that I had somehow engineered his sacking, like it was a coup. It was a ridiculous claim, but a malicious parting shot that helped poison some of my professional relationships. I always had high opinions of coach Sadler and I thought he was a hell of a football coach. I knew that he was frustrated and I did not take it personal. Coach Sadler had been very good to me. He would learn in a few days that there was no coup and I did not stab him in the back.

Meanwhile, my phone rang off the hook with congratulatory calls. "Thanks," I told everyone. "But it's not official." With all the hoopla, I hadn't heard yet from Coach Morrison.

A few days after the news broke a group of community leaders who were big fans and team supporters treated me to lunch. They'd watched what I'd accomplished with Sterling and were excited to hear what my promotion might mean for the team's performance in the future. It had been a heady year for the Gamecocks, for our players, and for me. The team had a winning season in spite of the late slump. The home games were packed with rabid fans and we gave them what they came for, a winning team.

Sterling and our quarterback, Todd Ellis, had worked so well together for most of the season that *Sports Illustrated* ran a profile of them under the headline "A Pair Extraordinaire." The writer called Ellis and Sterling "one of the most exciting passing combos in the college game." Todd Ellis was a great field general.

Although I wasn't mentioned, I was proud to read that, "Precious few colleges had even heard of Sharpe when he was growing up on his grandparents' farm near Glennville, Georgia. Those that did wanted him to be a defensive back. All except one—South Carolina."

Now he was a record-setting wide receiver, a school hero, and a Heisman Trophy finalist. He didn't win the Heisman, but there were plenty of objective observers who thought he should have. It made me feel good and gave me renewed confidence in my judgment and my ability to transform the lives of others. I was so proud of Sterling, as proud as any father could be of his son.

Sterling was on everyone's radar screen and I began to hear from more NFL scouts sizing him up in preparation for the next draft. Those same scouts were asking about my other star wide receiver, Ryan Bethea. Ryan may have been the best athlete I would ever coach. He could have been a number one draft pick. But his heart wasn't in it. He was 6-4 210lbs and ran 4.3 in the forty. He caught the ball with ease and the game just came easy to him. He was a *Parade* magazine first team high school All-American from Richland Northeast High School in Columbia.

It was telling that Sterling, who came from a poor black family, was hungry and willing to work hard and play by the rules, while Ryan, who came from a middle-class black family and for whom everything seemed to come easy, was often in trouble, smoked marijuana, skipped practices, and lacked passion. I tried my best, but he didn't have the fire. These are the intangibles that coaches often come up against when trying to get the best from an athlete. It's much more than sinew and muscle and good hand-eye coordination. Sometimes it's not meant to be, no matter how gifted the athlete and how good the person. I loved Ryan but it just was not in the cards for him.

After all this great publicity and the public endorsement of my work by Coach Morrison, some of the calls I got were from head coaches at other colleges trying to hire me away. It felt good to be pursued, but I told everybody my future was set.

The days passed and still I had no word from Coach Morrison. We were in the thick of the busy recruiting season, so I guessed that he had decided to wait to make my promotion official until after national signing day, in early February. That's the day each year when all high school athletes who have received scholarship offers from NCAA colleges have to choose where they want to study and play. Things calm down after that.

Sure enough, I finally got the call right after signing day.

Morrison wanted to see me in his office. I had an extra spring in my step as I hustled across the hall. In those moments, I thought about how I was about to make African American history, in my own small way. My status in the community would rise, and I'd be one step closer to my goal of becoming a head coach.

Although I had been in it a hundred times, I noticed with different eyes the symbols of success that decorated his enormous office: A photo of him as a young player in his New York Giants uniform; his NCAA College Coach of the Year plaque; autographed footballs; and pictures of him with famous people all over the walls.

Morrison let his tall husky body tilt back in his executive chair, lit a fresh cigarette with the butt of the one he was about to put out, crossed his thick arms, and said "Tank *if* you were the coordinator here, what would be your offensive strategy?" But instead of congratulating me, he was asking me about my offensive strategy."

The blood rushed to my head as I tried to figure out what was going on. *If* I was coordinator? And what did he expect to hear from me that he didn't know from my having worked for him for nearly six years? My strategy had evolved and been executed under his leadership. But I kept those thoughts to myself and for the next three hours reviewed every detail of our offense, giving him my personal take on the strengths and weaknesses of each of the players and coaching staff.

The meeting ended without a congratulatory handshake, and no mention of my promotion. It would have been awkward to bring it up, so I was left to try to read his mind. My analysis was solid, but it was a strange exercise to put someone through if you've already promised him the job. There was something cat-and-mouse about it that made me uneasy.

A few days later I heard through the grapevine that Morrison had interviewed another candidate. Al Groh had been head coach at Wake Forest, a school we had crushed a year earlier by 30-0.

After six years and a 26-40 record, Wake Forest fired Groh. His new job was assistant coach with the Atlanta Falcons. Getting fired as a coach is not always a disgrace. My high school coach Roy Gregory often said, "There are two kinds of coaches: those who have been fired and those who will be. It doesn't matter how good or bad they are."

He had been coaching the Falcons' tight ends. I couldn't see the match—him and offensive coordinator. Maybe it was a ruse, I thought. Maybe Morrison had to satisfy some alumnus with a connection to Groh and go through the motions of interviewing him.

One Thursday evening, a week or two after national signing day, I was at home with my family when the doorbell rang. I was surprised to find standing on my step Teddy Heffner, a sports writer from *The State* newspaper with whom I was on good terms. He had a funny look on his face as he huddled in his winter coat.

"Teddy, what's up? Come on inside. It's cold out there."

"Uh, Tank, if you don't mind I'd prefer to speak outside."

My chest tightened. What had happened? Had Sterling been hurt, or one of our players ? Had one of my players been in an accident? What was so bad that instead of calling me Teddy drove out to my house, where he'd never been before, to tell me in person? What was so bad he didn't even want to tell me in my house?

We walked into the front yard. Teddy stopped, looked at me for a long moment. "So, you haven't heard the news?"

"What news?"

He cleared his throat. "Coach Morrison just hired Al Groh as offensive coordinator."

My stomach flip-flopped. My ears began to roar. A wave of prickly heat rose up my neck.

"Are you sure, Teddy?" It was a stupid question, but I couldn't think of anything else to say. My head was spinning.

"Tank, I know how much this meant to you, and I know you turned Mississippi State down for it, but I have it from Morrison himself. Groh is gonna be your new coordinator. I'm really sorry, man. I hate to be the bearer of bad news."

I shook my head in disbelief. After the promises and the news coverage and the good wishes of friends and colleagues, how could this be happening? How could Morrison have yanked the rug out without even the basic courtesy of telling me first? Morrison had blindsided me, and what Teddy said next made the whole thing seem utterly callous. "I told him you'd quit if he didn't keep his promise. But he said you'd never quit, on account of how close you are to your players. He said you'd stay no matter what."

That was one of the worst nights of my life. I felt like a condemned man restlessly awaiting his dawn execution in the public square. Surprisingly, Morrison had not kept his promise and had left me swinging in the wind for all to see. My friends, family, colleagues, and the Gamecocks football community would all be scratching their heads trying to figure out what went wrong, so was I.

Coach Morrison was like a father to me in some ways. I was the youngest coach on the staff when I came to South Carolina (26) and the youngest one the whole time I coached there. Coach treated me with great respect and he and I had a very close relationship. He and I bet on everything for fun, usually one dollar just for bragging rights. I loved and respected Joe Morrison and at the end of the day I just believe people close to him talked him out of giving me the job. Maybe because I was young, maybe because I was black, who knows but I know in my heart Joe Morrison was a good person. Even after I resigned he and I stayed in touch and talked on a regular basis.

I am a college football fan through and through and especially a fan of the Southeastern Conference. The big debate over why black coaches do not get many major college football head coaching jobs is the same today as it was twenty years ago. It is just a very thick glass ceiling.

Mack Strong is the best of examples among many. I believe he is one of the top ten college coaches in the game. He is currently the defensive coordinator at the University of Florida. They have won two national championships in three years. Mack is great with young athletes and is an excellent role model for kids. My personal opinion is Mack has two strikes against him in this arena. One he is black and two he is married to a white woman. You would think that anyone who is the absolute best at what they do would not have to be concerned about such prejudices. College football has a long history of precluding black coaches from advancing and the progress has traveled at a snails pace for sure. This is no knock against white coaches or anyone for that matter.

The cold hard fact is that it is ridiculous that blacks dominate the game on the field yet are deemed unqualified to lead as head coaches at major universities. Hopefully Mack Strong and many others like him will get an opportunity to prove what most of us already know and that is, he is the best of the best and will bring unprecedented value to the university that has the courage and intelligence to make him the leader of their football program.

The next three months were miserable. Life went on, but it was a very different life from the one I had been living before Teddy rang my doorbell. The offensive team was busy implementing Groh's new strategy and tactics. I discovered off the bat that I had become the odd man out. Groh seemed irritated or resentful of comments or suggestions I had to offer. Then he stripped me of some of my responsibilities. The end game was clear. He wanted me out.

Having had the experience of being fired as a head coach, I'm sure he felt threatened by an underling who the press had praised and had anointed as Sadler's logical replacement. It was a toxic situation, but I did my best to grin and bear it while mulling my next move.

When spring practice ended it was time to make a decision, before the new season got started in earnest. I had coached college football nine years, six at South Carolina. Now I was up against a glass ceiling. The statistics were dismal (and remained so for many years): out of 117 NCAA College and university football teams, only four had head coaches who were black.

A coaching job in the NFL would have been an easy route for me. I had met plenty of NFL scouts who knew what I had accomplished with Sterling. I was confident I could find a good-paying job without too much effort.

But professional coaching held no appeal. College coaching was my passion, working with young athletes just coming out of high school, especially black kids. I had a lot to offer at a critical time in their lives when they're exploring the limits of their abilities, developing character, learning teamwork, and bettering themselves by getting an education.

The kids I worked with were playing because they loved football, not for a paycheck. They listened well and played hard. They were there to grow and have fun, not for the bragging rights of having an NFL logo sewn on their jerseys.

Also, nothing the NFL had to offer could compare with the sense of family you get at a school with a long athletic history, hundreds of thousands of alumni, and an army of local supporters who show up at home games 80,000 strong and raise the roof every time. There's nothing on earth louder than Williams-Brice Stadium in Columbia during a Gamecocks' football game. There's nothing quite as stirring as the sound of a brigade of drummers pumping up the stadium as the Gamecocks take the field.

Most importantly to me, there was nothing more rewarding than being a coach and seeing the affection and support of 80,000 people pour down on your players. I had been one of those players once, so I knew just how good it feels to make a great play and hear the stadium explode with approval. The Gamecocks had been my family for six years and the more I thought about it, the less appealing it was to think about starting over at another school.

From a number of sources came job offers outside of football, some of them with six-figure salaries. It made me sad to think about leaving the game behind, but I had a growing family to support. I consulted Coach Gregory, Sterling Sharpe along with others and everyone agreed that in order to move, I needed to move on.

In June of 1988, I finally threw in the towel and accepted an offer from Tony Dutt, co-owner of an insurance agency in Houston, Texas that catered to professional athletes. It was a way to stay in touch with sports and make more money than I ever had before. Dutt warned me that I'd be working long hours and spending a lot of time on the road. But I liked working hard, I'd get to meet a lot of players, and get to see a lot of the country.

On June 6, 1988, my father's birthday I walked into Coach Morrison's office with my letter of resignation in hand. "I've put a lot of thought into it and I've decided it's time for me to get out of coaching and start another occupation. I appreciate all the opportunities you've given me and I wish you and the team the best of luck."

Morrison stood up and came from behind his desk.

"Now Tank, let's just slow down here a minute, I think you might be overreacting to the changes we've been through. I know the situation isn't the easiest at times, but we need you on our staff, you are one hell of a coach. Why don't you sleep on it before you decide."

It struck me as absurd that he could imagine I'd accept things as they stood.

"I have slept on it, Coach. That's all I've been doing, sleeping on it. But I suppose one more night can't hurt."

My mind was already made up, so I went home and relaxed

with my family for the first time in months. I could turn away from the past and look toward the future.

That evening after dinner one of the team's wealthiest backers, a local businessman, phoned and asked to come by to talk. Morrison had recruited him to try to persuade me to stay. Good manners dictated I see him, even if the die was already cast.

He sat in my living room and talked to me about how important I was to the Gamecock program, and promised he would personally help me in my career. Coach Morrison just told me I was a great young coach and I needed to just be patient and I would eventually get what I wanted.

It was another absurd moment. On one hand an influential donor had taken his time to come to my house, lavish me with praise, and beg me to stay. On the other, I was being demoted and insulted. I listened, politely thanked him, and went to bed with a clear conscience.

The next morning I went straight to Morrison's office and told him my career as a college football coach was officially over. Considering how hard I had worked to get where I was, it was an unexpected relief to let it all go. I had answered the question I asked all my players: what will you do when your football career is over?

My new job in the insurance business would be a fresh start, but I sensed that bigger opportunities lay just over the horizon and I was eager to see what they were.

Me at my Gamecocks office door, 1984. I could have coached there forever. Gamecocks fans are the best!

Coach Ricky Diggs, Head Coach Joe Morrison and me after the Notre Dame victory in South Bend, October 20, 1984.

Chapter **10**

WE HAVE A PICK

STERLING FIDGETED with his glass of scotch and I perched on the edge of my seat with a soda in hand as we watched the broadcast from Madison Square Garden of the 1988 NFL draft, on April 24. We were in the living room of some friends in Columbia, Jim and Melva Boulware.

It was a big moment for each of us, but especially for Sterling who was about to learn where he would start his professional career—which team would soon be cutting him a very large check to play for them. It was an important moment for me as a coach, the ultimate payoff for years of working with him, and it came at a turning point in my career just as it came at a turning point in Sterling's.

He was the number one ranked college player in the country going into the draft that year. The Georgia farm boy who no one but the gamecock coaches took seriously had morphed into the hottest ticket in town. I was proud of him and proud to be his mentor and friend. We had done it together.

Sterling's ranking virtually guaranteed he would be among the first players picked, possibly first but certainly within the first ten or so of up to 256 top college players to be hired by draft. As a wide receiver, Sterling would be a good catch for any team, but not every team needed a wide receiver.

The draft takes place during multiple rounds over two days. Each of the thirty NFL teams is allowed to pick one player in each round. Experts prepare by poring over player statistics like Wall Street analysts and mocking up combinations of players into possible teams. Like a human chess match, there's a lot of horse-trading that goes on as teams swap picks and try to outsmart each other for the best players in the positions they need to fill.

The draft is designed to give poorer teams the same chance as rich teams to grab the most promising athletes, so rich teams can't dominate the sport the way the New York Yankees have done in baseball. It's no accident that the richest team has gotten into 40 percent of all the World Series match-ups in history, and won nearly 25 percent of them.

The other two of the three top-ranked college wide receivers in the country that year were Heisman Trophy winner Tim Brown from Notre Dame, and Michael Irvin from the University of Miami. It was a good year for receivers—all three went on to outstanding careers and Irvin became a Hall of Famer.

Sterling and I had been spending a lot of time talking about the draft, and gossiping about what was happening with the Gamecocks. My days with the team were ending, but I was still considering my options for the next step. Over time our conversations evolved into a discussion about us working together after the Gamecocks. It seemed our lives and careers were destined to remain linked.

After coaching him for four years, advocating for him with NFL scouts, and advising him through the draft process, I wasn't surprised when Sterling asked me to help him with the business side of his career. He was a hard guy to get to know, and had an aloof, cocky streak. He'd been getting a lot of advice from a lot of new people.

He loved the limelight but disliked the opportunists and groupies that came with it. "You're the only person I really trust, Coach," he said. "You know about all this contract and money stuff. I want you to handle everything for me." It was a natural extension of the partnership journey we'd been on since that day I first met him at Glennville High School five years earlier. We shook hands. I didn't know it then, but I had my first client.

The initial piece of business to tackle was getting some money in his pocket. Although players of Sterling's caliber are national celebrities by the time the April draft rolls around, the teams wait to cut their first checks until the season officially starts, in July. It can take a year from the time a top college player begins to see the pot of gold at the end of the rainbow to the day he cashes his first check.

This gap—so close but so far away—frustrates many college athletes, but none more so than those with backgrounds like Sterling's or mine. Patience is a lot to ask of a 21-year-old who spent many hours of his childhood hoeing onions under a hot Georgia sun. It's asking a lot of a son to be patient when his mother can't make the mortgage payment; or his brother's car died and he needs a new one to keep his job; or he's just eager to spoil his loved ones, as I was when I gave Mama most of my $5,000 signing bonus from the Atlanta Falcons.

NCAA rules prohibit high school and college players from accepting money or gifts, even if a good-hearted team booster wants to help a kid out with a used car or some extra pocket money. The idea is that in exchange for a free college education, free room and board, free professional coaching and mentoring, frequent travel, and all the other advantages, the college or university gets the services of the player that they can make money on by selling tickets and team merchandise, attracting alumni donations, and getting the school a boat load of free publicity.

It's a fair trade, in theory. It's a great bargain if you're a middling player who gets all the benefits but sits out most of the games. It doesn't feel so good when you're a star and you know that plenty of NFL teams are lining up for the chance to pay you millions to do what you've been doing for room, board, and an education.

This disparity between what they're worth and what they're paid gets a lot of promising college players, recruiters, agents, and so on in all kinds of trouble. The problem is that it's difficult to detect improper payments when it takes the form of paying the rent or buying a car or funding a wedding for the relative of a player. The rules are hard to enforce. Violations are usually discovered when some student who used to drive a beater car shows up in a sporty new convertible, or does something else equally obvious.

The prohibition ends once a college player has finished his last season. At the end of his last season, Sterling asked me to help him borrow against his expected signing bonus to buy his sister Libby a car and a very expensive BMW M3 for himself.

We went to meet the manager of my bank Tommy Bone and he arranged for the car loans and a $25,000 cash credit line. Two months before the draft, he'd maxed out the credit line, and needed another advance.

I was certain the bank would raise his credit limit. Sterling was a safe bet. But for some reason he didn't want to ask the bank. Instead, he wanted to borrow it from me. I had about $85,000 in investments and savings, so I cashed in enough to lend Sterling $25,000.

By the time we found ourselves in front of a television watching the 1988 draft, I was managing Sterling's career and deeply involved in the chess game. I couldn't represent him as an agent because the rules at the time required a law degree, so I hired an attorney named Rick Mostak to negotiate Sterling's first NFL contract.

The Tampa Bay Buccaneers had drawn the fourth pick in the first round. They'd lost all of their last eight games of the 1987 season, a crazy year that had been marred by a player strike, and they needed a good receiver.

Ray Perkins, Tampa's head coach, had called Sterling a couple of hours before the draft to express the hope that he would be "wearing a Tampa Bay jersey for many years." We assumed Sterling would be the first receiver drafted, and Tampa would get him. I guessed that receiver Tim Brown would go to the Oakland Raiders, which had the sixth pick, because Raiders owner Al Davis liked Heisman Trophy winners. The Green Bay Packers, with the seventh pick, would probably take Michael Irvin.

But the draft is not an exact science so Sterling and I were glued to the tv set as the NFL Commissioner Pete Rozelle began the process. There was a lot of history in the making that day, more than any of us knew at the time.

Our hosts were Jim and Melva Boulware, I had known Jim and Melva since I came to Columbia. In one of the those improbable-but-true twists of fate, watching with us that day in 1988 were their sons, twelve-year-old Peter and five-year-old Michael, mesmerized by Sterling and the atmosphere of drama.

Nine years later, I would be back in that same living room with the Boulwares, watching the 1997 NFL draft as Peter became the number four pick, by the Baltimore Ravens, as a linebacker. And seven years later, his younger brother Michael was drafted by the Seattle Seahawks. Sterling's younger brother Shannon would also become a notable NFL player. Looking back on it, the Boulware's living room was sort of a Big Bang event in football.

The first three picks that day were all defensive players. Then Rozelle stood at the podium and announced, "With the fourth pick of the 1988 NFL Draft the Tampa Bay Buccaneers select Paul Gruber, offensive tackle from Wisconsin."

Sterling's head jerked as he shouted, "What the hell?" Jim Boulware poured Sterling a fresh glass of scotch. What had happened to "wearing a Tampa Bay jersey for many years"?

Just then the phone rang. Jim answered and called out, "Tank, it's for you."

"Tank, hey, it's Tom Braatz." I knew Tom because he was general manager of the Atlanta Falcons and he signed me to my contract with the Falcons in 1979. Now he was the General

Manager of the Green Bay Packers, a team that had shown a lot of interest in Sterling. The Packer's receivers coach Buddy Geis worked Sterling out on campus and loved him. Green Bay had been the home of the legendary Vince Lombardi but the team had been struggling for years and had just completed two losing seasons in a row, one of them by a dismal 4-12. I could hear the draft broadcast in the background at the other end of the line.

Braatz said, "put Sterling on the line and tell him to wait until we get to our pick at number seven. Cincinnati is number five and they're taking a defensive back. Oakland is six, and they're taking Tim Brown. We're gonna draft Sterling seven." And that was exactly how it happened.

But the moment lacked the feeling of celebration. I was exhausted from the anxiety of it all, my first NFL draft as an interested party and glad it was over. Sterling's enthusiasm was dampened because he was already living in warm, sunny Tampa in his mind, relatively close to his hometown. And he was miffed that he wasn't the first receiver chosen. Instead of grinning with pleasure that his career was finally beginning, he was scowling.

Sterling was on the phone all afternoon, talking with his family and friends, his lawyer, and so on. He also sat for an interview with *The State*. I went out very early the next morning to get a copy of the paper from a machine in front of the newspaper office. I sat in the car and read. Sterling was a good student, intelligent and well-spoken. Among the many players I had worked with over the years, he was intellectually far above average. But he had a tendency toward narcissism and I found myself wincing at some of his reported comments.

He was quoted talking mostly about money, nothing about looking forward to playing for Green Bay or getting to know the people there. Just, "Hopefully, I'll make enough money to buy a coat." That one sounded doubly ungracious to me, especially combined with his statement that he intended to spend his off-season in South Carolina, not Green Bay. The rest of his comments just sounded bad.

> *"I hope to sign soon," he said. "I don't like negative publicity hanging over me going into camp. I hope it will all go smoothly and I will get paid what I'm worth. I don't want to be the highest paid wide receiver ever. I just want to get paid what I'm worth."*
>
> *Sharpe wouldn't put a number on his worth, but he did say he expected a salary along the same line of what Notre Dame's Tim Brown would receive. The Heisman Trophy winner was the first wide receiver taken, going to the Los Angeles Raiders with the sixth pick.*
>
> *"The pros made a mistake, saying Tim and I were about the same," Sharpe said with a big smile. "I want to make at least what he makes. If not, I don't want to be too far off."*
>
> *"They've got some good wide receivers. I don't want to try to start. I want to drop my first 30 passes so the guys don't think I'm after their job."*

For their part, the Green Bay folks were generous in their praise. Packers head coach Lindy Infante told the press that Sterling "is a potential point-scorer any time he touches the ball. You can't throw it into the end zone all the time. You've got to have guys who will catch it and take it there. I've seen enough of this guy to know if we can get the ball into his hands, he's a threat to go the distance."

Sterling flew to Green Bay the next morning. Before he left I advised him to try to tone down the language and forget all of that first-receiver-picked business. "You already see in the local paper how the press can turn everything you say into something negative. You just brag on the Packers, and thank them for selecting you."

He had his first press conference right off the plane, and said all of the right things. But I knew that what was on his lips was not in his heart.

A few days after the draft, I arranged for Sterling to spend a couple of hours with a troubled seventh grader whose teacher had contacted the Gamecocks. She was at her wits end to find a way to motivate this boy and thought it might inspire him to meet a famous, successful athlete.

I volunteered Sterling hoping he'd find some inspiration in the experience as well. I couldn't see how anyone in his shoes could be untouched by the hero worship he'd see in that kid's eyes.

Sterling took the boy for a ride in his new BMW, and gave him and his teacher each an autographed photo. One of the local newspaper columnists wrote about it a few days later. I'm sure that youngster never forgot the experience, and kept that picture in a special place.

But Sterling was unmoved. Not only was he disinterested in being a role model, he actually resisted it. "Why should I, for some kid I don't even know?" he argued. "Their Mom, Dad, teacher, or whoever like that should be their role model." It was a strange thing to hear from a guy who grew up without a male role model.

"Sterling, you've got to understand that the uniform you wear, because of who you are, automatically makes you a role model. Especially for black kids who need role models." It was inconceivable to me that he could be so cold about it. I tried to get him to join me in coaching some grass-cutter kids, the beginner's league where I got my start. I loved working with kids and never stopped coaching the little guys in my spare time. I loved it but Sterling wanted no part of that.

We remained friends throughout his professional career, but I could never understand Sterling's disdain for football fans and neither could the fans. In the years ahead he would earn a deserved reputation as a player who refused to sign autographs for kids. He would also become known for an ego on the field that sometimes rubbed people the wrong way, none more so than his quarterback, a young man with a golden arm named Brett Favre.

Sterling Sharpe at the Pro Bowl in Honolulu, Hawaii in 1990.
The Tampa Bay Buccaneers should have selected him in the
1988 NFL Draft. Sterling is as good as any receiver who ever played.
He belongs in the NFL Hall of Fame.

Chapter 11

BARRY'S FUTURE IS OUR FUTURE

THE SEEDS OF MY CAREER as an NFL agent were planted during a period of civil war in professional football. The 1987 season, before the Packers drafted Sterling, the NFL Players Association—the players union—had called a strike when negotiations for a new contract with the NFL broke down over demands that players be granted the right to become free agents.

This was a long-standing grievance—the way player contracts were written, a team could prevent a player whose contract had expired from signing with another team, leaving him in limbo. It was blatantly anti-competitive but the owners had dug in their heels, also rejecting demands that players get a bigger share of football's growing revenue.

The professionals initially honored the strike and refused to play, causing the cancellation of one week of the season. Then the owners tried to rescue the season and starve the union by fielding teams made up on players cut during training camp, plus a few veterans who refused to honor the picket lines. The public was turned off by what was perceived as player greed, and disgusted by team owners trying to foist on fans bush-league teams playing bush-league football. Replacement-player teams got mock names, like the San Francisco Phoney-Niners, New Orleans

Saint Elsewheres, and Seattle Sea-Scabs. Attendance plunged and television audiences quit watching.

In the end, the players blinked. The union had no strike fund so before long the pros started going back to work. They had to make a living and risked losing their pensions and other benefits. By the time that crazy season ended, the players had returned to work having won nothing but a defunct, toothless union that was formally decertified. It would take several years of litigation for the NFLPA to get back on its feet and resume collective bargaining.

In June 1988, on the heels of the strike, I left the Gamecocks and went to work selling disability and life insurance to professional footballers with Tony Dutt, who operated an agency out of Houston, Texas. He and his partner, Ron Kocian, agreed to add my name to theirs on the company's letterhead. So I became a partner in Kocian, Dutt and Black.

I'd met Tony when he came to South Carolina selling policies to our players, including Sterling. The premiums for this type of insurance were steep, about $25,000 for a million dollars of coverage, payable in the event of a career-ending injury. Many of the players who bought this insurance were juniors who were already high on the list of those likely to wind up being drafted their senior years.

The commissions for selling the insurance were high as well, because the payout risk was low. In my years selling career-ending disability insurance only two players collected—Sterling suffered a neck injury in 1994, and another player was injured in a car wreck. The only way the policy wouldn't pay was if the injury was self-inflicted or connected with a crime.

There aren't many college juniors who can get their hands on $25,000, so they usually ended up borrowing the money from a bank. It's a low risk loan because either way he's likely to have the money to repay it: if he's injured he collects, and if he's drafted he gets his signing bonus. Local banks in the communities where the players attend college like making these loans because of the public relations value and the chances the player will do all his banking with them once he's been hired.

Tony Dutt was one of very few insurance agents that focused on professional athletes, and the disability policy was popular as a safety net. Once they became professional players, we would also offer them life insurance.

In the year or so that I worked with Dutt I was on the road six out of seven days a week, sold a lot of insurance, made a lot of money, met hundreds of top athletes and coaches in basketball and football, and learned the sports business from the inside out. Because we were selling insurance and not acting as player agents, we could talk to players anytime during their college careers. Agents, prohibited by the rules from contacting players before they finished their last college season, would call us to help them get in good with the hot prospects when they were eligible to sign. I helped a number of agents with whom I would later compete.

My business plan was to let the agents be agents and concentrate on the business of managing players' lives, helping them budget their income, make sure they paid their taxes, pay their monthly bills, handle their travel needs, and negotiate major purchases like cars. Some agents offered those services as well, but few were any good at it. Their bread and butter was negotiating million-dollar contracts, not getting their client the best deal on a Mercedes.

Just as my background helped me recruit and coach black players like Sterling, I knew I'd have an advantage over my white partners selling to black players and their families. I knew they would be more comfortable doing business with someone who shared their cultural experiences. It had little or nothing to do with racial prejudice. It seemed to me the same as Mormons choosing to do business with Mormons, or the preferences of any other affinity group.

But the race issue in football was a constant subtext for African-Americans. If you're not black, you wouldn't notice it. After all, there have been plenty of black players on the field for years. But behind the scenes the game and the business is still dominated by whites while blacks continue to do the heavy lifting. It wasn't until 1988 that the first African-American was appointed as an NFL referee. It wasn't until 1989 that a black man, Art Shell, became the head coach of an NFL team, the Oakland Raiders. And he only got the job after twenty years with the Raiders, fourteen as a player and six as a coach.

The future continues to look brighter, but it must be said that black NFL players and coaches have long felt they have to meet higher standards to achieve the same success as whites. It's worth recalling that Rush Limbaugh was forced off an ESPN sports show in 2003 after he complained that Philadelphia Eagles quarterback Donovan McNabb "got a lot of credit for the performance of this team that he didn't deserve," because "The media has been very desirous that a black quarterback do well."

In 1988 I was one of very few African-Americans offering services to black professional athletes. This gave me a big leg up, as I discovered when I flew to Wichita that fall to meet the father of Barry Sanders, an outstanding running back from Oklahoma State.

The Wichita trip was my first big test in the insurance business. Sanders was an All-American, having a phenomenal season, and on the short list for the Heisman Trophy. Word was going around that he intended to forego his senior year and declare himself eligible for the 1989 draft. I had arranged a meeting with his father, Willie, who was handling his son's business affairs.

I knew something about Barry from my early coaching days at South Carolina. We were to face Nebraska again during the 1987 season. We had played them in 1986 and we were breaking down film from all of their 1986 games. Our defensive line coach Jim Washburn wanted to show me the play of a tailback named

Thurman Thomas who went on to play for the Buffalo Bills and became an NFL Hall of Famer.

Washburn said this guy Thurman is really good but sometimes this other guy number 20 comes in for Thurman and he seems even better. That number 20 was a freshman named Barry Sanders. I have no doubt I was the only person selling insurance who could say to Barry's father that I had studied his son's films.

Mr. Sanders had asked me to meet him at a pancake place at eight o'clock in the evening. I flew from Charlotte, North Carolina and, as was my habit, arrived early. Willie Sanders showed up right on time, wearing a black shirt, well-worn jeans, and cowboy boots with an unlit cigar clenched in his teeth. He looked me right in the eye, unsmiling, as we shook hands. He was all business.

Mr. Sanders ordered a huge meal—scrambled eggs with cheese, grits, T-bone steak, hash browns, the works. I wasn't hungry but I felt compelled to do the same. For the next hour or so I told Mr. Sanders my story, from my school days in Tennessee all the way up to leaving the Gamecocks.

Then it was his turn. He talked for several hours about how he and his wife had raised their children. Mr. Sanders owned his own roofing and carpentry company, and Barry and two brothers worked as his assistants as soon as they could handle tools.

"I'll never forget when Barry came home from school one day and said a boy in his class got an allowance from his parents, for doing nothing. My boys never got a cent they didn't sweat for. Even in college Barry had a part time job at a supermarket paying minimum wage.

"I taught my kids to respect their elders, work for everything they get, study the Bible and go to church, and keep their complaints to themselves. In high school when his friends were out partying on Friday and Saturday nights, Barry was running the stadium stairs. So you see, Tank, Barry's future is the future of our family."

As he talked I realized that Mr. Sanders was a "real" black man—he had lived through all of the hard times of segregation and discrimination and never forgot what that was like.

As much as I enjoyed chewing the fat with him, I wanted to meet the star of the show. I'd only spoken to Barry once on the phone. "I'm a little concerned Mr. Sanders, that I haven't met Barry face-to-face, or more importantly I should say Barry hasn't met me face-to-face. I want to be sure he's comfortable with me."

Mr. Sanders pointed his cigar at me and said, "Tank, I wear the big boy pants in my house and Barry isn't gonna make these decisions, I am. He wanted to play professional basketball but I told him he'd better stick to football because there are more scholarships. So you don't have to be concerned with meeting Barry. I'll tell him all about you and it'll be just fine."

This was a phenomenon I would run into often over the years, never more so than when I became the agent for Vince Carter, the Toronto Raptors basketball star. Carter's mother Michelle dominated Vince and ran his career. I've seen the best of behavior in parents—those who never ask their sons for a nickel and are grateful for anything they receive.

When it's bad, it's usually because there's a parent who cares more about the money and the proximity to fame than anything else. Vince's mother was the worst. Mr. Sanders was a man that I admired because of his strong work ethic and for being a strong father figure and husband to his family.

We sat in that pancake house booth for about six hours and even then Mr. Sanders showed no sign he was running out of steam. He lit and relit his cigar dozens of times.

Finally he sighed. "You're probably tired and I need to get home. We're all set here. Barry's insurance will all go through you. Now maybe you can help me with one more thing. Do you have a really good black agent you can recommend? I didn't raise my son his whole life to turn him over to some white people and let them run his life."

I understood perfectly where he was coming from. He said he had heard from white agents who bragged about how well they knew all the owners, how they played golf with them, and so on.

"That's the worst thing for a player, if the agent and owner are that close," he said. "I'm looking for somebody honest, somebody I can talk with and go to church with. I just feel more comfortable with blacks. Some people might say that's prejudice, but it's not. "Hell, White kids don't sign with black agents so why should ours sign with white agents?"

As it turned out, I did know a good black agent, an Atlanta-based lawyer named David Ware who represented a number of high profile players. I recommended David Ware to Barry' s father and Mr. Sanders told me right then and there that if I felt David was the right agent for Barry then Barry would sign with him. Barry's father wanted to meet David and I set the meeting for a couple of weeks later. Barry's younger brother Byron was being represented by Lamont Smith. Mr. Sanders wanted Lamont to be able to share in representing Barry as a favor for him working with Byron but only on paper and only at a distance. I called David Ware and told him that I had met with Barry Sanders father and he had agreed to let David do the contract negotiations for Barry. David could not believe it. "You're telling me that it is a done deal and all I have to do is show up and sign Barry. Tank you might be in the wrong business!"He could not believe that the deal could be done without him meeting Barry or Mr. Sanders.

Barry won the Heisman Trophy that December 1988, declared himself eligible for the NFL draft in January 1989, and signed with David Ware as his agent. He was the number three draft pick, by the Detroit Lions. David became the first black agent to sign a Heisman winner.

The 1989 draft was another big turning point for me. Of the top six draftees that year, three of them were clients: Barry, Derrick Thomas, and Broderick Thomas (unrelated). Barry Sanders remained my insurance client throughout his career, and as I got to know him I found him one of the most likeable players I'd ever met or worked with. He was humble with a gentle soul, even after he'd become a superstar. He came to visit me in Columbia once and I brought him with me to my weekly Bible study group. I introduced him by first name only and it wasn't until we were about to leave that one of the other participants asked if he was THAT Barry Sanders. He never traded on his fame.

Barry had an amazing career, culminating with his election to the Pro Football Hall of Fame. *Sports Illustrated* once described him as "indestructible." But he is also remembered for a shocking decision. In 1999, with four years to go on a $35 million contract, he suddenly announced he was quitting, and he did it in an odd way—he faxed a letter to his hometown newspaper. There'd been rumors, but the Lions learned it officially from the press.

The team begged him to stay and offered him more money. David Ware, myself, and others talked to Barry about it. He was only one season away from becoming the all-time leading rusher in the history of the NFL.

But none of that seemed to matter to him anymore. He told me once he'd grown tired of taking all the hits and carrying the load for the whole franchise, and the team only got into the playoffs once in his nine years. But there was something else he mentioned on numerous occasions that may have had more to do with his decision than anything else. Not long before he quit he had been invited to play in a golf tournament in Texas with one of his idols, Hall of Famer Earl Campbell, a retired running back for the Houston Oilers.

Barry came home from the tournament deeply disturbed to find that Campbell had been so badly injured during his career that he could barely walk, not even enough to play golf. Barry mentioned it more than once. I realize that he had decided the chance to rack up more records wasn't worth the risk of ending up like Campbell, crippled and middle aged. I was convinced he had chosen to preserve his health over the chance to rack up any more records.

Barry Sanders had learned something that few players learn while they are still playing "There's more to life than football."

Coach Jim Washburn, the games best defensive line coach, pictured here at South Carolina in 1984.

Barry Sanders and me at Sterling's Camp, Columbia, South Carolina, 1991.

Chapter **12**

JUST THROW IT to NO. 84

"**W**HO DOES THIS GUY Tank Black think he is?"

Terry Bradshaw was ranting on Fox's new "NFL Sunday" show in September 1994. "He's been holding Sterling Sharpe out before the season and now he says he might not play in the first game. That's gonna hurt Sterling and it's really gonna hurt the Packers."

It was the first time my name had come up in a national sports story but it wasn't the way I would have preferred. Sterling and I were on the receiving end of a torrent of outrage in the press and among the public that portrayed the Packers' star wide receiver and my marquee client as a greedy, selfish athlete prepared to betray his team and fans of six years for a few extra bucks. There was plenty of truth to it, but the real story was much more complicated.

Sterling and I had been working together for almost a decade, from the time I met him at Glennville High School to the peak of his career in the fall of 1994. Until 1993, when the NFL Players Association and the league finally agreed on a new contract, my business had been confined to managing the monthly budgets, purchases and personal affairs of top NFL players like Sterling. Until then, you had to be a lawyer to act as a player's agent.

The new rules adopted in 1993 loosened the requirements and allowed me to add agent to my list of services. This meant I could negotiate for players with their teams. There was less car shopping and more discussing big-money salary issues with team owners, and endorsement deals. The Players Association controlled who could and could not be an agent, and set the commission rate at four percent. Once I got my agent certification, Sterling became my first client.

By that time he had established an astonishing record of consistent success. He led the NFL in receptions in three of his first five years with the Packers. Sterling Sharpe deserves to be elected to the Pro Football Hall of fame based on his on the field accomplishments. His numbers are comparable or better than any receivers currently selected to the Hall of Fame.

In 1992 Sterling caught 107 passes which broke the NFL's single season receptions record set by Art Monk in 1984. That season Sterling became one of only seven players in NFL history to win the "Triple Crown" at the receiver position: leading the league in receiving yards, receiving touchdowns and receptions. A year later in 1993 Sterling broke his own record with 112 receptions. This made Sterling the first player in NFL history with consecutive seasons catching 100 or more passes.

In 1994, Sterling's last season in the league his 18 touchdown receptions were the second most in league history at the time behind only Jerry Rice. Sterling played seven seasons before suffering his career ending neck injury. He was named All-Pro in 1989, 1990, 1992, 1993, and his last year in 1994. I would challenge anyone to find a receiver currently in the NFL Hall of Fame with better numbers than Sterling Sharpe. Maybe Jerry Rice, Maybe. Yes, Sterling has rubbed a lot of people the wrong way, me included and he can be a real asshole in many situations but the Hall of Fame is about on the field accomplishments. Sterling Sharpe laid his heart on the field of play and was simply the best of the best the league has ever seen.

The NFL Hall of Fame is simply a fan club, if they are not going to elect the greatest performers on the field. It will always be grossly incomplete without Sterling Sharpe. Sterling was inducted into the Green Bay Packers Hall of Fame in 2002.

So Sterling was the star of the Packers show in 1992 when the team made a trade with the Atlanta Falcons that brought them a promising 25-year-old quarterback from the University of Southern Mississippi named Brett Favre. The word at the time was that Favre had been doing a little too much partying and drinking and when the Falcons had run out of patience with his behavior, they decided to make him somebody else's problem.

When Favre arrived, the Packers' leading quarterback was Don "Majik Man" Majkowski. The team had been struggling with the quarterback position for years and Majkowski had looked like he would be the team's salvation when he turned in a stellar 1989 season. But he was injured the following year, sat out 1991, and was injured again in the middle of a game against Cincinnati early in the 1992 season. The Packers were losing badly as a result of a series of pass interceptions and left for dead. Head Coach Mike Holmgren sent Favre in to replace Majkowski.

Packer's lore has it that Holmgren told Favre, "Just throw the ball to Sterling. He'll catch it and run with it." Favre, the new kid, asked what he should do if Sterling wasn't open. Holmgren said "Throw it to number 84".

The start was horrible for Brett as he fumbled four times during the course of the game. It was so bad that the crowd began to chant for back up quarterback Ty Detmer to replace Favre. Down 23-17 with just over a minute left in the game with the Packers on their own 8 yard line, Brett Favre completed a 42 yard pass to Sterling Sharpe. Three plays later Favre threw the game winning touchdown pass in the right hand corner of the end zone to Kitrick Taylor.

The legend of Brett Favre was born that day. Overnight he became the hero and the toast of the town, the new starting quarterback for the Green Bay Packers.

That day began a three year love-hate relationship between Sterling and Brett that produced a lot of big plays and touchdowns and also a lot of tension. Sterling, whose haughty attitude was always a problem, was the first team All-Pro Packers veteran and he was having to share the stage with the new kid on the block.

Sterling hated that Brett spread the ball around among all the receivers. He'd scream at Brett when a play failed or he had some other criticism to make, even in the middle of the huddle. In the beginning Brett didn't say much but his body language —turning his back to Sterling—showed how irritated he was.

As Brett became more confident in his role as quarterback and leader of the team, it became easier for him to shrug Sterling off. But there was always a lot of friction and power games between the two, virtually all of it was provoked by Sterling. Sterling wanted the ball and he wanted it pretty much all of the time.

After his first full season with the Packers, the team agreed to renegotiate Brett's contract, making him their highest paid player. This drove Sterling over the edge. He called me to tell me he had complained to head coach Holmgren and Mike Reinfeldt, the Packers' VP of Administration, and won a promise that they would rewrite his contract before the season started and he wanted to be earning more than Brett.

The Packers needed Sterling more than Sterling needed the Packers, but Reinfeldt, who'd played safety for the Houston Oilers before earning an MBA and becoming Chief Financial Officer of the LA Raiders, had been hired by the Packers to turn around the team's anemic financial condition. He was doing it with a sharp pencil and some stalling tactics which are a necessity in dealing with the fresh new NFL salary cap. Mike Reinfelt was and still is as good a team financial officer as there is. He is very intelligent, hard working and honest.

It was always my aim to resolve contracts well before the start of training camp and definitely before the start of the season, to avoid hard feelings or misunderstandings interfering with a player's performance. I called Reinfeldt to move the process forward.

"Training camp is going to start soon. Let's make sure we get on this contract business because if the season gets close and I don't have a new contract, Sterling's gonna be unhappy with me and you, and we're both gonna hear about it."

Reinfeldt sounded like he was on board, but the weeks passed without an offer. When I called to remind him he asked if we could wait on the contract until after the season got started. It was the first year of a new NFL rule setting a maximum pool of money, known as a salary cap, that a team could pay for all its players. The cap that year was $34.6 million, and teams that violated or circumvented it could be fined and forced to cancel contracts. It was new territory and all the league's financial managers were learning how to massage their rosters and their budgets to stay inside the boundaries. As a result everything was taking longer.

I understood all that, but I told Reinfeldt, "I consider you a friend and I know you're on the up-and-up, but I can't ask Sterling to wait after you've promised him that we're going to get this done on time." Sterling was in no mood to compromise and it was my job to represent that to the team.

He and I talked about it and I got him to agree to a show of good faith by going to practice, to avoid any negative gossip in the press, or anxiety on the team, while we sorted things out. But still there was no offer.

Finally, Sterling insisted that I lower the boom. I called Reinfeldt and gave him ten days to get the new contract done. "If we don't, I'm going to pull Sterling out of practice and he's not going to play until we do. It doesn't make sense for me to have him in there and practice all those plays when you can practice someone else and get them ready."

"Jesus, Tank. You can't be serious. We'll work this out, I promise. I just need a little more time."

My threat was bold, but I was a Christian holding four aces. Not only did the Packers need to keep Sterling happy, but their next-in-line wide receiver, Robert Brooks, was also my client and, like Sterling, someone I had recruited for South Carolina. The Packers needed to keep me happy, too.

"You gotta know Sterling's not bluffing, Mike," I said. "I'm just telling you the truth."

Two weeks before the first game of the season against the Vikings, I flew to Green Bay to talk to Sterling and try to fix the situation. He'd been showing up to practice, working hard, but we were getting nothing out of the Packers to suggest any progress. I arranged a sit-down with Reinfeldt on a Friday and threw down the gauntlet.

"Monday morning Sterling's not going to be at practice. I'm giving you a head's up so you can be ready to speak to the press about it. We're not going to talk to the press other than to say it's between Sterling and the Packers and we're sure it'll be worked out. That'll be our only comment."

"I understand, Tank. I appreciate you letting me know and I'm sorry it's gotten to this point, but there are other considerations." We shook hands and agreed to keep meeting.

Monday morning Sterling didn't show at practice and the story broke nationally, with Sterling getting the worst end of the press as the greedy, selfish player. This is one time Sterling did not deserve the negative publicity. The stories ignored the obvious hypocrisy, that when a team withholds a promised contract it is called a dispute but if the player then doesn't show up to work it's called a holdout.

There were two weeks left before the first game against the Vikings, and Sterling stayed out of practice the whole time. The second week, Reinfeldt and I began talking about details of a new contract but by the time Friday, September 2, rolled around, the deal wasn't done.

I let Reinfeldt know that Sterling would refuse to play

that Sunday. "I'm going to put Sterling on a plane with me tomorrow and we're going to go down to Columbia to go to the Georgia-South Carolina game Saturday night. If you watch it on tv you'll see us in the press box. Good luck on Sunday. I hope you win."

"Damn!" was about all Reinfeldt said.

Sterling and I packed our bags and headed out to the airport the next morning, reading the press accounts. *The Milwaukee Journal* reported:

> STERLING SHARPE has walked out on the Green Bay Packers and will not play in the team's opening game against the Minnesota Vikings at Lambeau Field Sunday...General manager Ron Wolf said weeklong negotiations with agent William 'Tank' Black had broken down.
>
> "We are announcing today that the Packers' efforts to satisfy Sterling Sharpe's contract demands have reached an impasse," Wolf said. "Contrary to reports that have recently circulated, the Packers have not reneged on any promises made to either Sterling or his representative. Under his existing contract, which runs through 2000, Sterling is receiving compensation befitting both his talent and stature as one of the premier offensive performers in the National Football League.
>
> "Coach Holmgren and his staff are preparing to play Sunday and the remainder of the 1994 season without Sterling Sharpe."
>
> Sharpe, 29, will miss his first game in six years. Also, Sharpe will forfeit one-seventeenth of his $1.3 million base salary, or $76,471. His cap salary of $1.990 million in '94 includes likely-to-be-earned incentives of about $600,000.
>
> Black intimated this week that Sharpe was irked because other wide receivers in the league had surpassed his compensation, and four of his teammates now had higher average salaries than him.

Once again, Sterling's focus on money was causing him terrible press deserved or not, and it wasn't helping me much, as demonstrated by Terry Bradshaw's ridiculous comments on "NFL Sunday."

We were sitting in the airport waiting for our flight to board when my cell phone rang. It was Reinfeldt.

"Look, have you got on the plane yet?"

"I answered my phone, didn't I?"

"Tank, look, this just can't happen, all right? I promise that if you come over here now, we'll work all day and stay up all night if we have to and get this done."

I was wary of a ploy. "Mike, don't be putting me through this just to stop us from getting on this plane. If Sterling misses one game it's not going to hurt." That wasn't true, of course. It was the big inter conference game against the Vikings and the Packers needed their best players on the field.

"Please, Tank, let's try to knock this out now."

So we left the airport, and Sterling went to the apartment he kept in Green Bay while I sat down with Reinfeldt in his office. It was clear the team was dead serious about fixing the problem.

We were still working at dinner time when I told him I needed to take a break to visit some of my clients on the Vikings. I went to their hotel and hung out for a while with running back Terry Allen and linebacker Ed McDaniel. Sterling's threat was topic A.

"Man, we already know Sterling is gonna play," Terry said.

"We'll see," I was careful not to give any clues.

"There's no way he's gonna be in town Saturday night and not play on Sunday. If he wasn't gonna play, you wouldn't even be here! You'd be gone!"

Terry was right, of course. I spent about an hour with him and returned to the talks with Mike Reinfeldt. It took us almost all night but we got it done. That Sunday, with the stands packed and the newspapers and the television commentators all reporting that Sterling would not play, the announcer at the stadium read off the starting lineup, announcing Sterling's name with a flourish at the end. The fans roared.

Sterling gave the hometown folks a great show, redeeming himself by catching the only touchdown for a 16-10 Packers win. With Packers VP Mike Reinfeldt, I watched from the press box quietly counting my blessings and feeling my oats—I had four of my favorite players in one game: Green Bay wide receivers Sterling Sharpe and Robert Brooks (who would one day make it to the Super Bowl); and Vikings running back Terry Allen and linebacker Ed McDaniel.

Sterling's victory would prove to be the high water mark of his career as a player and his reputation in Green Bay.

"On the verge of extreme selfishness…[Sterling] chose greatness," a sports reporter wrote in the *Milwaukee Journal*. "It made for the most frantic Opening Eve in Packer history." While the writer complimented Sterling for showing up, there was plenty in the article to make me squirm and remind me of what I found troubling about Sterling's attitude.

> For most of the day, much of Wisconsin had the record-setting wide receiver figured for a greedy lug. From the talk shows to the backyards, people were trashing Sharpe. Now he can return to his rightful position as a star on the field. Hey, Sterling, we take it all back. Well, we take most of it back.
>
> Sure, he was maximizing his leverage, but it was not exactly his best moment as a team guy. The first reaction to the news that he would not play was…utter, all-encompassing disbelief. This sort of thing just doesn't happen with a player of this stature. The second reaction is anger. There was too much at stake for this player, or any player, to pull a stunt like this.
>
> The team owes Sharpe some money, but he owes the rest of the guys something, too. In a perfect world, a guy in this situation might even consider some loyalty to the fans, who, when all is said and done, pay his salary. Wisconsin fans, who displayed patience and devotion and a willingness to keep paying for their tickets through a quarter century of disappointment, have suffered a long time to get to a season

such as this one. Now it's here and the notion that the biggest star on the team was walking had to be galling.

He is a great football player. He is tough and talented. He makes plays where none exist. He plays with pain. It doesn't matter how many people the other guys put on him, he still catches passes.

This was far from a selfless episode, but it apparently won't end in disaster.

This would also prove to be the high-water mark in my relationship with Sterling. I had treated him like a son from the beginning. He even lived in my home off season for two years after he signed his million-dollar contract with the Packers. He ate most of his meals at my kitchen table. He was family.

But as my business began to grow, Sterling became jealous of my time and attention. In the beginning I might be able to make it up to Green Bay for seven or eight games, but as time went on, I couldn't manage to make more than a couple.

One of the big turning points involved a young lady named Valerie Pringle who he'd gotten pregnant when he was in college. Much like the girl I had gotten pregnant when I was young, this girl had kept it a secret until several years later, until he signed his first professional contract. Then she showed up, there was a DNA test, and it was established that Sterling was the father of this boy. The boy Brooks Antuan Sharpe was about four-years-old at this time.

Sterling felt like he was being shaken down and he refused to help her. I sat him down and tried to get him to see the bigger picture.

"This is a little child we're talking about. We're not talking about a feud between a woman and a man. We're talking about a child that needs care and needs a mother and a father. Let me talk to her and negotiate with her, and I'll see what she wants, and I'll get it settled."

The mother said nothing to suggest she intended to go to the press. She just wanted some support for raising the boy.

"I know you think I'm here for the benefit of Sterling but I'm just here to make sure that whatever this child needs, this child has. That's the only thing that matters." This was the lesson I had learned from Mama when I thought I was a father out of wedlock.

The state law in South Carolina required fathers to pay up to $1,500 a month in support, so that's what we offered her. She also wanted back child support but Sterling was having none of that.

"It was her decision to not tell me," he argued. "Why should she get support now?"

In the end we did paid for her insurance, back child support, ongoing child support, medical expenses, and so on. But Sterling wanted nothing to do with his son Antuan. He didn't even want to meet him, which struck me as incomprehensibly cruel for a man who, like me, had grown up without a father.

I met the boy and he seemed like a great kid who would have benefited so much from having an engaged father like Sterling as a role model. As he got older, one of the saddest things I learned was that he knew Sterling was his father, and would brag about it at school. But Sterling wouldn't give him the time of day.

I was outraged and I let him know it." You're going to have to answer for this some day. How can you justify having a daughter that you'd give anything to while you've got your own flesh and blood son a few miles away that you won't even talk to? How can you punish a child like this?"

Sterling had a live-in white girlfriend named Susan that he met in Green Bay in his first year. Susan got pregnant and had a little girl they named Summer. Sterling treats Summer like she is the queen of the world which he should, but then he does not want to see or talk to his son Antuan. In my opinion Sterling got involved with Valerie at a time when he first came to the University of South Carolina. He had no status as a performing athlete and I believe most people would not consider Valerie Pringle to be a physically attractive lady although she was very friendly and has a very attractive personality. By the time Sterling found out about this child, he had become a superstar and had a brothel of women willing to sleep with him. I believe, in a large part, Sterling was embarrassed. Now, people would see that he slept with someone considered physically unattractive. Valerie was the main reason he wanted nothing to do with his son, Antuan.

Sterling got so upset with me that he stopped coming by the office as much and we lost the glue of our relationship. He had become an embarrassment in public as well. Kids who saw him coming and going to practice at the stadiums would ask for his autograph and he'd sometimes yell at them, "Get outta my face!"

I couldn't understand it, refusing an autograph for a five-year old kid who's got big googly eyes just being around you. He got to wear that Green Bay Packers uniform and be on national TV in front of millions of people, get paid millions of dollars, but didn't want to accept the rest that comes along with it. It wasn't right and we had a major fallout.

Sterling had gotten his wish in the 1994 contract. The Packers not only agreed to pay him more than Brett Favre but he also had a clause in the seven-year $29 million dollar deal that assured he would always be the highest paid wide receiver in the game. If any other receiver signed a more lucrative deal, the Packers would have to raise Sterling's annual compensation to top the deal by at least one dollar. It was the first time an NFL team had agreed to such terms, and the last.

Then fate stepped in. Sterling suffered a neck injury that season that was bad enough to end his career. The packers rec-ommended that he have surgery to hopefully fix the problem. He had the surgery that lasted 12 long hours. I went to the hospital, Carolina Medical Center with Sterling and went to surgery prep with him. I stayed in the room with Sterling the whole fours days he was there and slept on a cot.

When Sterling became conscious, I was the only one with him. He had bandages everywhere and he could only eat liquid food. I ask him how he felt he said he was sore and hungry. I ask him what he wanted to eat and he said "a chicken sandwich", I busted out laughing and said I might be able to get you some chicken soup. Susan came by one time for a few hours and that was it. No other visitors. Sterling was at a low point in his life and I was the only one there for him. His brother and mother called a few times, but otherwise Sterling had clearly burned a lot of bridges. Meanwhile, the surgery failed to restore his health to the point where the doctors would give him permission to play again. His playing career was finished.

The team could have paid him the $3 million or so that he was entitled to by contract, but Sterling had burned that bridge as well, and the team ended up with the last word. They offered him three hundred thousand instead of the $3 million, and cut him loose. Fortunately Sterling had followed my advice to buy a disability policy and he ultimately received $3 million from the insurance company, tax free.

Sterling had gone a long way from Glennville to the height of professional football, and then fallen a long way back down. I stuck by him long enough to help him get a commentators slot on ESPN, but Sterling is the first example that comes to my mind of the adage that "what goes around comes around."

Me and Sterling at the Rivery Ranch, Linton, North Dakota, 1993.

PART III

Penalties and Time-Outs

Chapter **13**

"BAD MOON" AND "LEFT EYE"

"T-TANK. OH MY G-GOD, Tank! I messed up real b-bad. Andre…he's gonna kill me for sure!" Lisa "Left Eye" Lopes' voice dissolved into uncontrolled sobbing.

This was a phone call I had been expecting all day. "Now Lisa, you've gotta get hold of yourself. Everything's gonna be all right. I ain't sayin' Andre's happy you burned his house down, but he still loves you. He told me so. Now you tell me where you are and let's get this sorted out."

By the time of Sterling Sharpe's late-summer game of chicken with the Packers, 1994 had already provided me with more than enough drama. I had another client-player in the news, and his story was messy. It started one day in early June when my pager went off in the pre-dawn darkness.

It was the builder I had worked with on a $200,000 renovation of a 12,000 square foot Mansion owned by Atlanta Falcons wide receiver Andre "Bad Moon" Rison. The house was in an exclusive golf community called Country Club of the South, in Alpharetta, Georgia, a half-hour's drive north of Atlanta.

"Tank, Andre's house is on fire, and it looks like it may burn to the ground. He's okay, nobody's hurt, but there's no way they're gonna be able to save much."

I jumped in the shower and dressed for the drive to Atlanta from my home in Columbia, South Carolina. It would only take me two and a half hours in my V12 600 Mercedes Coup. I turned on CNN as I pulled on my shoes. There it was, a live shot from a helicopter. Andre's trophy home, the pride of his career and stuffed with memorabilia and all his belongings, was a boiling mass of flame from one end to the other.

The phone rang just as I was about to leave the house. It was Andre. A siren wailed in the background. His voice trembled with anguish. "Tank, my damn house is burning up. I couldn't save nothin' but a coupla old footballs. And Lisa did it! Man, how could she do it? I'm worried, Tank. This is fucked up. This is the worst day of my life."

We arranged to meet at an out-of-the-way budget motel south of Atlanta where Andre took a room, hoping to avoid being recognized. We went for lunch at a local seafood restaurant and I listened as he told me what had happened. The more he talked, the worse it got.

Andre had been a client of mine since he was a first round draft pick in 1989, by the Indianapolis Colts. In the 1989 draft I had Barry Sanders the number 3 overall selection as an insurance client to the Detroit Lions, Derrick Thomas as an insurance client to the Kansas City Chiefs, Donnell Woolford as a management client chosen number 11 overall to the Chicago Bears, I had Andre as a management client chosen number 22 overall to the Indianapolis Colts and Louis Oliver an insurance client chosen number 25 overall by the Miami Dolphins. Andre, who'd grown up fatherless and poor like so many young black athletes, was intensely competitive and hot tempered.

As the number 22 pick overall that year, he was the third wide receiver drafted. Yet he had the confidence to publicly complain that he was better than the two picked ahead of him: Oklahoma State's Hart Lee Dykes, an All-American, and Eric Metcalfe of University of Texas.

"I was the best athlete in that entire draft," he crowed. He'd even claimed to be as good as Jerry Rice, the Forty-Niners wide receiver who was well on his way to being recognized as the greatest wide receiver in the history of football. So right off the bat, Andre Rison made a lot of team owners nervous. Andre was cocky but he was also very talented. As talented as any athlete in the draft as he claimed.

The next year, 1990, the Colts traded Andre and two other players to Atlanta. He flourished with the Falcons—four years in a row he had been selected both All-Pro and a player in the Pro Bowl. But by the time his house burned down in 1994, he had established a reputation as one of football's leading bad-boy superstars, dubbed "Bad Moon" Rison by an ESPN commentator, a play on the Creedence Clearwater song, "Bad Moon Rising." In retrospect, the lyrics seem prescient.

> *I see the bad moon arising.*
> *I see trouble on the way.*
> *I see earthquakes and lightnin.*
> *I see bad times today*
>
> *Hope you got your things together.*
> *Hope you are quite prepared to die.*
> *Looks like were in for nasty weather.*
> *One eye is taken for an eye.*

Among his bad press notices were two speeding tickets for driving over a hundred miles an hour, including one with a suspended license.

He mocked the "so-called, quote-unquote superstars" he played against in the Pro Bowls. He performed a frenzied dance in the end zone when he made a touchdown, until he started getting racist hate mail. After a game against the LA Rams, during which the fans booed and heckled him, he proclaimed, "You know you're large when the whole stadium acts like that."

Andre's love of provocation was matched only by his love of Atlanta's active night life and its subculture of rappers and other celebrities. He enjoyed the limelight and his starring role with the Falcons put him right in it.

It was the night life that introduced him to Lisa Lopes, one of three performers in a red-hot girl rap group called TLC. Lisa had beautiful eyes and someone had told her once that her left eye was more beautiful than the right. Thus she acquired the nickname "Left Eye," which she promoted by sometimes wearing her hair covering her right eye and wearing glasses during performances that had a condom in place of the right lens. Eventually people started calling her Left Eye.

Lisa fell hard for Andre. She had his jersey number, 80, tattooed on her arm and on her foot she had tattooed a moon with a face—for "Bad Moon" Rison. She became a regular in Andre's bloated entourage.

He was making a lot of money, more than a million a year, but he made the mistake that many young players make when they hit the jackpot. For a range of psychological reasons—guilt, generosity, narcissism—they acquire a retinue of hangers-on who treat them like princes when deep inside they still feel like paupers.

Andre had his crew—family members; people who took care of his house and pool and washed his cars; decorators; builders; and security services. When he was out in public, there'd also be some groupies, usually young women with all sorts of unhealthy motivations.

A Falcons teammate once observed, "Andre takes care of his mama, his brothers, his sisters and his cousins. If you or I were making the money he's making, we might invest it, but in Andre's eyes it's, 'What can I do to get what I want and also take care of these people?' He's living for now."

He often committed little random acts of kindness. He'd once given a parking lot attendant a $500 tip. Another time he saw a homeless woman and her child, picked them up, and brought them to his aunt's house for bacon and eggs, then gave a cab driver $200 to take them to a shelter.

My company, PMI, handled Andre's management business and I watched with growing alarm as his monthly expenses swelled to more than fifty thousand dollars. He was spending so much of his cash that he didn't have enough to pay his taxes and I had to loan him money for that and other expenses to keep him out of trouble. Around that same time, his mother was getting married and he borrowed $25,000 from me to stage a lavish wedding. The loans were to tide him over pending his becoming a free agent, when he'd be signing a new contract and getting another big payday.

Andre ended up re-signing with the Cleveland Browns, for $5 million up front, and he was into me for about $500,000. He paid me back and bought a home in a prestigious neighborhood in the Atlanta area, Country Club of the South, a gated community of new mansions built around the greens of a golf course. It cost him $861,000 in 1992, and he soon began building a massive addition.

I knew Lisa was a big star, but she was young and her music meant nothing to me until one day Andre showed up for a meeting at my office in his $100,000 Mercedes 500 SL convertible with Lisa. They stopped by my house afterward and my two children, eleven-year-old Jeremy and nine-year-old Shayla, were dumbstruck with awe that Lisa Lopes was in their house. The kids had met dozens of leading football players, but none of them could hold a candle to the bragging rights they'd have at school the next day having met Lisa "Left Eye" Lopes of TLC, one of the most successful musical trios of all time.

Andre's mother Merdice played an important role in his life. It was she who encouraged Andre when they lived in Flint, Michigan to pursue football in college. His first love was basketball but, she once explained, "He wasn't tall enough for the NBA, and he needs to hear the crowd cheering him on. So I told him he ought to play wide receiver. He wouldn't much like playing defensive back. Not enough glory." Merdice understood her son and she understood football.

In a 1990 profile in *Sports Illustrated*, Andre explained his provocative behavior: "Everywhere I've gone, I feel like I've disappointed people. I feel like I have so much to prove. I want to show the NFL I should have been drafted higher. I need to show the Colts they made a big mistake trading me."

His mother had been a 20-year-old single parent, a secretary who lived with her mother and father in Flint, Michigan, when Andre was born. "I didn't have any material things," he said. "I used to spend my time rippin', runnin' and havin' fun."

Andre plunged into sports convinced he had what it took to make it big. Whenever money was tight at home, he reassured Merdice, "The Lord put me on earth to go pro." He had a mission in his heart and a chip on his shoulder. To his credit, he understood himself, even if he couldn't control his impulses.

"I talk big to hide my insecurities," he'd explain. "People were always jealous of my athletic ability but I couldn't figure out what they were jealous of. They had the nice clothes, nice house, a mother and a father, a car.

"I had to talk myself up. Somebody had to believe in me. Somebody had to say it out loud." So he said it for himself.

Andre had fallen hard for Lisa, although it was a stormy relationship fueled by heavy partying, drinking, and all the rest. Lisa was the jealous type, and Andre was unprepared to settle down to domestic life. He'd already been through one failed marriage, to a girl he'd met in college and with whom he'd had a son. He wasn't anxious to do it again.

All these influences converged the night of the fire in early June 1994. Andre told me that he and Lisa had an argument and separately went out on the town. He said he ended up at a club surrounded by a group of young women. Lisa came in with some of her friends, and an altercation started with one of the girls sitting with Andre.

Andre left in a huff and went to another club. When he got home in the wee hours of the morning, Lisa was home, awake, drunk, and waiting like a bear trap. She attacked Andre, which explained the scratches I'd seen on his arms, neck and face as we sat having lunch that day of the fire.

Tears ran down Andre's face. "I left for maybe a half-hour and when I got back, the flames were shootin' out the windows. All I got was some game balls I had in the garage. And the windshields on all the cars were busted. The Range Rover, the Porsche, my Mercedes.

"Tank, I don't care about none of it. I just love Lisa and I'm so scared for her. I know she didn't mean it. Now nobody knows where she is, and my phone and pager got burned up in the fire. I'm sick, Tank. What if she, you know, did somethin'?"

I tried to calm him down and allay his fears. "She's probably just scared, is all. Let's take a ride and see if we can track her down."

We spent the day riding around Atlanta, dealing with the practical matters of police reports, renting him a car, and finding him a place to live. All he had left was the clothes on his back and a few signed footballs.

Everyone was calling my cell phone, including his mother, who was sputtering mad. "Tank, you tell Andre to leave that girl alone. Don't call her, don't talk to her. If she tries to contact him, you call the police."

I passed the message on but Andre just shook his head. "I'm not doing that with her. I'm not acting like that."

That evening, after I'd left Andre, Lisa called me using a friend's cell phone for fear her phone could be traced. She was blubbering so violently I could hardly make out what she was saying at first. The story I finally pried out was that she was in a rage when Andre left. She took a baseball bat and smashed all the car windshields.

Then she got the bright idea to burn some new sneakers Andre had just brought home. She put them in an empty whirlpool tub, poured lighter fluid on them, and threw in a match. It hadn't occurred to her that the tub was made of fiberglass, and in a few minutes the tub had turned into a noxious inferno of highly flammable plastic. It quickly spread and she ran off.

She sounded so lonely and afraid. She asked me to tell Andre how sorry she was and how she loved him and she never meant to burn the whole house down.

"You don't have to worry about that," I said. "Nobody got hurt. It's just stuff. Whatever you can say, you say. If you didn't mean to burn the house down, say it. But don't go on the run. It'll only be worse."

Lisa turned herself in the next day and was charged with arson. She got probation and court-ordered therapy. But their love for each other did not survive the fire. Andre's mom, family, and friends never forgave Lisa. Still, the two will be forever linked in the public's mind, especially after Lisa died at the age of 30 in a car wreck in Honduras in 2002.

The fire scandal had barely died down, and I had just settled Sterling's very public camp holdout with the Packers in September 1994, when Andre landed back in the news. This time it was an on field incident with another superstar, Cornerback Deion Sanders, during an October Falcons home game against San Francisco.

Deion had been drafted the same year as Andre, 1989, although Deion was the fifth pick of the first round and Andre was 22nd pick of the first round. I had been looking at Deion Sanders as a potential client but I happened to witness an exchange between him and a New York Giants official that scared me off.

It was before the draft, at a tryout event when eligible players run through their moves so the NFL scouts and coaches can get a better sense of their abilities. I was hovering near Deion and another player when a Giants coach approached him.

"Deion, we'd like to talk to you. We'd like you to come to our suite, and we'd like to talk to you this evening if you've got some time."

Deion sneered. "Shit, man, when're y'all draftin'? Y'all got like, what, tenth, eleventh? Shee-it! I ain't gonna be there when y'all get to your pick. I'm gonna be gone by then. What y'all wanna talk to me for?"

The Giants coach was unflappable after years of wooing arrogant players. "You know, Deion, we do pick tenth but we can always make a trade and go to first. You just never know what's gonna happen with the draft."

Deion snorted. "No, man. Y'all go ahead."

I immediately crossed him off the list of possible clients. If that's how he talks to coaches, I thought, I want nothing to do with him. I was only doing management at the time and it takes a lot of time and energy and really cocky players are the hardest to do management for. Deion was reportedly a teetotaler and religious, but he had a vice and it was ostentation. He attended the 1989 NFL Draft covered in jewelry with a leather outfit embroidered with his nickname "Prime Time." He was also known as "Neon Deion."

Deion and Andre played together with the Falcons for four years until 1994 when Deion became a free agent and signed with the 49ers for a record amount of money.

Deion Sanders was an amazing, unique athlete, starring at Florida State in football, baseball, and track. A month after he'd been drafted by the Falcons, he was drafted by the New York Yankees as an outfielder, and played professional baseball part-time between football seasons.

He was traded in 1991 to the Atlanta Braves, so he could literally drive from his football job to his baseball job. Three of the four years he played for the Braves the team got to the National League Championship series, winning twice and losing the World Series both times. One of those golden seasons he skipped the first four games of the Falcons football season because the Braves needed him for those crucial playoffs.

He became the only pro athlete to ever hit a home run and

score a touchdown in the same week. He also became the only athlete to appear in both a World Series (losing with the Braves) and a Super Bowl (winning two times, XXIX and XXX, first with the 49ers and then the Cowboys).

Andre and Deion seemed to get along great when they were on the same team. They practiced against each other, and there was no hint of friction between them. But Deion's defection to San Francisco irked a lot of Atlanta fans and his first time on Falcons turf in a 49ers uniform turned into a grudge match. He was booed when he came on the field.

The game was going badly for the Falcons and for a play in the second quarter Deion and Andre faced each other on the line of scrimmage. It was a rushing play so instead of running for a pass, Andre shoved Deion in the chest to block him. Deion responded by whacking Andre on the side of his helmet.

A brief fist fight broke out that a ref had to break up, and the two became the lead story on the sports pages the next day. The NFL penalized Deion as the instigator, but both players pulled a $7,500 fine.

The 49ers crushed the Falcons 42-3, and Deion taunted the Falcons fans during one full-field touchdown run. After the game Deion told the press " I built this" referring to the Georgia Dome. After that one season with San Francisco, he next signed a record-breaking contract for a defensive player, with the Dallas Cowboys: $35 million over seven years, with a $13 million signing bonus.

I don't think Andre ever quite got over his jealousy about that. In my opinion he was not jealous of Deion getting paid as much as irked by the fact that in his heart he felt he was just as great an athlete. It is normal for players to have shades of jealousy toward each other. They are constantly competing and most of them want to be Mr. Big. Andre was very unique however in that he had a heart of gold and would give anyone in need the shirt off of his back.

As stressful as dealing with some of these dramas could be, I liked my players. I understood the game from the inside out, so I had a big advantage as a recruiter. I could quickly tell which players had what it takes to play in the NFL, and which ones did not.

Because I thought like a player and a coach, I tended to treat my players as members of my team. If they had a crisis, I wanted them to call me twenty-four hours a day. Whatever they needed, I wanted to be there for them. Too often, the problem was irresponsibility regarding money or women.

It was a constant frustration to see so many of them get into financial trouble, and I often put my own credit on the line to help them pay bills, or advance them money for purchases like cars. My banker, Tommy Bone who handled all these transactions, would often ask me, "Why are you doing all this? What happens if things don't work out?"

"I know all the people I work with aren't going to be successful players," I explained. "Things aren't going to work out for some of them. But I make a good living and this is my way of giving back. It isn't just about making money. These are guys who grew up a lot like me. They never had anything, and they never had anybody give them a chance." Like many of my players who felt a great obligation to family and friends once they started making money, I also had a hard time saying no once I could afford to say yes.

The public and the press are quick to condemn the professional athlete who gets caught acting badly or living ostentatiously. I agree that there's no excuse for players who misuse guns or abuse drugs or any other sort of narcissistic or antisocial behavior.

But it's worth noting that these very young men for the most part have never held a real job, never managed real money, never had to think about taxes, and all the rest. They have been treated like Princes all of their careers because they are great athletes and have not had to answer to the same rules and then they are punished by the same people who hold them up so high when they do something that hits the national spotlight.

One day someone hands them that much anticipated six- or seven-figure check, the one they have been busy spending for months, and suddenly people start coming out of the woodwork— family members, girlfriends, homeboys, investment advisors, accountants, and sales people. Commonly the first thing they do is buy mom a new house or pay off the mortgage on the one that she has, then new cars for siblings and friends, then clothes and jewelry for their multiple girlfriends, and on and on in pursuit of their concept of what it means to be rich. They don't realize that a huge chunk of the money has to be set aside for the government, and they can't do everything they want at once.

I always told players, "You need to be setting money aside for taxes, set up a savings plan, and don't be buying all this stuff for people. You don't need a 15,000 square foot house. Buy a used Mercedes instead of a new one that loses twenty percent of its value the second you drive it off the lot."

Some players got it, but too many didn't and I often became the bad guy among family members who would sometimes call me and say, "You just need to worry about staying in the agent business. Stay out of this other stuff." In addition to everything else that suddenly comes at them, players with manipulative families have to deal with power trips, greed, and all sorts of bad behavior.

I had always been a saver and it made me sad to see players allow family members, sycophants, and predatory sales people manipulate them into making bad choices that robbed them of future financial security. I would never have predicted that one day I'd fall into that same trap.

All-Pro wide receivers Andre Rison and Sterling Sharpe at my surprise birthday party, March 1993.

Sterling and my son, Jeremy.

Chapter 14

THE FIRST BAD CALL

MY RELATIONSHIP with Andre Rison became a catalyst for a major turning point in my business—when my first partner Bill Bradshaw and I parted ways in 1995. I sometimes wonder if Bradshaw and I had stayed together whether he might have helped steer me away from the catastrophes that followed.

The parting was amicable, but it was a big change. We'd been in business together for six years as Professional Management Inc. (PMI) and I'd known him for nine years before that. He'd been a freshman at University of South Carolina playing football and earning a broadcast journalism degree. After he graduated and before he came to work with me, he had coached college football.

His family was in the restaurant business, but he enjoyed being around athletes and I recruited him to join Tony Dutt's insurance agency before Bill and I decided to go out on our own together as PMI. We had put a lot of thought into the company and between the management of players' business affairs and selling insurance, we had become very successful with a long roster of leading NFL players. Bill had brought on an investment and insurance professional named David Rodarte who was a top notch business professional and an excellent peoples person. David was great with our players.

Bill was the real financial expert, and I trusted him completely. He had become a registered investment adviser as well as a real estate broker, so he was able to handle a lot of affairs for clients that we would otherwise have had to farm out.

Bill's decision to sell out his share to me had a lot to do with Andre. On the one hand he was a hot player whose contract was up and would certainly be the subject of a bidding war that would net a major new deal. But he had been spending with reckless abandon on cars, homes, jewelry, clothes, women, and family, and neglecting to pay his taxes. I persuaded Bradshaw that PMI could afford to advance Andre $250,000 to tide him over. Then, later I personally loaned him another $225,000 .

We expected Andre to fetch an offer of at least $15 million, but Bradshaw became uncomfortable having our money at risk, especially with a player nicknamed "Bad Moon." I understood Andre and could relate to him even if I disapproved of his irresponsible behavior.

Bill came from the other end of the social spectrum. He was white, and hailed from a football family. His father, Charlie Sr., had been a star quarterback at Wofford College in Spartanburg, South Carolina. Bill's brother, Charlie Jr., had followed in his father's footsteps, playing quarterback at Wofford during the same time Bill was playing for the Gamecocks.

The senior Bradshaw was a wealthy entrepreneur who made it big in the fast-food business. The boys' parents made a point of attending all of their games, even if it meant chartering a private jet to get from one to the other when they were scheduled to play on the same day. They once showed up at a Gamecocks home game wearing matching mink jackets.

Bill had grown up wanting for nothing but he was down to earth and, like myself, a family man of deep faith and a strong moral compass. He was sick of babysitting football players, uncomfortable lending money to them, and tired of the long hours that kept him from his family.

I had good instincts with this situation, as became apparent when Andre finally got his new contract, with the Cleveland Browns. His signing bonus was $5 million against a $17 million five-year deal. Between the money I lent him from PMI, and my personal loans, he owed about $500,000.

By this time, as often happens with young players, Andre's mother, Merdice Brown, had become the boss of his affairs, much as Barry Sanders' father dominated his. Because the checks went directly to the players, it was up to the players to make good on their obligations.

After Andre signed and got his $5 million, PMI got a check for the roughly $250,000 the company had advanced to him and the $200,000 he owed me for my fee but there was no check for my personal loans which was $225,000. I had paid for his mother's wedding in Michigan. It was a beautiful wedding and a festive day for their family. I never charged players interest on funds I loaned them. They were always interest free loans. I called Andre to find out what the holdup was and he passed me off to his mother.

Merdice said "Well, you know, we just got a lot of other things we're lookin' at, and we just wanna make sure how we're gonna do it and how much we might wanna pay now and maybe we may wanna try to pay some later. Let me get back to you." There is always a dilemma with what to pay with players and their families. About a week later Merdice called me to tell me I could pick up my check for the personal loans from Andre in Atlanta. Merdice was a perfect mom for Andre. She was intelligent and a very kind lady with a very positive spirit. We all enjoyed working with moms like Merdice. Yes, Andre kept her and all of us busy trying to keep up with his lavish lifestyle but at the end of the day Merdice and Andre are just really good people and a joy to be around.

There were other players who I loaned money to who failed to break into the big time and were unable to pay me back. But it was never the kind of money Andre borrowed, it was for real emergencies and not luxury cars, and business was good enough that I could afford to be generous. When you've grown up as poor as I had—learning math by counting nickels, dimes, and quarters on my grandmother's kitchen table and eating fried bologna sandwiches for dinner—you know how few dollars it can take to change a life or ease someone's suffering. I had it and I was glad to be able to pay it forward.

By the mid 1990s, PMI had become the dominant agency in recruiting players drafted from schools in the Carolinas. We still handled only management services for some players who had agents but those who didn't increasingly trusted us to negotiate their contracts.

Our roster included Mark Clayton of the Miami Dolphins, Carl Banks of the New York Giants, Terry Allen of the Washington Redskins, Keith Jennings of the Chicago Bears, Ed McDaniel of the Vikings, Harold Green of the Cincinnati Bengals, Corey Miller of the Giants, Donnell Woolford of the Bears, Robert Brooks who played with Sterling Sharpe for the Packers, Natrone Means of the San Diego Chargers and Sterling's younger brother Shannon, who played for the Denver Broncos.

We grew our staff to include a financial adviser and rented new, larger offices. I moved into a new large home with two basketball courts, a swimming pool, and an upstairs sauna in the master bedroom. I traveled half the year, but it was the price of managing a fast-growing business and I was still in my prime, just about to turn forty, and making more money than I had ever dreamed of earning.

Before Bill Bradshaw sold his share of PMI to me, a large husky young black guy named Brantley Evans showed up at my house one day in a beat-up compact car with the rear seat removed and the driver's seat shoved into the back to accommodate his girth. Brantley had been a South Carolina State center on the football team and he wanted to come work for us. He had competed in high school and college against a number of players who went on to the NFL and he thought he could help us sign players.

Brantley was persistent but Bradshaw was skeptical. Something about Brantley bothered him but after Brantley called me repeatedly over several weeks, I persuaded Bradshaw we should hire him to recruit. He did well, bringing in Natrone Means and several others. When Bill Bradshaw sold his share of the business to me, I made Brantley vice president of PMI. I decided Bill had misjudged him.

Instead, hiring Brantley would prove to be the first in a series of bad calls I would make over the next several years.

Natrone Means, runningback San Diego Chargers.

Barry Sanders, Bill Bradshaw and Ira Hillary.

Me and Carl Banks at his wedding reception on a cruise ship in New York.

Me and Mr. LSU, James Carville at the Rivery Ranch, Linton, North Dakota, 1998

Chapter 15

GATOR RAID

BY 1995, THE TWELVE universities in the Southeastern Conference—covering nine Southern states—were surging in the number of their players being drafted by NFL teams. The reasons were money, political muscle, and doing whatever it took to sign the greatest players. The political clout had long been there: about two-thirds of governors and U.S. senators have been alumni of Southeastern Conference (SEC) schools. When Southern Republicans dominated the GOP takeover of Congress in the 1994 elections, these fiercely loyal regional alumni gained a lot of influence that they used to help and protect their alma maters.

That same year the conference had become the first in the nation to exploit an overlooked NCAA rule allowing championship games. These hotly contested matches generated millions of new dollars in ticket sales and broadcast rights. That money went into the pockets of the conference schools' athletic budgets allowing them to spend more on recruiting the best players, which in turn, attracted more alumni donations.

With so many good players coming out of Southern colleges, the number of NFL scouts and agents looking for bankable talent surged. For everyone involved, the SEC became a football goldmine.

With all that money and influence, the Southeastern Conference earned a reputation for playing fast and loose with NCAA rules. Top recruits and players got caught accepting money, cars, apartments, and so on, usually arranged by "helpful" alumni or outside sources in an effort to avoid detection.

Bribes and other inducements were paid to influencers to steer high school stars into choosing one school over another. Academic fraud—faking a player's grades to keep him eligible to play—was common. It was well known in the business of agenting and managing professional athletes that at most Southeastern Conference schools, the ends justified the means—as long as you were discreet.

For every one that was caught dozens of instances of cheating have went unnoticed or ignored. It is important to note that this is not a Southeastern Conference problem. I am speaking about the Southeastern Conference because I recruited these schools so heavily. This is a problem throughout the NCAA in all major conferences. Without rules violations I feel very strongly that the Southeastern Conference would still be the best athletic conference in our nation.

CNNSI.com's Mike Fish said in 2002 that "If you look at football programs guilty of major violations since 1990, the SEC has been found to have committed three times more than any other conference. He says this is true in basketball as well. Most of these major violations involve over zealous boosters with unprecedented passion for collegiate competition.

Ike Hilliard and Reidel Anthony were my first recruits from the University of Florida. I never gave money to either of them while they had college eligibility. Fred Taylor and Jacquez Green never really ask for anything. Ike and Reidel helped them with the little things they needed.

The hotbed of recruiting activity was Florida, whose schools were turning out more professional football players than any other state. My agency, PMI, hadn't cracked that market until

1996, when Brantley Evans came back from a recruiting trip to the University of North Carolina all wound up about a tip he'd received from one of his friends.

Brantley told me that Alfred Twitty—everyone called him "Tweet" or just Twitty—were buddies with Ike Hilliard, the All-American wide receiver for the University of Florida Gators.

Twitty told him that Ike, a junior, had decided to forego his senior year and declare himself eligible for the NFL draft at the end of the '96 season. Ike Hilliard was a red hot prospect, and would be a big catch for us. That would also give us an opening at the University of Florida, a tightly knit football community. Twitty claimed he could persuade Ike to become a PMI client, for a fee.

Paying fees to "runners" like Twitty is common but controversial. Runners do the legwork for agents, going to college towns, picking up gossip, getting to know the hot players, and trying to influence who they sign with. Some runners are bona fide employees of agents, paying their dues until they can become licensed agents themselves.

Others, like Twitty, get a finder's fee if a match is made. The problem is that agents and their runners have every incentive to corrupt the process to get the deal done, offering money, gifts, girls, and so on to competitive young athletes living on scholarships and what they can earn from part-time jobs. The NFL Players Association rules prohibit agents from offering players money or gifts to sign before they are eligible, but neither the agent nor the player has any incentive to blow the whistle on himself.

Like virtually every other agent, I played the game too. College athletes I was interested in recruiting would sometimes ask me if I could help them with Christmas money or cash for some other incidental need. In most cases I gave them what they ask for with the verbal understanding that they would pay me back whether they signed with me or not. I knew it was against the rules, but I enjoyed the role of benevolent provider, always mindful of that long-ago night when Mr. Isbell pressed $50 in my hand after I was robbed of my MVP award in high school. The money mattered, but the gesture mattered even more.

I also broke the rules in a more organized fashion, providing through Twitty and other runners monthly support of several hundred dollars to some University of Florida players including Jevon Kearse, Reggie Mcgrew, and Johnny Rutledge, as well as Kevin Faulk of LSU who went on to a long career with the New England Patriots. My runners often took players out to eat and I made sure they had plenty of cash to entertain players and their families.

All of the top sports agents were doing the same. We all knew that players wouldn't decide whether to sign with a particular agent because they got a couple of hundred dollars here and there. But the largesse gave us an opening to get to know the players and vice versa so that when decision day arrived, we knew each other well enough to make an informed decision.

Players who didn't sign with me often made no effort to pay me back, but those who did tended to be appreciative and conscientious—Jevon Kearse reimbursed me $1,000 I'd lent him as a student so his mother could pay some bills. The whole system is utterly corrupt, but no one talked much about it, unless someone got caught.

Brantley met with Ike Hilliard at a motel in Gainesville, Florida in October 1996 and reported back that Ike was certain he would turn pro at the end of that season, and confirmed that he trusted Twitty to help him choose his agent. I flew Twitty to Columbia so I could get a read on him and discuss compensation. I liked him from the start. He was friendly, with a warm, ready smile, and a sincere demeanor.

We agreed that Twitty would receive 20 percent of the income that PMI received as a result of Ike Hilliard signing with us. I began calling Ike once a week, to get to know him better, and introduce myself. The Hilliards seemed to have a knack for football. His uncle Dalton had been a running back for the New Orleans Saints for seven years. Ike's older brother Ivory had been an outstanding player in high school and college. Many years later, Dalton's son would become an outstanding college player.

Ike and I found plenty to talk about, and he struck me as level-headed. He had the perfect profile for the kind of athlete I could help better than any other agent. Being black like Ike was an obvious advantage, but it also worked against me in some ways: his college team was managed and coached largely by whites; the big established NFL agents were white; and the NFL teams were owned, managed, and coached by whites. It was 1996, but this was the Southeastern Conference, the last region to actively recruit black players—in the 1970s—and only then because their teams were getting beaten by schools from places like California where they did recruit black athletes.

Like Sterling, I had played Ike's position in high school, college, and briefly for the Falcons. I had coached dozens of wide receivers. We had lived similar childhoods—he had been raised by his mother in Patterson, Louisiana, a small bayou town in the Mississippi River delta below New Orleans that had become famous for turning out All State teams.

Ike's roommate was also a Gators wide receiver and All-American—Reidel Anthony. Reidel was from South Bay, Florida, a small rural town of about 5,000 at the southern end of Lake Okeechobee, and his father was the mayor. Mayor Clarence Anthony had been a past president of the Florida League of Cities, and was a respected black political and community leader. Unlike Ike, who seemed to be calling his own shots, Reidel's father played a big role in his son's life and I knew it was important to show my respect by calling him instead of Reidel. I first asked Reidel if he minded my calling his father to introduce myself. He gave his blessing.

When I reached Mayor Anthony I explained, "I'm interested in signing your son and I just wanted to know how you're planning to make that decision." Reidel's father said he'd heard of me, which was no surprise because I was becoming well known in professional football because of my well-known clients, and I had been active in black causes.

"First things first," he said. "I don't want you talkin' to him. I want everybody to go through me and if you don't do that, you won't have a chance."

I assured him I would abide by his wishes. Then I added him to my weekly calls. As with Ike, we had plenty to talk about between life, politics, and football. He was a country boy like me, from a background even poorer than mine.

Clarence had been one of six children born into a family of poor farm workers. His father had abandoned them and then he himself became a father at the age of seventeen. Now he was 37 and had already been mayor for a dozen years of a town of mostly black and Latino families with a third living below the poverty line.

He had worked in the fields and canning factories as a child before the family settled in one place long enough for him to get serious about school. He had put himself through Florida Atlantic University while working in a supermarket, and went on to earn a master's degree in public administration. He started a consulting business and supported the family from that and his $3,800 salary as mayor.

Mayor Anthony told me he'd grown up nearby in a housing project called Okeechobee Center, a shanty-town featured in a famous 1960 television documentary about the lives of migrant farm workers called "Harvest of Shame." Legendary CBS News correspondent Edward R. Murrow had narrated the program and it caused a huge public and political stir as America became conscious of just how much grinding poverty still existed in the country.

"You know, Tank, I never knew how poor we were until I got

to college and saw that show," he said. "I mean, all the kids had to work. That was just the way it was." I knew exactly what he meant. Although eastern Tennessee was not as poor as South Bay, we black kids all had to work when we were young, often picking tobacco.

By the time we started talking in late 1996, the town was in rough shape because the only major employer, South Bay Growers, had just closed down after almost half a century. The town lost 1,300 agricultural jobs, including his mother's, and unemployment was higher than 50 percent. He had persuaded the state to site a new minimum-security prison nearby that would provide about 350 jobs, although most of the former farm workers wouldn't be skilled enough to qualify for the majority of them.

Clarence Anthony and I bonded early on, and our friendship would deepen with time.

The Florida Gators finished the regular 1996 season with a 10-1 record and were to face Alabama for the big conference championship game in Atlanta on December 7. Twitty arranged for me to meet Ike's older brother, Ivory, and their mother at a downtown Atlanta hotel where they were watching Texas play Nebraska in the first-ever Big 12 championship game.

It was a big day for Ike and his family. The Southeastern Conference title would be decided that evening, after the Big 12 game. If Nebraska lost to Texas, and Florida beat Alabama, it meant the Gators would be going to the Sugar Bowl in New Orleans for the National Championship.

Ivory, who played football at Louisiana State, and his mother were so excited that I left the brochures and sales materials I'd brought in my briefcase and decided to relax and enjoy the game with them. Nebraska lost, and the Gators won. Ivory, Ike, and their mother went out to celebrate that night. I had agreed with Tweet to rent a limo for him and Ike to go out on the town and celebrate. After the championship game I had the limo driver come to the back of the Georgia dome and wait. I got in the limo and waited for Tweet and Ike. When they came to get in the limo it was actually a group of them. It included Ike, Tweet, Ivory, Reidel Anthony, Fred Taylor and Jacquez Green. The limo took me back to the hotel and I told everyone to enjoy themselves and keep the limo as long as they wanted. Eventually all of these players became my clients and went on to successful NFL careers.

The next morning we all met for a late breakfast: Ike, Ivory, their mother, Ike's roommate Reidel, and another outstanding Gator's player, running back Fred Taylor from Pahokee, Florida, a village just north of Reidel's home town on Lake Okeechobee. They were stoked because now they would get to play rival Florida State in the Sugar Bowl.

I was very impressed with Fred Taylor. He had a calm friendly demeanor about him. Fred walked outside with me after breakfast. He saw my Mercedes 600 S v12, and asked how much it cost. I said about $135,000. Fred commented that he would never spend that much money on a car no matter how much money he made. I told him he would change his mind about that and the last I heard he was driving a $200,000 Bentley.

Not only was the national championship at stake, but this would be an all-Florida blood feud. The Florida State Seminoles had handed the Gators their one and only loss that whole year, by a spread of only a single field goal. The Sugar Bowl would be the Gators' chance to punish the team that robbed them of a perfect season.

I was excited because I just had breakfast with three of the best players on one of the best college teams in the country. All three had first-round draft potential. If they all decided to declare for the NFL Draft and I managed to sign all three, my company would be in the center ring with the big boys.

So the Sugar Bowl was shaping up to be my Super Bowl. A college player can only sign with an agent once he has played the last game of his last college season. The Sugar Bowl might be that last game for Ike and Reidel if they chose to forego their senior year and declare themselves eligible for the draft.

Every top agent would be in New Orleans for the meeting of these two high-octane teams. More than three dozen players in that game would be selected in the NFL draft before their careers were over.

Just before New Year's, 1997, Brantley Evans, Twitty, and I flew to New Orleans where I lunched with Reidel's father. The mayor and I got along well and shared growing-up stories. Reidel had gotten some extra game passes that allowed holders onto the field. Mayor Anthony invited Brantley and I to watch the game from the sidelines with the passes. I had fifty yard line seats in the stands that I gave to Mayor Anthony and Tweet.

The Gators demolished Florida State 52-20. Ike had an outstanding game that pushed his potential draft status up the scale. The next morning when we met, I didn't have to say a thing. He just blurted it out: "I'm going to declare and I want you guys to represent me." It was a big moment for us both.

It was a thrill to see the shine in his eyes and the grin on his young face. I knew how much it meant to him to see that all those years of hard work were finally going to pay off. I knew how much it meant to him to finally be able to spoil his mother after all those years of scrimping. I was glad to make a good living at what I did, but the biggest thrills were moments like that.

We arranged for Ike to come to Columbia with Ivory, to work on details, get to know me better, and meet my staff. As I'd done with other players, I took him to my bank to arrange a credit line. He got a line of $50,000 and was astonished when we drove right to a car dealer so he could buy his dream car, a Lincoln Navigator. He was impressed with how quickly everything got done.

Ike wanted to help his mother buy a house so I promised to fly to Patterson and help her with the details of arranging a mortgage. When we'd finished our business and dinner in Columbia, the Hilliard boys drove happily off to Patterson in Ike's new wheels.

Next I flew to South Bay to see Reidel's father and go through all the details and answer all his questions. We spent a day together, he showed me the town and where he'd grown up, and I stayed over.

The next morning he asked me, "When are you planning on heading back to Columbia?"

"Mr. Anthony, I'm not planning on leaving. I plan on staying here with you for however long it takes until you tell me that your son's gonna let me be his agent. It's that important to me because I know I'm the best person for Reidel."

I returned to Columbia the next day after Clarence told me he was 99% sure that I was his choice. A couple of days later he called to make it official.

About a week later, Reidel and his father came up to Columbia for the same drill I'd gone through with Ike. I told them that I estimated Reidel would be offered somewhere in the neighborhood of $5 million. As I had with Ike, I took Reidel and his dad to my bank. His father thought a credit line of $25,000 for a twenty-year-old kid was plenty and allowed him to buy a Chevy Tahoe. Then the smiling father and son drove home to South Bay. I had done the unthinkable. I had signed both All-American wide receivers from the University of Florida Gators.

Clarence Anthony had an entrepreneurial spirit and in the next two years would become a sort of runner for me, leveraging my relationship with Reidel to help me recruit other Florida players. We became so close that when Clarence married his second wife, I paid for his honeymoon in Cabo San Lucas. I also paid for his season tickets to the Tampa Bay Buccaneers games.

I went to Mayor Clarence Anthony's wedding in Florida and the night before the wedding Clarence rented a limo and me, Clarence, his son Reidel and a couple of other friends of their family went out on the town in West Palm Beach. Clarence actually had us go to a local black strip club which I thought was interesting especially with him being a Mayor and his son Reidel with us.

When they signed with me the betting was that Ike and Reidel would be drafted in the last third of the first round—a respectable showing. But a good agent doesn't sit around waiting for the draft. Players headed for the Draft have to go through a process of being physically tested and take the Wonderlic Personnel Test, a twelve-minute, fifty-question intelligence test used to assess the aptitude of prospective employees for learning and problem-solving. It's used in a wide range of occupations but in football it is controversial and I disliked my players having to take it. I never thought it was of much use in discerning skills that were instinctive.

Most of this poking and prodding takes place at the annual NFL Scouting Combine, a job fair for prospective new players held over six days each February at the RCA Dome in Indianapolis. Players are put through drills, tests, medical exams, and interviews with more than six hundred NFL personnel including head coaches, general managers, and scouts.

A player may look good coming out of college, but a smart agent and coach puts his new clients on strict work-out programs to improve their results. I always took our players down to New Orleans to a preparation clinic run by Tom Shaw, a former strength and conditioning assistant in the NFL. I always paid the cost out of my own pocket because it was so valuable in improving a player's draft chances, and I'd stay there with them to see how they were doing and add my own coaching knowledge.

Although all serious draft contenders show up at the NFL Combine, they can opt out of certain tests and arrange to do them at another time and place. I never let my players do the athletic skills testing in Indianapolis because they were all from Southern states and I didn't want cold weather to put them at a disadvantage.

Because I had so many players going into the draft, I had the clout to hold them out of the physical tests and set up private workout days when the NFL scouts could come and see them do their stuff on their home school fields, in warmer weather. My players would simply tell the NFL personnel that on the advice of my agent Tank Black I am going to wait and workout on campus in March. When I had players from the University of Florida, Louisiana Tech, University of Tennessee, Clemson and the University of South Carolina, I set up four different private workout dates, one at each school.

All the teams send scouts to these events and have the players run 20- and 40-yard dashes, do vertical leaps, and standing broad jumps. Receivers run routes and catch balls and do the things they would normally do in a game. The scouts film the players' performances for later study. Both Ike and Reidel ran 4.4-second forties, a good showing, and did well in their receiving exercises.

Meanwhile, I was on the phone to almost every, general manager and receiver coach in the NFL to let them know why I thought I had the two best wide receivers in the April draft.

Draft day 1997, April 19, finally arrived and as I had become accustomed to doing, I stayed home, and I insisted my players do the same, explaining, " you should enjoy the experience with family and friends." Staying away from the draft site also eliminated the possibility of any television footage of a player saying or doing something embarrassing in the heat of the moment.

Ike was picked seventh by the New York Giants and Reidel was picked sixteenth by the Tampa Bay Buccaneers. They had been drafted earlier than expected so I would be in a position to negotiate outstanding contracts for both. It was a huge day for me.

One of my advantages as an agent was making sure my players had all their paperwork done by the first day of training camp. It's a distraction to have a player drafted but not know exactly where he stands the first day he's supposed to show up for work.

George Young, president and general manager of the Giants

had a reputation for being difficult to negotiate with. The Giants had not had a first round pick sign in time for the first day of training camp in more than a decade. But Ike signed at 7 o'clock the morning of the first day of training and became the first-ever number seven draft pick to get a $5 million signing bonus.

Ike officially signed with the Giants in New York and we both appeared at a press conference afterwards. Brantley Evans was with me that day and, for the first time, I sensed resentment toward me. I didn't think much about it at the time, but when I look back on it now, it's clear that he was starting to feel like he wasn't receiving enough respect for having brought Ike and Tweet to me in the first place.

As soon as we had signed the deal with the Giants for Ike, I flew to Tampa to finalize Reidel's deal. Tampa's management was much easier to negotiate with and we signed a six-year, $7.3-million contract a couple of days before camp started.

Rich Mckay was in charge of the player contracts for Tampa Bay and Rich was as good as they come. He was very intelligent and very level headed. He did not bullshit and he knew where he could go to get to a fair place with players.

Jerry Angelo was his right hand man back then and Jerry and Rich are just first class people. They were in the class with guys like Ozzie Newsome of Baltimore and Michael Huyghue of Jacksonville. These guys are "the best of the best" in their professions.

Reidel's father insisted his son set up a foundation to provide scholarships and attract private investment to South Bay. He wanted Reidel to learn early to give back, especially to those where he'd come from. It was a view I shared, and put into practice. I had given large sums to causes in my home town of Greeneville, Tennessee and in Columbia, South Carolina.

Ike and Reidel were big additions to the PMI family, they were happy, I was proud as a new father, and our Florida Gator connection was up and running full speed ahead. I was certain that nothing could stop me from becoming the best and the most successful agent in professional football.

The following year in 1998 I would sign the top two NFL prospects from the University of Florida in Fred Taylor and Jacquez Green. Fred was my favorite player. He was extremely talented with a height, weight and speed index that was off the charts. We just got along really well and I would have done anything for Fred and I know he would have done the same for me.

The time would come in the future when Fred would be told by the government that I stole money and misappropriated his investment in Cash 4 Titles. That was *never* true! To make matters worse, the government would not allow me to call Fred to explain what really happened. Leaving him with only the government's version. Knowning that made me want to throw up. The last thing in the world I would have ever done would be to steal money from my clients. Afterall, I loved Fred Taylor like my own son.

Alfred Twitty, the Rivery Ranch Linton, North Dakota, 1997.

Chapter 16

SUCKER PUNCHED

THERE WAS A bittersweet moment during my 1997 draft triumph that had its roots nine years earlier, the day Sterling Sharpe was drafted by Green Bay and became my first client. Sterling and I had watched the draft in 1988 on a television in a living room in Columbia with a dazzled fifth-grader named Peter Boulware, and his four-year-old brother, Michael.

Peter's parents, Jim and Melva, were close friends. Jim was a doctor, Raleigh James Boulware, who was known by his middle name. Their eldest son was Raleigh Jr. Their only daughter was Kayla who was an All-American high school track star and attended Notre Dame on a track scholarship. Our families were as close as could be, we often visited each other's homes, and we even started a local church together—First Northeast Baptist Church. I spent most of my spare time at their home, along with my wife and kids, Jeremy and Shayla.

In the years that followed the 1998 Draft that Sterling and I watched in the Bouleware living room, I treated young Peter and all of their children like members of my own family. I often played basketball with them, and I would show Peter little tips about football. I played rough with Peter on the basketball court because I knew it would make him tougher and as time passed he got tougher. Early on he would sometimes go in the house and cry to his mother Melva about how I was playing against him. He could never beat me but I knew someday he would be able to take me inside and have success. Melva would laugh and say you "just have to keep trying".

Throughout my career, I always enjoyed coaching young-sters. I always volunteered on some grass-cutter or community league team. It was fun and it felt good to be giving something back for the advantages I had gotten from my early influences in Greeneville.

Making money in the football business was exciting, but I've always been most content on the field helping young players reach their potential. It's a profoundly creative process that has as much to do with building character as it does with developing physical ability and winning games.

Peter had real potential and showed strong interest so I went out of my way to encourage him. Sterling Sharpe had lived on the first floor of my house in Columbia for two years and then bought his own place in town, so Peter got to see quite a bit of him. Peter also got to know two other of my NFL clients who were members of our church: Giants linebacker Corey Miller and Bengals run-ning back Harold Green. I made it a point to introduce my clients to the Boulware family because they were like family to me. I arranged for Peter to attend Sterling's summer football camps, so he got to meet a lot of other professionals and learn a lot of valuable techniques.

Peter's father, a radiation oncologist, had status in the com-munity, but it was Melva who ruled the roost and she did so with an iron hand. She insisted her boys address adults and authority figures as "Sir" and "Ma'am," adding "Yes" and "No" where ap-propriate. She was tough on her boys whenever she felt they had failed to meet her high standards. Peter would later say she was tougher than his toughest teacher or his toughest coach. Melva rarely held her tongue, always without apology. Her philosophy was, "If somebody has a dirty face and you don't say it's dirty, then they don't know to wash it." I actually admired the way Melva kept a close hand on her kids.

With all that encouragement and expectation, Peter did well. He was All-State in high school, and graduated first in his class. He went on to Florida State University and in his junior year led the Atlantic Coast Conference in tackles and was named Defensive Player of the Year.

That was the same year as the 1997 Sugar Bowl, so Peter Boulware—who I thought of as a son—ended up competing for Florida State against two other college juniors from the Gators, Reidel Anthony and Ike Hilliard. All of them appeared likely to bypass their senior years and declare themselves eligible for the draft at the end of the big game.

As I reviewed my list of prospective new clients, Peter's name was first. His parents were close friends, and after a decade of getting to know Peter, I needed no introduction. But I wanted to avoid appearing presumptuous, so I decided to confine my discussions with him to good luck and congratulatory calls.

At the beginning of Peter's junior season I talked to Jim and Melva after church one Sunday and we agreed we'd wait until the season was winding down to work out the details and get Peter started as a PMI client if he decided to forego his senior season. After Thanksgiving, I called Jim and Melva about setting up a date to get together. Melva was curt. "You're way behind, Tank. You should have been talkin' to Peter all along. We're gonna interview some other agents."

"Wait, Melva. You guys told me that, you know, don't worry about it, don't say nothin'. Just let Peter play. And we were gonna sit down at the end of the season. What's this all about now?"

She insisted that she wanted to go through the proper steps of choosing an agent and I would have to be interviewed just like everyone else. This was devastating news. I felt the only reason to put me through such a charade was because his parents had decided against signing with me.

I did my best to suck it up and play the game, hoping that once the Boulwares went through the formalities, they'd come to their senses and see why I was the right choice. But I got a bad feeling when I called Peter to try to find out what was going on.

"You know, Mr. Black," he said apologetically, "really it's up to my family what I'm gonna do. You know what I'm sayin', Sir?"

"I understand, Peter." But the "why" made no sense.

My bad feelings were confirmed when I learned from the grapevine that they had signed with my principal competition, Eugene Parker, an agent from Indiana. Parker was also black and also had marquee clients, including cornerback Deion Sanders and the star running back Emmitt Smith, both with the Cowboys at the time. Parker had made headlines two years earlier when he got the Cowboys to give Sanders a seven year, $35 million contract, with a $13 million dollar signing bonus, making him the highest paid defensive player in the NFL. Eugene was definitely a top quality agent and I had a great deal of respect for his professionalism but I was family to the Boulwares and Peter was like a son to me.

I felt sucker punched, and I needed to know why it had happened. When I finally pried out of Melva what really had been going on, I was furious. Sterling had betrayed me.

Over the years Sterling had grown increasingly jealous of the time I spent with other players as my roster grew. After he suffered his game-ending injury in 1994, I helped him with some connections so he could land a job as a sports commentator. But he'd made occasional sly remarks about how busy I was that suggested he felt forgotten. Every star player grieves for his career when it's over. Sterling was selfish by nature and chose to take out some of his unhappiness on me. Sterling also had a short memory and seemed to forget that I drove to Charlotte Medical Center with him when he had his neck surgery and I stayed in the room with him for four days never leaving his side until he was released. While there I spoke with the ESPN executives and had Sterling an audition for an analyst job waiting when he was able to travel. He'd told Peter and his parents, "If it was me, I wouldn't go with Tank because he has too many clients and he's busy all the time. I can hardly get him on the phone anymore."

Between Sterling's poison and Parker's success on behalf of Deion Sanders who like Peter graduated from Florida State University and was an All American defensive player, Parker probably looked good to the Boulwares on paper. But there is no question in my mind that I would have done a better job because Peter was family to me, and I would have been a more loyal advocate for Peter, and later for his brother Michael. I have a high opinion of Eugene Parker as a person and as a professional. He did do a good job for Peter.

This episode broke my heart, not because of any money I might have made but the coldness I now felt from people I had considered family. I was angry with Sterling, but I was used to his narcissism and bad manners.

It was the distrust of Jim and Melva that crushed me along with the way that they handled the whole situation. I had been family to them and they could have ask any favor of me and I would have come through for them. I would have negotiated Peter's contract for free. Had things been reversed there is no way I would have allowed my son not to sign with Jim. But they never came clean with what was on their minds, after I'd been nurturing their son's dreams in one capacity or another for a decade. That hurt the most.

So it was with mixed feelings when NFL commissioner Paul Tagliabue stepped to the microphone in Madison Square Garden on April 19, 1997 for the fourth time that day and announced, "We have a pick." With the fourth pick of the 1997 NFL draft the Baltimore Ravens select linebacker Peter Boulware of Florida State University.

I immediately went to the Todd and Moore sporting goods store and purchased 10 Baltimore Ravens caps and came back and gave them to Peter and his family. I was genuinely happy for him, but it was a sorrowful ending to the long friendship I'd enjoyed with his family.

Peter excelled in Baltimore as he had everywhere else. He became the 1997 NFL Defensive Rookie of the Year, and played in the Pro Bowl four of his eight years with the Ravens. He also earned a super bowl ring in 2001. After the episode with Peter, Michael told me when he went pro he wanted me to represent him. Michael followed in Peters footsteps. He went to Florida State University and was drafted in the 2004 draft by the Seattle Seahawks. By then my world was upside down.

Dallas Cowboys cornerback Clayton Holmes and me in Dallas, Texas.

Libby Saylor and Debbie Kanipe escort me into my surprise birthday party, March 1993.

Peter Boulware (center), his sister Kayla (left) and brother Raleigh (right).

Peter's mom, Melva and me.

Chapter 17

RAE CARRUTH'S SHORT, SAD CAREER

EVEN WITHOUT Peter Boulware, the 1997 Draft was a big success. I had both ALL-American wide receivers from the University of Florida. Ike Hilliard the 7th pick of the first round and Reidel Anthony the 16th pick of the first round. I signed wide receiver Rae Carruth after the draft, a player from outside the South who would have a bright but short career and then become a poster boy for the dark side of the NFL dream. Rae was the 27th pick of the first round. That signing gave me three first rounders as clients from the 1997 draft. I also had Duce Staley running back from South Carolina who led the South Eastern Conference in rushing and Marcus Robinson a very under-rated wide receiver from South Carolina who was also a first team track All-American. Both in my opinion were as talented as the first rounders I had.

Rae Carruth was in his senior year as a wide receiver for the University of Colorado. He'd grown up in a crime-plagued inner-city neighborhood of Sacramento and I met him through one of my scouts, Oliver Lucas, a former Colorado running backs coach.

I'd known Oliver from my days with the Gamecocks when he'd been a visiting coach with his team. We got to talking, made a connection, and kept in touch. When I started PMI I tracked him down because I knew he'd left coaching and might be looking for an opportunity. He knew a lot of athletes from his college days and was used to dealing with athlete's families, a valuable skill.

Oliver brought to the fold two Colorado players: cornerback Deon Figures from California, a first-round, twenty-third pick in 1993 by the Steelers; and a round two pick in 1991, running back Eric Bieniemy, chosen by the Chargers. He had identified Rae as a hot prospect and a senior headed for the Draft. Since he was a wide receiver, my specialty, I wanted to go to Boulder to meet him and take his measure.

Rae's mother, a social worker, had come in from Sacramento and Oliver and I took mother and son out to dinner. Rae seemed younger than his twenty-two years. He was quiet, respectful, and articulate. His mother, Theaudrey Carruth, was warm, friendly, and protective of her boy. Rae had been born Rae Wiggins but his father abandoned the family early on. When his mother remarried, he took her new husband's last name. The second marriage hadn't lasted, but they kept the family name anyway.

Theaudrey told us that Rae had wanted to be a famous football player since he was little. He excelled on his high school team, was named an All-American, and was so popular with the other students that they twice voted him prom king. His grades were middling but he managed to squeak by and win a scholarship to Colorado where he'd maintained a B average and a clean disciplinary record.

"I practice hard, work hard, and I think I'll get a good shot," he told me.

I needed no convincing. "You're gonna get a *great* shot."

Rae expressed the same aspirations I heard from most of the college players I worked with: he wanted to play pro football, make a lot of money, retire and go into business. I was glad when the Carolina Panthers drafted him. We did not negotiate his contract with the Carolina Panthers. We signed Ray as a full managment client and handled all of his day to day business out of our offices in Columbia. He signed a $3.7 million, four-year deal. Rae's professional dream had come true and he opened his pre-season line of credit, bought himself a nice car and took care of his mother.

Many players get themselves in trouble with girls once they've become millionaire athletes. Rae had gotten a head start. He'd left a girl pregnant back in Sacramento and was now on the hook for child support.

It's a mighty temptation for a young man when so many women seem to love the idea of having sex with and maybe getting pregnant by you. Some of these women are true predators, willing to do just about anything to make it happen. It's a sad truth of pro sports that most players get rich before they get smart, and become stars before they can tell the difference between a fan and an opportunist.

Millions are paid each year to women who become pregnant by professional athletes. Sometimes the money buys silence about an abortion, sometimes to settle a paternity claim. More than once was I asked by a client to arrange money or a car for a mistress or casual date that turned into a potential embarrassment for a player.

Rae was earning about $900,000 a year so his child support payments weren't a great burden. But just as I had with Sterling, I encouraged Rae to try to have some sort of relationship with the child, not to repeat his own father's mistake of abandoning the family.

Rae had grown up going to church with his mother every week so when one of his first visits to Columbia fell on a Sunday, I thought it might be good modeling to take him with me to my church. I hoped he might be inspired by meeting some intact black families and see how important it is for a child to have a mother and a father in their life.

He hadn't brought any dress clothes with him. "I can't go to church in this sweat suit."

"Okay, I'll wear a sweat suit, too," I offered. "And since I'm on the board of the church, nobody's gonna mind a bit. Besides, church is church. The Lord doesn't care what we're wearin'."

So we both went to church in sweat suits. The congregation fussed over Rae like the celebrity he'd become and had a good laugh when I explained why I was wearing sweats.

Rae's rookie season, 1997, he started in fourteen games, led all rookie receivers in passes received, and was named along with another client Reidel Anthony to the all-rookie team at wide receiver. The next season should have been his breakout but in the first game he fractured his right foot. He hardly played after that, ending the season with just four catches. He got himself back in shape for 1999, and started off with a respectable 14 catches in the first six games, gaining a total of 200 yards.

By this time Rae had a couple of girlfriends, including Cherica Adams, a beautiful, outgoing, 24-year-old. She was supposedly working as a real estate agent but when Rae made a point of introducing her to me, my radar picked up right away that she had an agenda.

She'd grown up in North Carolina and while she was in high school in Charlotte she interned for the Panthers and babysat for the children of some Charlotte Hornets basketball players. She'd gone to college for a couple of years, done some modeling, gotten her real estate license, and she'd worked as a stripper in clubs and topless bars. Strip clubs and sports just seem to go together, and strip club owners love it when professional athletes hang around—they always bring along their posses and give the place a buzz.
Rae had met Cherica in one of those clubs.

I checked around and discovered she'd met quite a few professional athletes in those clubs. She claimed she'd dated Shaquille O'Neal, the NBA star, and that he'd bought her a car. The more I heard, the worse it sounded.

In the fall of 1999 Rae told me Cherica was pregnant with

his baby. She was due near the end of the year. He sounded okay about the prospect of becoming a parent and had even gone to a Lamaze class with her.

Rae wanted to throw himself and Cherica a big party in November that year. Rae smoked pot occasionally and Cherica had introduced him to a shady character who Rae hired to build a fence at his house. His name was Van Brett Watkins and he also supplied Rae with weed. Rae told Cherica he was going to buy a lot of pot for the big party, so there'd be plenty to go around. Cherica in turn told Watkins.

Rae had hired Watkins at Cherica's urging. Watkins had been in jail, was down on his luck, and needed some work. But Rae had no idea that the guy was seven kinds of bad news—three years in prison in New York in the early 1980s for attempted assault and possession of a weapon; back to prison in 1987 for criminal mischief and grand larceny of an auto; and in 1997 he had been accused of threatening a woman with a meat cleaver, forcing her into a car, and beating her.

Now Watkins was working part time as a bouncer in a strip club, running drugs between Atlanta and Charlotte—and detailing Rae Carruth's cars.

In one of the conversations at the time, Rae told me about the big party he was planning and mentioned in passing his plan to buy a supply of marijuana. I don't know why he told me but I was glad he did. "Rae, I don't smoke marijuana and I don't judge what other people do, but in your case, this is a really bad idea. What the hell are you thinkin' about?"

"You think it's a bad idea?"

"Yeah it's a bad idea, and you shouldn't be smokin' marijuana in the first place. If they ever spring a urine analysis on you, you're gonna get caught and maybe suspended for some games, which could cost you a lot of money, maybe $200,000. Are you gonna tell me gettin' high is worth all that?"

I talked him out of getting the marijuana. But when Cherica

told Watkins that Rae had changed his mind, Watkins blew his stack. He'd apparently already laid out the dough and somebody was going to have to pay, one way or the other.

Watkins small time drug deal was halted, Watkins was furious, and it all exploded one night in the middle of November. Watkins and two cronies were waiting for Rae at his house when he came home from visiting a teammate. Watkins demanded to be paid for the pot but Rae told him, "I never said I was gonna do it for sure. I just said I was thinkin' about it." Watkins was pissed off but he left with his sidekicks. Rae was going to get together with one of Watkins' friends later to play video games, after he and Cherica went to the movies.

Cherica drove to Rae's house, and together they drove in his car to see "The Bone Collector" at a Charlotte movie theater. Afterward, Rae packed a bag and they were going to drive in their separate cars to Cherica's house. Rae was going to spend the night because she lived closer to the stadium where he had practice the next morning. Rae left his driveway first and Cherica followed right behind in her BMW.

On the way Cherica pulled up alongside Rae's car at a traffic light, rolled down her window and told him she'd changed her mind about him staying over and she was going home alone. So Rae drove to a teammates' house to play video games. That's where he was when he got a phone call—Cherica had been shot four times at a stop light by someone in another car.

Rae went straight to the hospital where the police told him that Cherica was in bad shape. Cherica's distraught family accused him of being involved in the shooting. Before she lost consciousness, she'd called 911 and told the operator that Watkins had pulled up next to her car at a stop light and shot her. She had said something about Rae's car being "in front" of her, and when the operator asked if Rae was involved, she had answered, "I think so."

Watkins and the two cronies who'd been in his car with him

were arrested and charged with attempted murder. Rae was also arrested, for conspiracy to commit murder. The cops thought they had a murder-for-hire.

I was at my office the next day when I heard about it and was blown away. Why would Rae go with Cherica to Lamaze classes and then conspire with Watkins to have her killed? It was crazy. Why? What would the motive be? Child support payments? That is ridiculous.

He was able to make the $3 million bail and called me in a state of hysterical terror. "Tank, those cops in Charlotte, they told me that if she dies, 'Your nigger ass is gonna get the death penalty.' Honest to God, I had nothin' to do with this. Those guys, Watkins and them, they're trying to save their asses by saying I had somethin' to do with it. And Tank, man, she's in bad shape. She's in a coma and they say she could die for real."

Rae couldn't explain Cherica's statements implicating him, but the cops seemed to be building the case that he wanted to avoid getting stuck with more child support payments and wanted her out of the way. Rae had been making good money, so that motive rang false. The most he'd have to pay her under state law was $1,500 a month, which was nothing for someone earning the kind of money Rae was making.

The only person who could clear things up was Cherica and she had gone into a deep coma soon after she arrived at the hospital. Doctors performed an emergency caesarian to save the pregnancy and discovered twins. One died and the other, a boy, was born with birth defects. Technically, it was now a murder case. It became official a month later when Cherica died without ever waking up.

Rae was ready. Before the cops had time to pick him up, he jumped bail and vanished, triggering a nationwide manhunt. He turned up a week or so later in Tennessee, hiding in the trunk of a car parked at a motel where a friend had taken a room so he'd have access at night to a toilet and shower. The friend had called

Rae's mother to find out what was going on, and his mother had pried out of her where he was hiding. Terrified her son would be gunned down if the cops had to chase him, she tipped them off in return for a guarantee of his safety.

Rae's career was over. Now he was fighting for his life. His 2001 trial produced a tangled story with Watkins as the prosecution's star witness testifying against Rae in a deal to beat execution. Watkins told varying versions of a story that had Rae directly or indirectly involved.

But a jailhouse guard testified that a month after the shooting, which was nine months before Watkins cut his deal to testify against Carruth, Watkins confessed that he shot Cherica because, "She flipped me off and I just lost it. I just lost control and started shooting."

The guard testified that Watkins, who was so psychotic he threw feces and urine at his jailers and had to be kept doped up on Thorazine, told her the shooting was Rae's fault. "If he'd just have given us the money none of this would've happened."

Defense experts testified that Cherica's supposed accusations against Rae could have resulted from suggestions by the 911 operator who took her call, and interference from family members who didn't like Rae and were trying to protect Cherica's reputation. And the cops seemed to be too eager to nail a big fish. All Cherica's statements had been made in the minutes after she was shot when she was in shock, or when she was heavily sedated after she got out of surgery, just before she slipped into her coma.

In spite of all that, the jury convicted Rae (Carruth) Wiggins of conspiracy to commit first degree murder. The judge gave him twenty-four years in jail, with his earliest release date in 2018. He had the best defense lawyer in the state who took the case up on appeal as far as he could but got nowhere.

Knowing Rae as I had, having had the conversation in which I talked him out of the marijuana deal, knowing how much his career meant to him, knowing the kind of kid he was, I think

Watkins told the truth the first time. He shot Cherica in a blind rage. He'd demanded money from Rae earlier that night, Rae brushed him off, and when Cherica did the same, he just lost it. In Watkins' twisted mind, Rae's refusal to pay for the marijuana he never got was the cause of Cherica's death.

Cherica's implicating statements were vague and uttered under extreme stress or while heavily sedated. With her distraught relatives at her bedside badmouthing Rae to anyone within earshot, it's easy to imagine her getting mixed up and highly susceptible to the cops' leading questions.

I often wonder if my testimony might have saved Rae, but by the time his trial rolled around I was in jail too, fighting my own battle for the truth.

Rae Carruth (left) and son, Chancellor.

Shannon Sharpe in college at Savannah State.

Ryan Black's college graduation celebration.

Chapter **18**

WHAT COULD GO WRONG?

MY BUSINESS had become so complex by 1998 that I'd hired a full time lawyer to manage the growing number of player and endorsement contracts I was negotiating. I had also been exploring other business ventures, including a travel agency that had started to boom.

Both decisions—to hire my own lawyer and diversify my activities—made perfect sense at the time. But each proved to be a Trojan horse harboring the agents of my destruction. I was making all the right moves but I had no idea that they involved some of the wrong people.

The travel agency came about early in the 1990s when I began to see myself as more than just a manager and babysitter for professional athletes. It was the dawn of a new age for African-Americans, the early days of the new black-entrepreneur class. Wally Amos—who launched "Famous Amos" and started the gourmet cookie industry—had become a national celebrity and motivational speaker, a black entrepreneur success story.

Oprah Winfrey was another new role model, a strong black businesswoman, and she introduced America to others by having them on her show. Jesse Jackson was briefly the front-runner for the Democratic nomination for president in 1988, earning nearly seven million votes. *The New York Times* called the election "the Year of Jackson."

This was the perfect environment for someone like myself: restless by nature, I enjoyed trying new things; ambitious by nature, I enjoyed the sport of capitalism; and charitable by nature, I actively used my growing resources to help others.

The pace of change began to accelerate in the early 1990s. After twelve years of Republican administrations that seemed indifferent to the black community, we were energized in 1992 with the election of a charismatic Southern president from an impoverished background who was as comfortable in a rowdy black church service as he was playing golf with a group of rich white bankers. Bill Clinton would have felt right at home in my grandmother's kitchen sipping her moonshine, hissing away the burn, and swapping tall tales.

It seems unbelievable that less than two decades ago it was considered a risky decision for Clinton to invite a black writer, Maya Angelou, to deliver a poem at his first inaugural. Clinton swept away the culture of exclusion in Washington. For the first time in history, four African-Americans—Ron Brown, Mike Espy, Jesse Brown, and Hazel O'Leary—held seats in the President's Cabinet. Black culture and black enterprise moved to the top of the national agenda.

All this electrified black business people like myself. I had my eyes peeled for new horizons. In the late 1980s I got involved with a small travel agency because we spent so much each year on travel for our staff, prospects, families, and clients. It added a new benefit to our booming sports agency and management business.

I had discovered that sports management was a hard way to make an easy living. Overhead was high, competition fierce, and it was labor intensive—I spent a lot of my time managing egos and expectations, and helping players solve private problems and avoid public scandal.

David Ware, the Atlanta-based lawyer/agent with whom I

had worked on behalf of a number of shared clients, explained it best when he told the *Los Angeles Times* in 1999:

> "[I] may not think the 1:00 AM phone call from a player is important, but obviously he does. An athlete calls you…and says, 'I've got a girl in my hotel room and my wife's here. What do I do?' Or, 'I've got my shoes in Detroit and I'm in Orlando. What do I do?' [I'm] agent, manager, social worker, family counselor, psychologist. All under one hat."

Amen, brother!

The best opportunity for an up-and-coming black entrepreneur in those days was to network with like-minded black entrepreneurs. I belonged to several African-American business groups and was active locally and nationally with community services organizations like the United Way and Red Cross.

My Rolodex was becoming more muscular all the time. I traveled the country half the year meeting leaders from all aspects of professional sports—college coaches to NFL team owners; from local political leaders like Mayor Clarence Anthony to national heavyweights like Rev. Jesse Jackson. I was meeting a lot of corporate executives who liked to hang around the college and pro football scene, and many who were college alumni, donors who took an interest in promising players. I was plugged in just about everywhere.

In the mid-1990s I was recruited to the board of a start-up marketing company based in San Diego that had the license to sell a *Trivial Pursuit*-style board game based on facts about famous and notable African-Americans. "Black Americans of Achievement, The Game" grew out of a school project aimed at teaching black history and introducing young people to black role models. The company hoped to sell the games through tele-marketing and in quantity to schools and other organizations.

Named for the game's acronym, BAOA Inc. had been launched as a penny stock, a term for companies listed outside the major exchanges. These are typically paper corporations with little more than an idea and high hopes. The shares are usually priced under a dollar, hence the term penny stock.

There are successful companies that begin as penny stocks—winning ideas hatched at someone's kitchen table. But for each success there are many times that number of failures and a high percentage of outright frauds. Many people buy penny stocks much the way gamblers feed slot machines—the cost of entry is cheap and with a lot of luck your 10,000 shares of 10-cent stock in a gold mine in Chile could be the one that pays off a hundred to one.

Making a pile of money was not my goal with BAOA. But I thought it was a worthwhile idea. It was good for the black community. I don't believe black achievers get enough recognition.

I was given 450,000 shares of BAOA stock as part of my agreement to become the President of BAOA. My players were never sold my stock. Several of them did buy stock in the company at 50 cents a share. The agreement was made in writing that if the stock did not do well I would personally purchase the stock back from them for what they paid for it. I did that. I purchased every players stock with a cashiers check giving all of the players their money back.

BAOA was an experiment that never got off the ground, but the travel agency turned into a major business success thanks to official support for minority-owned businesses. In 1992 the U.S. Commerce Department set up a high-profile pilot project in Chicago called the Minority Enterprise Growth Assistance Center that became a catalyst for similar centers around the country.

The federal government and many state and local governments enacted tax credits for businesses that earmarked a certain percentage of their expenditures for minority-owned vendors. The federal government's procurement policies included giving extra weight to minority-owned businesses in awarding bids.

The travel agency I invested in had been owned by a Michigan native, Linda Wilson, who I met on the phone through an adviser to Andre Rison. Her agency LWS Travel catered mainly to small corporate businesses, she was ambitious and smart. As we talked it hit me that collectively with her travel expertise and my corporate contacts we could do some amazing things together. "The world is changing but you still have to be two steps ahead of everybody else just to have a chance for success when you are a black American".

I told her how I'd built my company, and how much harder I had to work to compete with white agents. I told her how hard it was for a black agent to get business even from a black athlete because of the perception that white agents and lawyers had more access to power. Barry Sanders's father was one of the more astute parents who understood the inherent conflict-of-interest of agents bragging that they played golf with team owners.

Less astute parents and players, most of them, were impressed by such claims. They didn't understand that the agent who is cozy with the owners is more concerned about staying on management's good side for future business than in getting a single player the best deal possible.

"It's the old ice vendor joke, you put two ice vendors on a street corner on a good hot day, one is black and one is white, and black folks will buy their ice from the white vendor because they think his ice is colder."

It was a perfect match. Linda knew the travel business inside out, and I had access to big corporate prospects. We made a deal and I became CEO of the travel agency. A year later she moved the business and four employees to Columbia.

The big money in travel was to be made servicing Fortune 500 companies. One of our first big catches was E.I. Dupont which gave us about 5 million a year in billings.

I had a connection at E. I. Dupont, which spent nearly $300 million a year on travel. They were interested in giving us a chunk of that business and sent us to a Philadelphia-based company, Rosenbluth Travel, which had the exclusive contract to manage all of Dupont's travel needs.

Rosenbluth was the oldest and one of the largest travel agencies in the world. The CEO was Harold "Hal" Rosenbluth and his brother Lee was COO. They were great-grandsons of the founder and had followed the family tradition of working their way up from the bottom, starting as entry-level clerks and reservations agents.

When I met Hal Rosenbluth, we connected early on. Although we came from very different backgrounds, our values were similar, we both loved sports, and we both enjoyed the game of business. Rosenbluth had a long list of major corporate clients, so this was potentially a huge opportunity for us.

"You own a major travel agency, and we own a very small minority-owned travel agency," I told Hal. "We're no competition. If we made an alliance, you could fulfill all your clients' quotas for minority vendors."

Hal got it right off the bat and we made a deal—he, Linda, and I each owned a new agency called World Express International. Linda and I owned the majority which still qualified us as minority-owned. Hal got us set up with Dupont and we were off to the races.

Dupont started out giving us $500,000 a year in billings and then raised it in subsequent years until we were handling $5 million a year, with a commitment to grow it to 10 percent of their overall budget of $260 million.

The one office we started out with in Columbia quickly grew to more than thirty satellite offices around the country. The travel business turned out to be a smart move.

I flew up to Philadelphia several times a month to meet with Hal Rosenbluth to discuss business and, of course, sports. Duce Staley, a running back with the Philadelphia Eagles was a client of mine. We became really close friends me and Hal. He was laid back and easy going much like I was. I even got my friend The Reverend Jesse Jackson Sr. to come to Hal's main offices in Philadelphia and meet the employees one day. When the

Philadelphia Eagles flew into a deep slump in the late 1990s and needed new blood and rejuvenation, we discussed putting together an investment group to buy the team. I was in a position to recruit talent, and he could put together the financing. We could turn the team around and make it highly profitable.

As the travel business boomed, so did PMI. I had hired a financial manager and in late 1997 I added to our staff a very smart, 30-year-old, black lawyer with an impressive resumé. I'd first crossed paths with James A. Franklin, Jr. when he was a student at the University of South Carolina, during the years I coached Gamecocks football. Jim was a standout young man: he was elected president of the student body, and he went on to earn a law degree from Harvard.

He'd landed his first job working for a firm owned by my lawyer, former South Carolina Governor Robert McNair, a Democrat. McNair had the historical misfortune to have been in office during the 1968 Orangeburg Massacre, one of the worst cases of police brutality during the civil rights movement.

Students from all-black South Carolina State University staged a protest of a segregated bowling alley in Orangeburg. One night during a bonfire rally the white police force panicked and opened fire into the mob, killing three boys and injuring twenty-seven others. Most had been shot in the back. Then-Governor McNair had declared it "one of the saddest days in the history of South Carolina."

By the 1990s, McNair was regarded as a friend of the black community and his law firm had grown to more than a hundred lawyers, including Jim Franklin. McNair was in his seventies and slowing down, but he advised me on big picture issues and we participated together in community and University of South Carolina activities. Young Jim Franklin was assigned to do the actual work for me.

As Jim and I got to know each other I found him easy to work with and eager to succeed. I offered him a full time job as house counsel and, with McNair's blessing, he came to work for PMI.

New clients often asked for investment advice when they got their signing bonus checks, and we often referred them to my bank or other people who were experts. But we had never been in the business of recommending investments, other than the penny stock in the board game company, which was small beer and more about supporting a good cause than making a good investment.

In fact, I spent a great deal of my time trying to talk players out of bad financial choices, and trying to get them to stay within the budgets we created for them based on their contracts. A tremendous amount of time and energy went into making sure taxes were accounted for, and that the players were being realistic about how much house they could afford, and how many expensive cars.

Most of them couldn't do it. There was always something they wanted or someone they wanted to help that wasn't part of the budget. I gave so many players my standard lecture: "You have a golden opportunity to put away money so you'll have an income all the way up to when you retire. But it's a one-time opportunity. You don't know how long you're going to play so you can't sit around and give money away. You could play for one year, or it could be fifteen.

"You do know that when your money runs out, there's not going to be anyone there that's going to be able to pay your bills for you and take care of you and your family. The chances are very high that once you leave the game, you'll be lucky to earn more than $50,000 a year."

To most of the young men I represented, who were consumed with competing and seduced by the glamour and power of football stardom, those words meant nothing. Most had their own investment advisors and all we knew about how they were doing was when we got copies of their monthly account statements, often discovering that they'd pulled out a chunk of money for some luxury purchase or the advisor had moved their funds into some other investment.

Andre Rison was a spendthrift, with his fleet of luxury cars and the huge mansion that Lisa Lopes burned down. Mark Clayton, a wide receiver for the Miami Dolphins, was always short on money because he couldn't say no to all the family members asking him for money. They were sucking him dry. I would continue to pay bills for Mark Clayton years after he was out of the NFL because we were such close friends over the years. I thought the world of Mark and we spent a lot of time together back then just having fun. Mark Clayton's college receiver coach at Louisville was Kippy Brown, a close friend of mine and a hell of a football coach.

A few players were good with money. Sterling Sharpe was downright stingy, one of the few who I thought could have done more for others nevertheless Sterling was frugal with his money and not wasteful at all. I talked Sterling into making a large donation to the Eau Claire Pediatric Center in Columbia because I really believed in Dr. Stuart Hamilton and that turned out to be a great thing for the community in Columbia.

Carl Banks of the New York Giants was another who managed his money well. He was all about his family, concerned about providing a future for his kids. He was older than most of the other players and had already made and learned from his mistakes.

In 1998 at the Super Bowl I saw Carl Banks. I spoke to him and he seemed kinda cold and distant for some unknown reason. I ask him could I speak with him privately for a moment. He said yes. I told him that he seemed to be upset with me about something. He was not the friendly Carl Banks I was use to. He said that he was upset because the life insurance I had sold him— that he put $25,000 into—only had a few hundred dollars in it. I ask him if he had been funding it like he said he would for four straight years. He said no. I reminded him that as we had talked about when I sold it to him that if he did not fund the policy the policy would take from the cash value and automatically pay the insurance. I told him that the company should have been sending him notices to that effect. He remembered getting some notices but said he felt I should have been calling him to tell him.

I told him I only made $6,700 on his policy as a commission but I would check into it and if he felt I should refund his money I would or do something that was fair. He said he would be happy if I did something that was fair.

We laughed about some old times and had a non alcoholic drink. A few weeks later I sent Carl Banks a check for $25,000. He immediately called me and said he could not believe my gesture. I told Carl I had never caused a player to lose anything and I did not want him to feel that I had caused him to lose. His friendship was a lot more important to me than money. I always did right by my players in spite of what the government said or the press wrote.

Sometimes players would come to me with an investment offer they'd received to see what I thought. Few of them seemed very good and I told the players what I thought. But that didn't stop them. Mark Clayton, the star wide receiver for the Miami Dolphins, came to me once about a piece of land that some people wanted him to buy in Atlanta for $200,000. The city was supposedly going to build housing on it for people coming to participate in the 1996 Olympics. The promoters told Mark he'd double his money.

I asked the people pushing this project to send me a contract and any other related paperwork. They never did. I scolded Mark. "You don't have a contract, or anything that says how the deal's supposed to work and what they're going to do with your money, or anything."

Mark bristled. "Yeah, but I've been talking to the guy for a long time. I know him really well. He's made a lot of money doing stuff like this. I feel good about it."

"Mark, I've been around a long time and I still don't ever feel good when I don't have anything in writing. You don't need to do this. This guy was pressuring Mark to do the investment immediately. I told Mark that was a red flag because if it is a good investment today it will be a good investment a month from now. It's a real roll of the dice."

I was so vocal and relentless about my opposition that Mark quit bringing it up. That's because he went ahead and wrote the check for $200,000 to the promoters.

Mark had at one point been one of the three highest paid wide receivers in the NFL, making $1.2 million a year in the early 1990's. He and legendary quarterback Dan Marino were at one point the most prolific tandem in NFL history.

Mark Clayton's contract with the Dolphins was coming up for renewal in 1995 and he got it in his swollen head that he should be making $2 million a year. I was negotiating the deal for him with Miami Dophins front office executive Tom Heckert until we got stuck at $1,850,000 a year. I brought it to Mark and urged him to take the deal.

"Listen, you need to go ahead and sign this. You're in Florida. They don't have the state income tax in Florida. So it will be better than if you try to sign with another team in a state that has an income tax."

He dug in his heels. "I'm going to talk to Coach (Don) Shula because I've been here all these years and I've been laying my ass on the line for these people. They need to pay me."

I begged him to calm down and think it over, but he stormed into Shula's office and said something in such a way that the two of them got into a nasty argument that ended with Mark shouting, "If you ain't gonna pay me, I ain't gonna play!"

I got a call from Tom Heckert. He had bad news "Tank, Shula and Mark had a bad cussing match and Coach is so pissed off he doesn't even know if he wants Mark on the team now. I don't know what we're going to do, but the deal is off the table."

I wasn't surprised when the team came back with a new offer, to sign for no raise—$1.2 million—for four more years.

Mark blew a gasket and told Shula he was declaring himself a free agent. But Clayton had been playing for almost a decade for the Dolphins. Statistically, his years were running out.

There was no market for Mark at this time in 1993. He had just turned thirty two years old. He had only been with one team and that was the dolphins for eleven years. He was on his last leg as an NFL player. When the dust settled, I had managed to get him a one-year contract with the Green Bay Packers for $750,000. Clayton had managed to talk himself out of four more years enjoying the mild Miami winters, paying no state income tax on nearly $2 million a year and catching passes from Dan Marino one of the leagues greatest quarterbacks ever. In its place he got Green Bay's Arctic climate, playing on a team where he knew no one, making less money than he'd made in years, when before, he was one of the three highest paid wide receivers in the NFL. To make matters worse Mark was not a starter for the Packers. He was miserable and quit the game after the 1994 season.

And that hot Atlanta property investment that was going to double because of the Olympics? He lost every cent of the $200,000, right near the end of his career. It was a shame and a waste. After that Olympic loss Mark ran low on funds and I had to cosign for Mark to borrow $200,000 from First Citizens bank in Columbia. Later Mark was unable to pay off this loan and I paid it for him.

After all I'd been through with these players, I was skeptical when my new in-house counsel came to me days after he started work to tell me he'd come across a terrific investment vehicle for our players. One of Jim Franklin's corporate clients at McNair's law firm was a consumer loan company, Cash 4 Titles, which made small, short-term loans to desperate people with bad credit and a car title in their name. Cash 4 Titles also made paycheck anticipation or "payday" loans. The default rate was high, so they charged interest rates of more than twenty percent a month. But even with the default rate, Jim said the company made a huge profit.

Cash 4 Titles, based in Atlanta, had more than a hundred stores or sales reps all over the Southeast. The business was legally structured to avoid being subject to usury laws and other regulations.

Cash 4 Titles raised the money to make the loans by selling investors promissory notes that paid unheard-of annualized returns of 36 percent. Jim was pushing it because we would get a cut of any notes purchased by our clients as a kind of finder's fee. Cash 4 Titles would pay our clients about 20 percent annualized and we would get about 16 percent just for making the referral.

Franklin assured me "It's a great investment that your clients can make a lot of good, safe money out of, and we can make a lot of good, easy money out of, and everybody's happy. They've been in business for a long time and they're just killin' it. This is the real deal, Tank."

The company name rang a bell. I'd seen their ads on television, and then I remembered that a few years earlier someone from Cash 4 Titles had come over from their Atlanta office to see me. I had brushed them off at the time because I didn't know the people involved and I had no time to study it to see if it was legitimate.

Now that I knew McNair's law firm represented the company, and that my new in-house counsel had managed their legal work and knew the company inside and out, I gave it a closer look. I discovered I knew one of the Cash 4 Titles principals. Jimmy B. Roof had a successful Michelin tire franchise in the Columbia area and was a big Gamecocks booster. His son Mike had been one of my graduate assistants on the football team and Jimmy sometimes threw a big cookout for all the coaches, players, and their families. Jimmy was an easy-going country boy. I liked him, and I'd been buying my tires from his dealership for years.

Jim Franklin set up a meeting with Jimmy Roof and another Cash 4 Titles guy named Robert C. Ellenburg, also from the Columbia area. I remembered him as the person who had approached me two years earlier. Ellenburg was a retired teacher and high school athletic coach turned entrepreneur.

Roof and Ellenburg explained how it all worked, and that they were raising money to expand the business into new markets. It all sounded solid, although somewhere in the back of my mind I winced a little at profiting from predatory lending. I rationalized that it was a service much like a pawn shop, and I knew that a lot of those small loans never got paid back. For many people in the black and immigrant communities, it was the only place you could go when you needed money for an emergency.

Foremost in my mind was making sure there would be ready access to the invested funds. "I know my athletes," I told Roof and Ellenburg. "If they call me up one night and say they want their money, it means they want it now, not a month from now. They may give you a check for $500,000 today and a week from now ask for $300,000 back because they want to buy Mom a new house. I handle their businesses and I know how they are.

"Now I'm the guy they trust so I have to know I'll be able to pick the phone up and call you and say, 'Fred Taylor wants his money and here's where to wire it within 24 hours.'"

Roof and Ellenburg eagerly assured me that anyone who wanted to cash in their notes could do so anytime they wanted. Hundreds of millions of dollars were flowing through my business at this point. It was clear we could do a lot of business together and PMI could make a lot of money. It all sounded great, but I had never recommended an investment to a client before and I wanted to make sure I was on the right track.

I asked for a meeting with the top executives of Cash 4 Titles, and invited a friend I'd met through Hal Rosenbluth. Randy Thurman sat on Rosenbluth's board and they were friends. Thurman was (and still is at this writing) a well-known executive in the pharmaceutical and health-care fields, and he ran a private fund that invested in health-care companies. He had taken companies public, so I figured he would be the smartest guy to have with me in the room.

We all met in Columbia: our in-house counsel Jim Franklin and I, my mentor Randy Thurman, the local Cash 4 Titles guys Roof and Ellenburg, and the two men who ran Cash 4 Titles, Michael E. Gause and Charles Richard Homa—Mike Gause and Dick Homa. They were professional and persuasive. Their investors included the University of South Carolina head football coach, Brad Scott and his wife and former University of South Carolina football coach Jim Carlen. It also included South Carolina politician Nikki Setzler along with high-level government officials and many others. They described a blue-ribbon operation, with some 2,000 investors and counting.

As soon as they had finished their presentation and left, I got Thurman alone in my office. "So?" I said. To my relief, he smiled and gave me a thumbs up.

"It looks great to me, Tank. These guys clearly know their business and as long as the money can be accessed easily, it's an excellent short-term, high-yield place to park some cash. Beats the hell out of money market funds. I just don't see how it can go wrong."

Ike Hilliard wide receiver New York Giants on horse at the Rivery Ranch, 1997.

Me, Jesse Jackson and Hal Rosenbluth at Hal's offices in Philadelphia, 1998.

(Standing) Gerald Dixon, Shannon and Sterling Sharpe, Mike Jones and Harold Green; (seated) Mark Clayton, me and Andre Rison, March 1993.

Chapter **19**

A ROLLS ROYCE WITH WINGS

WITH JIM FRANKLIN and Randy Thurman giving Cash 4 Titles their blessings, we began to tell our players about the high-yield promissory notes. Over the next year or so they invested a total of more than $18 million. I invested millions of my own money, and some of my family and friends bought in as well.

Our players were happy earning their 20 percent, we were happy earning our 16 percent override, and Cash 4 Titles seemed to be happy earning its 120 percent or so on its car-title and paycheck loans. It was a bonanza for everyone. On an annualized basis, the $18 million our clients invested in Cash 4 Titles notes generated almost $3 million for PMI in overrides.

I made sure to stay in close contact with Dick Homa, Jimmy Roof, and "Bobby" Ellenburg. This was no set-it-and-forget-it deal. My players' earnings, my reputation, and a significant portion of my own wealth was on the line. I wanted to keep my finger on the pulse of Cash 4 Titles. As my business and contacts with them grew, my relationship blossomed with all four—Mike, Dick, Jimmy, and Bob.

As promised, when we called to have some or all of a player's money returned, the funds were transferred within twenty four hours. There were no hesitations and no glitches. It all worked like a finely-tuned Swiss watch.

In the late 1990s the economy heated up and I was in the thick of things, hitting on all cylinders. Emboldened by success, I was intrigued when my partner in the travel agency, Linda Wilson, brought me an opportunity to buy a large, older hotel near downtown Detroit with the idea of renovating it. In the 1996 elections, city voters had approved casino gambling, up to three licenses.

The hotel had been bought at a tax sale by a young real estate speculator who she knew because she had once been married to his father. John Bryant had been a child at the time and after Linda left his father they went there separate ways. It had been years since Linda had heard from or seen the son. Seven years later Bryant invited Linda to his wedding in Detroit. At the wedding Bryant mentioned the hotel and his real estate investment business. Bryant and a partner, Dean Parker, wanted to flip the hotel and he was promoting it as a good investment for us because when the new casinos opened in town, customers would need rooms.

It sounded promising, and as Linda and I talked it over, it occurred to me that I had political connections through people like Congressman James Clyburn, Jesse Jackson, Mayor Clarence Anthony and others that might help us get one of those three casino licenses. If that happened, the hotel's value would soar.

I sent Jim Franklin to Detroit to check it all out. He confirmed that Bryant had bought the hotel from the government at an auction. I flew to Detroit and met Bryant, who walked me through the property. They were both well-spoken, professional, and polished, young entrepreneurs with good business heads. Bryant said his business was buying and selling properties and his capital was tied up so he couldn't raise the estimated $3 million needed to renovate the hotel.

Once again, I called on my Cash 4 Titles mentor, Randy Thurman in Philadelphia and discussed it over the phone. Bryant wanted just over $1 million and at that price, it was hard to see much downside. At the least, a second wave of speculation would come along and we could flip the property ourselves for a profit. Jim Franklin and I started out planning to manage the renovations on our own, but as soon as I saw how complicated it was I reconsidered and decided it was safer to partner with a major hotel operator, leasing the building out to a lodging operator. We began talks with Marriott, but Detroit was low on their list of priority markets so progress was slow.

Meanwhile, the money kept rolling in from the Cash 4 Titles investment overrides, and Cash 4 Titles was booming with all the new money flowing in from PMI's clients. Gause and Homa lived in Florida and they were doing so well they bought a luxury "heavy" corporate jet for $15 million, a Bombardier Challenger 601. Gause in particular wanted to be able to visit potential investors and the loan stores and still be home for dinner with the family.

They gave me a ride and the experience was a game-changer. The plane had twin jet engines mounted at the rear of the fuselage, could fly at over 500 miles per hour, and had a range of about 3,000 miles. The Challenger is so robust and reliable it's used as a transport by military air forces around the world, including the U.S., Canada, and China.

This one was fully tricked out: seven windows along each side of a wide, walk-about cabin furnished with four massive leather easy chairs at the front, two long leather-covered sofas facing each other across the aisle in the middle, two more seats at the rear, a galley, a bathroom with a window, and all of it accented with dark wood-grain paneling and inlays. The sound system was amazing. It was a Rolls Royce bus with wings.

I'd logged millions of air miles, often running through airports to keep to impossibly tight schedules, and nothing I'd ever experienced in any first-class cabin could come close. "Boy, I could sure get some use out of one of these," I told Gause and

Homa. "I spend most of my life on the road." I quizzed them about how much it cost to buy one and how much to operate it.

By the time we'd gotten to our destination, I'd made a deal to lease a one-third share in the cost to operate their jet. By the hour it was $3,500, but for $18,000 a month, I could share the time equally. It made perfect sense. Even with our own travel agency, I was a hostage to airline schedules.

It also would be a real eye-popper for potential clients to be able to fly into their home town airports in "my" private 12-seater jet with its luxury appointments, and to send the plane to their home towns to fly them up to our offices. The cost would be more than offset if it helped me sign just one more major client or negotiate one more major contract a month.

Of all the luxuries that money could buy me, there wasn't much that could hold a candle to the sense of freedom and control of my destiny I got from being able to walk out of my office in South Carolina at two o'clock in the afternoon to attend a business dinner that night in Chicago, arriving with time to spare for cocktails at the bar. The stock market was gushing wealth. "The Millionaire Next Door" was a best-selling book, cab drivers were becoming day traders, and the country was obsessed with all the symbols of wealth—cigars, yachts, vacation homes, and private planes. In that world of smoke and mirrors, that jet was the ultimate symbol of success.

The next business opportunity Jim Franklin brought to me involved banking in the Cayman Islands, a growing international finance center in the Caribbean south of Cuba. He said the Cayman Islands laws offered substantial tax benefits, and the Cash 4 Titles guys were already moving money there. Offshore banking was all the rage at the time, thanks to IRS loopholes and corporate chicanery. The Caymans was a popular place to do it because it was close to the U.S. and the Cayman government and banks made it easy and profitable.

Jim, myself, and the Cash 4 Titles guys made plans to fly

there at the end of the 1997 football season, in January 1998. One of the Cayman bankers was Brazilian and had offered to escort us on a side trip to Rio after we did our business. I'd never been to Rio. It sounded like fun so we added it to our itinerary.

Linda mentioned to her step-son, John Bryant, that we were making this trip and Bryant asked if he could join us. I checked with Mike Gause and Dick Homa and learned there were several unoccupied seats. So John Bryant came along with a business partner named Dean Parker and two other men. They flew with us to the Caymans and sat in on the meetings with our offshore lawyers. They wanted to learn more about how it worked.

Private jetting to such an exotic and wealthy place, finding myself sitting in the sumptuous offices of an international bank talking about moving around millions of dollars, with panoramic views of an azure sea and gleaming beaches right outside the windows, I felt on top of the world.

Bryant's business partner, Parker was an impressive young light-skinned black man, handsome, tall and athletic, from a solidly middle-class background. He had been an aspiring basketball player who failed to break into the big leagues and decided to go into the real estate business.

Parker showed us a picture of his wife Kim and their two young sons, Dean Jr. and Dylan, who attended private schools. He and his family lived an upscale lifestyle in a secluded mansion complete with a man-made lake in the Detroit suburb of Kipp. As near as I could tell, he was a successful black entrepreneur like me, although our childhoods couldn't have been more different.

The Cayman Islands meeting went smoothly. The bankers explained how the Caymans banking business worked, guaranteed that monies deposited there would always be available on a moment's notice, described the tax benefits, and all the rest. Gause and Homa knew their way around all of it, and everything fit together seamlessly. So this is how the big boys do it, I thought.

When we'd finished our meeting, all of us except Gause and

Parker flew on to Rio. Homa explained that Gause was devoutly religious and a homebody who had no interest in visiting a notorious hedonistic playground. Parker lacked a Brazilian visa.

The party included Jim Franklin, Jimmy Roof, Dick Homa, the Caymans banker who was from Rio, John Bryant, two other guys he had brought with him from Detroit, and me. The flight distance was nearly 4,000 miles so we had to stop to refuel half way, in Manaus, Brazil, on the middle reaches of the Amazon River. We all got off to stretch our legs and take a group picture. Rio was spectacular, unlike any place I'd ever seen or experienced. It was a nonstop party. Rio was off the chain to say the least. Our first night in Rio we went to an area called Coco Cabana. They have this strip that is about 200 yards long that is filled with call girls and ladies of the night dressed like they are going to a ball. Sex for sale is as common as ice cream and apple pie in Rio. I could not help but think of Sodom and Gomorrah that night as I talked with the ladies of Coca Cabana. They spoke Portuguese, which is a broken Spanish. But they all understood the U.S. dollar.

It is a fact that the vast majority of rich businessmen especially in America have paid for sex at one time or another. At the end of the day, most men pay for sex in one form or another. The women in Rio were young and as beautiful as one could imagine a woman being.

I had players with women problems. Children out of wedlock and child support issues.

The truth is I was no different. I was relatively young, and rich. At the time money meant virtually nothing to me.

I was married and I had a son by another woman. Matthew Donovan Hampton was born December 28, 1995. I tried to keep it a secret from my wife and everyone, but eventually things got so stressful for me that one night I asked her to take a ride with me and I told her everything. However, I always made a point to spend quality time with Matthew from the first day he was born. Children are like precious stones to me and Matthew was the youngest.

On a trip to Atlanta, Natrone Means and Brantley Evans convinced me I should go to this strip club called Magic City, because we had several player clients going and I needed to socialize with them. I had spent 20 years in and out of Atlanta and I had never been to Magic City. I looked like a "fish out of water" it was obvious I was not a frequent patron.

I was about to leave when I saw this beautiful dancer who called herself Chastity. She came over and said I can tell you don't come to strip clubs often. I replied, "I didn't think it was that obvious". She sat beside me and I gave her twenty dollars. She did lap dances for ten dollars, so that was worth two lap dances. I was embarrassed to have her do a lap dance, so I told her I was paying just to talk to her for two songs. We talked and she said I should come back sometime to the club. I said "I just may do that".

A few weeks later I was back in Atlanta and I went to Magic City to see if Chastity was there. She was actually on the main stage dancing when I came in. She immediately noticed me and as soon as she finished her dance she came over and sat by me saying that she had hoped I would come back. We exchanged numbers and agreed to eat lunch the next day.

Chastity did not seem to fit the mold of what I thought of a stripper. She was intelligent and up to date on current news events and she had a very warm personality. I began to frequent this and other strip clubs for a period of time after my first trip to Magic City.

This is a prime example of how if you put yourself into life's forbidden fast lane shit will happen. I had no business in that strip club, the first time I went, my better judgment told me not to go but I was trying to get to the top of the agent business and I had several clients and potential clients who wanted me to go. And I must admit it was very tempting and exciting.

This is one of those things you feel you really need to do if you are going to be in with the top athletes. Don't kid yourself into believing that it's only Adam "Pacman" Jones and a few other athletes that like going to strip clubs. Most athletes go to strip clubs. They just don't get into any trouble and cause attention to come there way.

The nicest strip club I have been in is in Tampa, Florida. It's called Mons Venus. It's not a big place at all, but it has about 50 of the sexiest, most beautiful dancers that give lap dances.

The first time I went into Mons Venus was in the fall of 1997. I was there for a Tampa Bay Buccaneers game. Alfred Twitty took me there and the place was packed on a Saturday night. I turned the corner with my head on a swivel from glancing at all the sexy young women. Then I noticed, ESPN field reporter Sal Paolantonio laid back with a young sexy brunette on his lap. He had his shirt open and she was massaging his chest and giving him one of those erotic fully nude lap dances that make men want to come back for more.

Being in a strip club is no crime, and it is an adult activity much like gambling, the draw of those beautiful women cannot be underestimated.

Although I was always an early riser, a habit acquired as an athlete in training, and although I never drank much and never did drugs, I managed to keep up with the rest of the guys and never beat the sun coming up during our five days in Rio. Dick Homa was our eager and generous host, paying for everything. But I was ready to leave Rio. Being out every night until the sun came up we flew back exhausted, stopping in the Caymans for a day to tidy up our business there.

The way Homa and the Cayman folks presented it, the off-shore banking system was perfectly legitimate, you saved a lot in taxes, and we'd earn additional income on our deposits to boot. Cash 4 Titles was investing its money there, including funds belonging to some of my players, so I opened an account with about $1.5 million of my own money.

To make sure my clients were protected, I had Cash 4 Titles set up a special account in the Caymans under the name Ashford just to receive funds due our players. When requested, Cash 4 Titles would wire money from that account to the U.S. account of the player. No money was wired to my company account or my personal account, but I was to receive bank statements for Ashford so I could keep track of the flow of funds. We needed the information to make sure everybody was getting what they were entitled to, and that our players were properly reporting their interest income to the IRS.

Prior to the trip to Rio, Linda told me that Bryant wanted to invest in the Cash 4 Titles notes. "Do the Cash 4 Titles people accept cash? John wants to put in a hundred thousand."

That was an odd request. We never dealt in cash. If you had a cash business, retail or otherwise, you deposited the cash in the bank and wrote a check. If you had a business like Mama's, selling moonshine, the bank was the last place you put your money.

I grew up around people who did business in the gray zone because it was the only place they could pursue the American dream. You can't grow up black in America without knowing a lot of people who've seen the inside of a jail cell. You learn to withhold judgment because you know first-hand that plenty of people who have been to jail are basically good, kind, and productive people. But you also learn to watch your back.

I'd heard nothing to suggest her stepson had gone into his father's alleged line of work (when I first met Linda, she told me she had been married once. She said her ex-husband had been killed in the streets of Detroit. It was rumored that he was in the drug trafficking business. She told me she didn't know if the rumors were true or not because when she was married to him she was certain he was not in the drug business. There was nothing extravagant about their lifestyle to suggest any illegal drug activity. He worked as a Detroit Firefighter). Bryant presented himself as a real estate speculator, but $100,000 is a lot of currency in a business where most transactions involve cashier's checks.

"Where's John getting the cash from?"

"He says it's from his night clubs. And they do a lot of gambling in Las Vegas."

It wasn't my call, so I put the question to Roof who said they did have several clients who invested cash from time to time. Then I ran it by Franklin since we'd be earning an override. He assured me that Homa and Gause did accept cash.

"You're sure this won't present a problem for us? I mean, that's a lot of folding money and who knows where it's coming from."

"It isn't our money, so it's not our problem," he said. "If Bryant wants to invest cash, that's none of our concern as long as it doesn't go through our bank accounts."

On Franklin's legal advice, we agreed to arrange the deal and Bryant flew down to Columbia from Detroit with $100,000 cash in a cardboard box. We logged the transaction to keep track of the overrides due us and handed the money over to Jimmy Roof. In the space of just two weeks in January 1998, Bryant and his partner Dean Parker invested nearly a million dollars in the Cash 4 Titles notes, all of it delivered in boxes and garbage bags.

At this point, it was clear something sketchy was going on at the other end. Linda and I, using a money counting machine personally counted all of the money. It took all day, even though it was packaged in rubber bands according to denominations.

One final attempt to give us cash was rejected. Dean Parker's brother Donald showed up one day with $300,000 he said was Dean's and wanted it invested in Cash for Titles. At that point, we balked. Neither Dean nor John was there and handling all of that cash had started to feel creepy and uncomfortable. So we told him we couldn't do it and turned him away.

A shadow of worry fluttered across my mind now and then, but neither Linda nor I asked any questions, nor did Roof or any of the Cash 4 Titles people. Neither Parker nor Bryant volunteered any information, either. As the saying goes, when money talks, the truth is silent. What we didn't know couldn't hurt us. That's how we had it figured.

It was too easy to rationalize our role in these transactions, but no surprise in the context of the sports business. Just about every agent carried wads of cash that found its way into the pockets of promising college players, mostly to curry favor in advance of eligibility. You couldn't buy a player's promise, but the money got his attention long enough for an agent to make the case for why he'd be better than the others.

If I hadn't seen or heard enough of corruption in the business of football, during the hotel purchase and negotiations in Detroit it was clear that pay-to-play was a guiding principle in that city. It's one of those American cities where crime and self-dealing seems to flourish. So when two well-dressed young men from Detroit wanted to invest cash in somebody else's promissory notes, at a handsome profit to my company, it didn't seem like such a big deal. They might be dodging the law, but I wasn't the law, I had no proof the money came from an illegal source, and I had no obligation to ask questions.

As disastrous as these transactions would prove to be, at the time they were just a couple among hundreds we were involved in between the travel business and sports management. Our annualized billings exceeded $100 million. We had four dozen needy clients and faced a dozen crises or deadlines at any given moment. That left little time for moral reflection. My trusted lawyer said it was okay, and that was good enough for me.

The relationship with Cash 4 Titles operated like clockwork. Bryant called us one Friday from Las Vegas asking for $100,000 of his money to be wired to him so he could buy a car. Because it was the start of the weekend, it was impossible to arrange an international wire transfer overnight so I agreed to advance him the money from my account. Cash 4 Titles promptly reimbursed me by wire transfer the following Monday.

Everything I touched was turning to gold. We had so much money coming in that I decided to expand the agency business by building a state-of-the-art sports complex. We bought a piece of land along one of the interstates around Columbia where we planned to build offices and a training center for prospects and players. We hired architects to draw up sketches and start the site engineering.

The sports complex was to have enough extra space to lease for offices, restaurants, and retailers so the rental income would cover the operating expenses. That way we'd end up with our own offices and training facility space for free.

Linda, Jim Franklin, and I created a holding company for much of this new activity called Silver Line Development. I retained a majority interest. Silver Line owned the Detroit hotel, the sports complex project, and would own any other properties we might buy or develop in the future.

As my wealth and national visibility increased, I also became known as an active philanthropist and fundraiser in the community, fulfilling an obligation I always felt to pay my good fortune forward. I helped raise money for and made large donations to The United Way and the American Red Cross, sitting on their local boards. I also sat on the board of Columbia's nonprofit hospital, Richland Memorial, which provided free medical care to the poor and uninsured.

I was elected to the board of the local United Negro College Fund, and was active with the Urban League. I funded a scholarship endowment at my alma mater, Carson Newman College, and I pledged $300,000 to build a child care center in Columbia, to be named after my grandmother, Susie Black.

My core sports business was chugging along at high speed, and I was making bigger inroads into the Florida college football scene. I had signed one first-round pick and two second rounders in the 1998 NFL draft and the next year promised to be even more successful.

The first sour note came five or so weeks after Bryant and Parker had invested all that cash. Linda called me one day sounding uncharacteristically grim. "Tank, we might have a problem."

Linda had just received a phone call from Dean's wife Kim. Dean had been arrested and they needed some of his money. He and John Bryant were targets in a major investigation into a massive cocaine distribution ring.

Linda was furious. "How could John do this to us? How could he put us in this position?" Now we knew where all of that money had been coming from, and our involvement in helping off-shore all that cash made us feel dangerously vulnerable. Still I persuaded myself that because I was in the dark when the money changed hands, I was not responsible. See no evil, and so on.

Dean managed to make bail, which seemed like a good sign. What we didn't know is that he got out by secretly agreeing to wear a wire, to trap John Bryant. The cops didn't trust Parker to keep his word, and with good reason. He was plotting. Within days of his release, he loaded the car with essentials and his family and bolted, leading the Dearborn cops on a high-speed chase before escaping.

We learned Dean was a fugitive, when one day at the beginning of April Dean shows up unannounced with his family in Columbia. He needed to get his money out of Cash4Titles. Linda and I dreaded getting the phone call or visit from Dean or John looking to us to help them get there money, knowing that there every move was probably being monitored by the FBI or DEA. Linda and I felt like we were between a rock and a hard place. We had helped Dean invest his money in Cash4Titles, how could we not give him assistance and then on the other hand he was a fugitive on the run from the law. Whatever decision we made we appeared to be screwed. We were also worried about our business getting mixed up in his and hurting our reputation.

Parker took his family to Myrtle Beach for a few weeks and then wanted to go to Montego Bay, Jamaica, to see some real estate he was interested in purchasing. Linda and I flew with the Parkers and their kids to Montego Bay on the corporate jet. In Jamaica, we drove out to the property but Dean didn't like the location, but they wanted to stay a while and chill out in Jamaica. Linda and I returned to Columbia breathing great sighs of relief. Dean Parker was out of the country and out of our hair.

We had dodged a bullet, or so we thought!

My daughter Shayla, and my granddaughter, Kaylen (KK).

My son, Matthew Donovan Hampton, at his graduation (below, left).

My granddaughter, Kennedi Aleise.

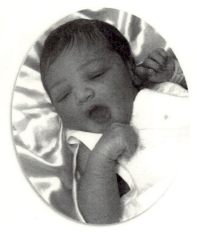

John Brown, Denzel Washington and Linda, at John's house in Columbia, South Carolina, spring 1996.

Me and Randy Thurman at the Rivery Ranch, Linton, North Dakota, 1997.

PART IV
End Game

Starting at the center: Coach Brad Scott, my banker friend Tommy Bone, and me at FCA golf fundraiser.

Chapter **20**

SAVING VINCE CARTER'S BACON

THE SHRILL BEEPING of my pager woke me at home one night in October 1999. The display showed an unfamiliar number in an Oakland, California area code. I rolled over to go back to sleep but the pager went off again—same number. What football player did I know in Oakland who'd be calling me in the middle of the night?

I picked up the phone and dialed. An operator answered—a hotel switchboard. I had no idea who to ask for and decided it was someone dialing a wrong number.

As I settled back into bed, the damn thing went off again, same number. I padded down the stairs to my garage and threw the pager on the front seat where it could beep all night without disturbing anybody. I'd sort it out in the morning.

After a pre-dawn breakfast I checked the pager and counted more than two dozen calls from the same Oakland hotel number. I wracked my brain as I drove to the office until it hit me that the recently franchised Toronto Raptors basketball team was traveling on the West Coast. The calls must have been from the team's star player, Vince Carter, my first and only basketball client. I went straight to my desk and dialed.

"I'm sorry, we have no Vince Carter registered."

Vince sometimes used aliases when he traveled, to avoid being spied on. I tried a few names I remembered him using before, and got lucky. The operator laughed. "Yeah, we have an Al Capone. Please hold." It was still middle of the night in California, but Vince picked up on the first ring.

"Hey, buddy. What's goin' on? You musta called me 30 times!"

"Tank, man, you gotta help me!" The stress in his voice was jarring in someone usually full of good-natured bluster and optimism. He sounded nearly hysterical.

"I got a serious problem. I don't know what to do. You gotta promise you won't tell my mom. Shit!" He started bawling. "I fucked up good this time."

Every horrible scenario ran through my head, including the one with a dead body in his room. That wasn't anything I'd expect of Vince, but I'd only known him about 18 months, since he'd signed with me at the end of a spectacular junior year at the University of North Carolina in Chapel Hill. It's more accurate to say his mother signed with me, because Michelle Robinson (she'd remarried) wouldn't let me near Vince until she and I had basically done the deal. All he was supposed to do was sign his name.

Vince Carter's sudden financial success had turned Michelle from a hard-working school teacher into a tyrannical dictator, living like a queen on her son's sudden wealth. Vince might be a beast on the hardcourt, but he was a mouse with his mom.

Vince, the multi-millionaire NBA star, once asked his mother for money to buy some custom clothes. When she turned him down, rather than stand up to her, he came to me and borrowed the money on the sly. Vince and Michelle made a successful but dysfunctional team. She was the most extreme example I encountered of a player parent run amok. I'm sure she loved Vince, but she loved his money more.

Vince made up for the oppression when he was on the road, away from family. That always meant girls. He often asked me to help him find female company in another city. He couldn't just go out to a night club and pick up a girl without risking finding himself in the gossip columns. He was the pride of Toronto's young NBA team, an up-and-comer who quickly became known as a dunk master, executing his signature dunks with ballet-like grace and accuracy. He'd go on to win the NBA Slam Dunk Contest in February 2000. He was a point guard with a real gift, and the fans loved him for putting Toronto on the basketball map.

We had a list of call-girl services we trusted and could rely on to find someone in most any city. These women tended to be the type that loved spending time with athletes and loved getting paid richly for doing it. They had every incentive to remain discreet, and always did.

We had negotiated lucrative endorsement deals for Vince with companies like Puma, Fleer Sky Box, and Gatorade to name a few. When I heard the terror in his voice that morning on the phone, I prayed that whatever he'd gotten himself into could be fixed without attracting attention from the cops or the press. Millions were on the line.

"Vince, Vince, slow down for a minute. First tell me what's going on and we'll sort it out."

It was one of many crazy moments in what had been a crazy year, 1999. It began with my signing a record-setting five first-round picks in the NFL draft. But it also began with an investigation by the University of Florida into loans I had arranged and cash I had provided to standout Gators football players who were close to becoming eligible for the draft.

The NFL Players Association, the union that also regulates agents, had instigated it. In the beginning it seemed like more of a nuisance than a threat. Most top agents were doing what I was being targeted for, and almost every player exploited the system by taking money from multiple agents. It was the worst-kept dirty little secret in college football. By all accounts it still is.

But the nuisance had escalated into a crisis, and it appeared

Vince Carter was about to hand me another. He'd gotten a Toronto girl pregnant. She'd called Vince to deliver the news and announced that she intended to keep the baby.

Vince was a wreck. He wasn't married or engaged, but he was going steady with Evonne Lopez from Florida who I was sure Vince's mother didn't think was good enough for Vince. He cared most, however, about keeping it from his mother. He was that intimidated.

Once I got him calmed down and off the phone, I booked a flight to Toronto to meet the girl. This young lady Cyndi I had met a few weeks earlier after a Toronto basketball game. I wanted to find out what was going on for myself, and see what we'd need to do to keep it out of the news.

Assuming she wasn't lying or trying to pin someone else's baby on Vince, Vince said he wanted me to offer this lady whatever she wanted to make this go away, for her discretion—silence. After fifteen years as a player manager I was used to dealing with women claiming they'd been impregnated or abused in some way by a millionaire athlete. My clients Fred Taylor, Ike Hillard and Duce Staley were all dealing with child support issues. At the same time that Vince's crisis popped up, another of my clients, Rae Carruth, was attending Lamaze classes with a woman carrying twins she claimed were his. As the stakes got higher and higher, with huge endorsement deals on the line, these secret dramas posed threats that needed to be dealt with quickly, before the press got hold of them.

I arrived in Toronto on a cold, late-fall day and headed into town in a rental car to meet with Cyndi-Vince's problem girl, hoping she wouldn't turn out to be crazy or greedy. The purpose of my journey was a stark reminder that being an agent for young athletes with big egos earning huge salaries looks a lot more glamorous than it really is. The work included sordid tasks like the mission I was on. In Vince Carter's case, it would be followed by a reckoning with his powerful mother who kept a tight rein on his money. Although Vince begged me to keep this news from reaching her ears, I knew she would find out one way or another, and I was sure she'd have plenty to say to Vince about it.

The stakes were high because a lot of people besides Vince had come to rely on his income since I first signed him in the spring of 1998. In less than a year and a-half he had become my most profitable client. Football had been my sport all my life and my career for two decades. Within the football world I had become known as an expert. I represented more than four dozen NFL players, many of them marquee names in their cities, and a number of them with national followings.

It was something to take pride in, especially for a black guy in a business dominated by white owners, managers, and head coaches. And I had done it during a period when player salaries grew and attracted a lot of new people into becoming player agents. Each year the field got more crowded and the competition fiercer.

I had been mulling how I might break into basketball when I got a call in early spring 1998 from Grady C. Irvin, Jr., a young, passionate, black attorney from Tampa who I knew well from my days with Sterling Sharpe, my first client. Grady had been one of the lawyers working for the NFL Players Association when Sterling suffered his career-ending neck injury in 1994.

The players' union was going to help Sterling in his dispute with the Green Bay Packers over how much he was entitled to be paid for his last, in-completed season. The team had ordered him to have surgery to see if the injury could be repaired to a point where he could resume playing. But after the surgery the doctors said it was too dangerous for him to take the field again.

The Packers then released him with an offer of only $300,000 in severance. He would have earned $3.3 million if he could have played the whole season. He had his career-ending injury insurance to fall back on, but there was still a lot of money at stake. The Packers were in the wrong to punish Sterling for getting hurt, but

Sterling had ticked off the owners more than once with his pay demands and ego battles with star quarterback Brett Favre. Now the Packers were giving him a taste of his own medicine.

In an effort to resolve the dispute, I flew to the NFL Players Association headquarters in Washington, DC. The honchos—President Gene Upshaw and his right-hand man, General Counsel Richard Berthelsen—were out of town so Sterling's grievance was assigned to a NFLPA attorney, Grady Irvin. We spent some three hours talking about the case and getting to know each other. I was impressed by his passion for the well-being of players and his knowledge of the system. He assured me, "We've got a good case against the Packers on this one."

A week or so later Grady flew to Columbia for a follow-up meeting that included Sterling. But in the midst of the legal maneuvering, Grady quit working for the union and went into private practice in Tampa, Florida. By this time Sterling was just as impressed by Grady as I was and we both wanted to keep him on the case. Upshaw and Berthelsen, Grady's former bosses, would have to give their blessing.

Sterling was in my office when I called Berthelsen, expecting a speedy and hearty approval. I hardly got the words out when he cut me off. "That ain't gonna be possible." Then he rushed me off the phone with some excuse about another call.

Annoyed as hell, I hung up and immediately dialed Upshaw. He delivered an equally unpleasant response. "We're gonna bring this case and Grady's not gonna be a part of it, at all. End of story."

"Gene, I don't get it. Why does it matter so long as we win? Sterling's payin' Grady's fees, not you. All he wants him to do is just be a part of the case and help out. He knows it backward and forward."

"We're not doin' none of that," he snapped. "If Grady's gonna be a part of the case, we're not gonna file it." I was getting a front-row seat to the Upshaw I had heard about, the one who was autocratic, territorial, and ruthless.

"Why would you not file it, Gene? You know you've got a case, and all Sterling wants is to make sure the same guy who started it is there to help finish it. I thought you'd be glad to have somebody share the cost. This is savin' you guys money."

Upshaw wouldn't give an inch. He expressed no particular interest in Sterling's fate, but it was clear he wanted the union getting all the credit for winning a claim against the Packers. Sterling heard my side of the conversation and when I hung up he was so infuriated he insisted on calling Upshaw himself, on speakerphone. He got the same brush-off: "Sterling, Grady's not gonna be a part of it. And if we're gonna file this, we're gonna file it and we're the ones who are gonna deal with it. Nobody else."

"But I'm the client. I'm a dues-payin' member of the union and I'm the guy who's hurt. I should be able to use who I want."

"Well, you can either use him or use us, but you're not gonna use both."

Sterling blew up and Gene responded in kind, setting off a long cussing match that finally ended when Gene hung up on Sterling and Sterling bellowed, "MOTHER******!!!"

He defied the union and hired Grady Irvin, so infuriating Upshaw and Berthelsen that they refused to lend any support to Sterling in his dispute, thereby undercutting his bargaining position.

This schism had even greater implications for me. I was licensed by the union and the bosses made it clear that I should support their position by using my influence with Sterling to get him to do what they wanted: forget Grady and use the Players Association. I was the man in the middle, but I couldn't do the bidding of Upshaw and Berthelsen without betraying the wishes of my client.

Sterling knew what he wanted, he had been my first player, and if he was willing to pay the freight, why should I interfere? Between the union that licensed me and the player who depended on me, my first responsibility was to Sterling, so I had to support his decision. That created some very bad blood between me and the Players Association, especially Berthelsen who treated me with disdain ever after that, like I was a traitor. Looking back on it now, it's clear that this episode planted a seed that years later would blossom into a catastrophe.

After speaking with Grady Irvin I learned what the real issue was regarding Sterling and his grievance. Grady had to file the grievance by a particular date or Sterling would lose his right to file a future claim. Berthelsen was out of the office and Grady filed the grievance on behalf of Sterling against the Packers.

There was a clause in the NFL collective bargaining agreement that caused 50% of Sterling's 3.3 million dollar salary to count immediately against the Packers salary cap once the grievance was filed. Berthlesen ask Grady did he know the effect this was having on the Packer's salary cap. Grady said that was not his concern because he was hired to protect the player's rights. Berthlesen had likely gotten a call from the NFL management council, the attorneys that represent the NFL teams and Grady thought Berthlesen wanted to appease the management council.

Grady would not change anything that would allow the Packers to get relief from the salary cap hit and from that day forward Berthlesen had disdain for Grady and he wanted Grady out of the NFLPA.

Grady was a very hard worker, coming in at 7am and staying most days until 7pm. He said that Berthlesen would come in at around 11am most days and leave between 3 and 4pm. They were cut from a totally different work ethic and certainly a totally different character. Initially, Richard Berthlesen had pursued Grady telling him he wanted a black attorney to be out front on some of their cases.

Grady had filed an antitrust suit against major league baseball called Morsani v Major league baseball. It was a high profile case and Berthlesen really wanted Grady out from that point on.

Grady turned the NFLPA offer down the first time and eventually agreed to accept the position after they agreed to fly him back and forth from Tampa and put him up in a hotel for six months. Now he wanted Grady out, it appeared because he could not control Grady. Grady would resign and go into private practice. He was fed up with the under the table shenanigans of Berthlesen and the NFLPA. Grady said that a couple of years later at the NFLPA super bowl party Gene Upshaw would apologize to him for how they handled him and the whole Sterling Sharpe situation. At the party Berthlesen approached Grady and ask him what he was doing there. Grady said he just came by to say hello to Gene and some other former associates. Grady said Berthlesen told him he should not be there and wanted Gene to throw him out of the party. Gene just told Berthlesen to relax and blew it off.

Grady Irvin went on to establish a reputation as a maverick, choosing to remain a sole practitioner rather than join a large firm. He was noted for taking on unpopular and hopeless cases, and unafraid to speak out about racism in the judicial system. He once told a Tampa business magazine that among African-American lawyers it was a common experience to overhear "demeaning and insulting" courthouse remarks by white attorneys and court staff. "I am sometimes disheartened when civility takes a back seat."

As mutual outcasts from the players' union, Grady and I became close friends, so I wasn't surprised when he called me one day and wanted to know if I represented any basketball players, or wanted to. He offered to arrange an introduction to Michelle and Harry Robinson, mother and step-father of the star shooting guard for the North Carolina Tarheels—Vince Carter. The Tarheels had been Michael Jordan's college team, and the coach for many years had been the legendary Dean Smith, who had just retired.

Vince Carter would be a great catch for my company, a move into a second sport with a high-visibility client on day one. I knew exactly what my pitch would be and why I had an advantage: we were not on the radar of any other basketball agent because we had never represented any athletes except football players. We also had established a track record for going out and actively marketing our players for endorsements and other deals. In 1997, I negotiated a $150,000 shoe deal with Converse for Ike Hilliard, while other first rounders were getting $10,000 to $15,000.

Sports agents are notorious for badmouthing and backstabbing each other—anything to get a leg up on the other guy. But being pegged in the media and the industry as an NFL agent, meeting with Vince Carter's family would be seen by basketball agents as a courtesy gesture or a fool's errand. The NBA field was dominated by billion-dollar sports management company IMG, and the likes of celebrity agents such as Michael Jordan's David Falk and Kobe Bryant's Arn Tellem. I was the only black agent, so the other guys may also have dismissed my inclusion as an empty equal-opportunity gesture. I saw it as the challenge and opportunity it had always been for me—a shared cultural background.

Hiding in plain sight and with fire in my belly I flew to Daytona, Florida with my in-house counsel Jim Franklin and PMI's marketing director Bill Shelton, to meet Vince's mother and stepfather—Michelle and Harry Robinson. We had methodically prepared ourselves, spending several hours in the office planning our presentation. We'd been forewarned by Grady's contact that Michelle was running the show, and Vince wouldn't be there at her insistence. The message was clear: I would meet Vince if, when, and where Michelle chose.

The Robinsons greeted us warmly with the engaging manners you'd expect in a couple of school teachers they were. They lived a solid, middle-class lifestyle in a well-kept but unremarkable Florida rancher. Harry's bright, ready smile and easy-going ways helped settle the butterflies in my stomach. But Michelle looked weary as we sat down around their dining table, which had been cleared to make a conference table for our meeting.

"I don't have a lot of time," she began, "but you had such a

strong recommendation I figured we ought to hear you out."
About a half-hour into our two-hour presentation, Michelle began to drift off. Her eyes grew heavy-lidded, her gaze wandered, and she seemed to be melting into her chair. Harry remained alert and engaged, but we needed to win over Michelle. It was time to change the pace.

I abruptly stood up and locked my gaze on Michelle, eye-to-eye. "Mrs. Robinson, we are the best company by far to assist your son in developing his career. There's a lot we can do for you that you might not have thought of that could bring in a lot of money, and pretty quick, too.

"All I'm asking for is an hour or so more of your time. But I need all of your attention." Then I pulled off my suit jacket and flung it across the room where it landed on the floor. Michelle snapped to attention and stared at me with wide eyes as I unbuttoned my cuffs and neatly rolled up my sleeves.

"Well, all right, then. You've got my attention now!"

That broke the ice. Michelle emerged from her haze and the meeting ran more than three hours, followed by dinner at a gourmet seafood restaurant. I explained agenting to them in a way no one else had—honest about the good and the bad, and making it clear that it was about more than money.

"Look, we don't have any basketball players. Now, you might look at that as a negative but because Vince will be our first, you best believe we're going to do everything we can to make sure that this works out for us as well because we want to build a reputation with a big splash.

"Furthermore, our players are like family. I'm there for them whether it's a business decision or a personal crisis, twenty-four hours a day, seven days a week. As Vince's folks, I can assure you I'll be keeping an eye on him."

They said they liked what they'd heard, and appreciated what they'd learned about the business side of a professional athlete's life. As we parted, Harry whispered to me, "She's impressed!"

A week or so later he called to say we were among the final three candidates of all the agents they'd met and that they wanted to visit our offices and talk some more. The next day Jim Franklin and two other members of my staff flew down to Daytona with me in the Challenger to pick up the Robinsons and bring them to Columbia. They'd never been in a corporate jet and the experience had the intended effect—they were agog.

The camaraderie established during our first meeting deepened as the day wore on. I had each of our staff members explain the services they performed for our clients. Michelle hit it off with Linda Wilson, my partner in the travel agency. I took the whole staff out to dinner with Michelle and Harry. The Robinsons spent the night in my home. The next morning after breakfast we boarded the Challenger and flew the Robinsons home. Harry told me on the sly that he thought Michelle had been sold, but I remained cautious. My competition—David Falk and Arn Tellum—were heavy hitters and would put up a fight.

I called the Robinsons every day for a week or so until one day Michelle asked if I could send the jet to pick them up and fly them to Columbia for a second visit. She said she'd prefer to meet me in Columbia rather than in Daytona, and I agreed to send the jet empty. She said she wanted to tell me something "face-to-face." I couldn't imagine her asking for such an elaborate favor if they didn't intend for Vince to sign with me, but I was on pins and needles that morning waiting for them to arrive in the limo I'd sent to pick them up at the airport.

Michelle grinned broadly as she stepped out of the car in front of my office. "Tank, I don't want you stressing anymore over this situation. I have good news. Vince is going to declare himself eligible, and we've chosen PMI to represent him. It's official."

It was a huge victory, won by thinking smart, working hard, and praying constantly. But it was also one of the oddest of my career. I still hadn't met my client, although I'd spoken with him briefly a few times on the phone. "So when do I get to meet the star of the show?"

"We'd like to go to Chapel Hill and pick up Vince and take him home," Michelle said. "Then we'll come back up with Vince to sign the papers."

A few anxious days later, Vince finally arrived in Columbia with his mother and Harry and signed his contracts. Vince was the well-spoken, polite young man he'd been on the phone, and completely deferential to Michelle. Vince was the star, but Michelle was the boss.

It was May 1998 when Vince came to Columbia to sign with me and PMI but it felt like New Year's and Christmas rolled into one. Everyone in the office was in a giddy mood. We broke out some champagne and the staff lined up to have their pictures taken with Vince and his family. I took a moment to send a text message to my man Alfred Twitty who'd bet me I would never land Vince. The message was simple, "15," Vince's Tarheels jersey number five times.

I couldn't wait for the basketball world to discover that one of the kings of football had snatched a prize player out from under the noses of the biggest guns in the NBA. My future just kept getting brighter. "15 15 15 15 15"

PMI guys (from left rear): Tweet, me, Jim Franklin, Banks, Bill Shelton, Oliver Lucas. (Front) Ivory Hilliard and Bralyn Bennett.

Me and Vince at marketing meeting in my office, Columbia, South Carolina, 1998.

Me, Vince and Swedish candy makers.

Chapter **21**

FRIENDS FOREVER

B Y THE TIME I flew to Toronto to fix the problem with his pregnant girlfriend in October 1999, just sixteen months after he first signed with me, we had helped to elevate Vince Carter from a gifted athlete with great promise into a superstar moneymaker. His announcement in Chapel Hill, in May 1998, that he was forgoing his senior year to declare himself eligible to play professionally had been big news. Then he was a hot prospect going into the 1998 NBA Draft, to be held June 24 in Vancouver, British Columbia.

Once Vince was our client, Michelle began calling me several times a day. Her main concern was money—how much was Vince going to earn? Michelle asked me one day "Do you think Vince could make as much as Michael Jordan, from endorsements?"

The question caught me by surprise. Vince hadn't even been drafted yet. Michael Jordan was retired, a well-established legend. "That's a tall order, Michelle. No NBA player has come close to making Jordan's kind of money. But," I added coyly, "no rookie has ever been marketed like we're going to market Vince, including Michael Jordan. So who knows? Let's see where he ends up in the draft first. That'll tell us a lot."

Michelle, Harry, some new PMI marketing partners and my senior PMI staff flew with me in the Challenger to Vancouver a few days ahead of time. Vince arrived separately with his girl-friend, Ellen. Vince dated Ellen in college and shortly after the draft they broke up. But Michelle remained in contact with Ellen and kept her updated on what was going on with Vince. He later met Evonne and began dating her. It was obvious Michelle preferred Ellen over Evonne. Vince and Ellen eventually married and then divorced.

I had arranged for Vince to participate in a work-out with the Oakland, California-based Golden State Warriors just before going to Vancouver. The Warriors had the fifth pick and Vince was expected to go early, especially to a team like Golden State which was desperate for talent after finishing an embarrassing 30-52 season. I wanted them to see what an asset he would be.

Professional sports drafts always have there moments of drama and that years NBA draft was no exception. The night of the draft in the green room there were tables for Vince and our group, Mike Bibby, Antawn Jamison, Mike Olawakandi, Keith Traylor, Paul Pierce and Raef LaFrentz. David Falk walked into the room and whispered into his client Mike Bibby's ear. Immediately after that Mike Bibby burst into tears, right there in the green room in front of everybody. He was being consoled by his mother and other family members and friends.

I had figured that David Falk had told Bibby he was gonna be chosen #1 overall by the Los Angeles Clippers and now had to give him the bad news, that the Clippers were taking Michael Olawakandi. That meant that the Vancouver Grizzlies would likely select Bibby with the second pick of the draft. This was the team he did not want to play for. Vince and I were seated right next to Bibby and his table and Vince was trying to figure out what the problem was. I told Vince the bad news Falk must have just had to give to Bibby. Vince simply replied " better him than me", at least he is from the west coast".

The draft started and sure enough the L.A. Clippers selected Olawakandi with the first pick and Vancouver selected Bibby who was totally shaken up. Denver took Raef LaFrentz with the third pick and Toronto selected Antawn Jamison with the fourth pick. I thought for sure Toronto would take Vince, I was shocked. Head coach Butch Carter of the Toronto Raptors had assured me that the one player they coveted was my guy Vince Carter. With the fifth selection the Golden State Warriors selected Vince Carter and we were all wearing Golden State caps at our table. Five minutes later we found out that before the draft Toronto had agreed to take Antawn and trade him to Golden State for Vince. Now we were all wearing the Toronto Raptors caps we preferred over Golden State. Butch Carter had held true to his word. Toronto loved its new team, but they were growing impatient after limping through its first three seasons, finishing the 1997-98 season with a dismal 16-66 record.

The steal of the draft that year was Paul Pierce falling to the tenth pick to the Boston Celtics. Several teams passed on Pierce who ultimately ended up being the best player of that draft. Vince would win the NBA Rookie of the year and Paul Pierce would come in second.

Vince had a third cousin who was already playing for the Raptors. Tracy McGrady had been *USA Today's* High School Player of the Year and was drafted the year before Vince, right out of high school. Tracy, only eighteen at the time, became the youngest rookie in the NBA.

From Vancouver our entourage flew to Toronto where we met with Raptors Head Coach Butch Carter, who appreciated that I had been a coach myself and a starring high school basketball player. We understood each other, got along well, and he was open to some suggestions I made about how best to groom Vince's performance. While there we also explored some possible endorsement prospects locally and across the border in the U.S.

We now knew where Vince would be playing, and we had an idea of how much he'd be earning. But we had to wait to negotiate his contract because of an unresolved dispute over a new collective bargaining agreement between the NBA Players Association and the league. The season was expected to be delayed. No one could say for sure when, or if, it would start.

Nevertheless, as I had with so many players and their families before, I went ahead and co-signed a loan so Vince could buy a new SUV, and Michelle could buy a Mercedes-Benz. On top of that, I advanced them about $30,000 in cash. Unlike many of my new clients, Vince came from a stable, middle-class background with responsible, caring parents. Although Harry was a stepfather, he had parented Vince from the age of seven and been one of Vince's biggest supporters, filming nearly every game he ever played. Michelle had earned an MBA degree in addition to her teaching credentials. She was motivated and ambitious. Unlike some of my clients there were no pressing financial emergencies. Michelle just wanted material things now and did not want to wait until the lockout was over and Vince could start earning his salary.

Under the circumstances, I thought I had been generous in sticking my neck out, especially for a player whose league was on strike and whose contract signing would be delayed. But Michelle wanted more, NOW. One day she called me and announced that Vince had "found her" a new home. I had no illusions that a twenty-one-year-old college boy had been out looking for a house for his mother. Michelle had been shopping for a new home that Vince would buy with the money he hadn't yet earned. The price on the house was $650,000. Michelle asked me to help facilitate this deal and I contacted my bankers and used my connections to get Michelle in that home.

The only financial guidance I gave my players was to encourage them to use some of their good fortune to help others. Beyond that I had learned not to interfere with their money decisions because it often led to friction. I'd been told to mind my own business enough times that I made it a habit to mind my own business.

Next she asked me to co-sign for a lakefront apartment in Toronto where Vince could live during the season and his family could visit him. That was $400,000, financed by my bank in Columbia. This was also purchased before Vince signed and I personally cosigned for this loan.

While we waited for the NBA contract talks, we helped Michelle set up a corporation to manage the endorsement deals, Visions in Flight, Inc. One of the first deals was with a trading card company, for about $100,000. Michelle made herself CEO and 51 percent owner of Visions in Flight and immediately started spending that money to furnish the new home that Vince her junior partner at 49%, had "found" for her.

Vince said nothing to me about his mother's controlling behavior until January, just before the lock-out ended. One night I took him, Michelle, and Harry out for dinner at the exclusive Capitol City Club in Columbia. During the meal Vince mentioned that another player had taken him to a tailor that specialized in making suits for professional athletes who had a hard time buying clothes that fit their tall, bulky, or long-limbed bodies. He'd already been measured and knew what he wanted.

Michelle sipped her wine and gave Vince a narrow-eyed look. "How much is that going to cost?"

"I don't know. I guess maybe about $15,000. But that's for a whole wardrobe, so I wouldn't have to buy anything else for a long time." Vince had that hangdog look, like he was begging for scraps from the dinner table.

"Well, we got a lot of expenses now, Vince, and you need to wait 'til this lock-out is over before you start spending money on fancy clothes and whatnot. It's not like you've got nothing to wear."

It was such a shameful, embarrassing moment for Vince I felt a wave of empathetic heat rise up my neck. How could a mother treat her son with such callous indifference, like he was her personal ATM machine? The hurt on Vince's face was painful to see.

Later, when we all got back to my house, Vince quietly asked me to take him out for a drive. As soon as we left the driveway he said, "Tank, my mom has everything she wants—a new house, a new Mercedes, new clothes, jewelry, and all I want is some nice clothes that fit me right. It's just not fair."

"Why don't you talk to her about it? Just tell her how you feel." I didn't dare take sides, or say what was in my heart—it's your money, you'll earn it, and you shouldn't let your mother bully you about it. I had learned the hard way not to get in the middle of family squabbles.

Vince shook his head glumly. "No, I'm not gonna say anything to her. I can't. I'm just gonna go on and order the suits. They won't be ready for a month anyway. I want you to pay for them, and I'll pay you back." Instead, I loaned him the money to pay the tailor with the understanding that he would pay me back after he got his signing check.

The NBA dispute was finally resolved in mid-January and a week later, just before the abbreviated season was to start, Vince celebrated his twenty-second birthday. I bought him a diamond and platinum Rolex watch that set me back $60,000, inscribed with the words "Friends Forever." My jeweler is a really great guy from Chicago named Mark Engel. Mark always dealt in high quality jewelry and could be trusted to always do what he said he would do. His character is impeccable and he is just a down to earth good person.

Vince lived up to the expectations everyone had for him. He and Tracy helped the Raptors win forty-six percent of the fifty games played in that lockout-shortened season. Vince was named NBA Rookie of the Year. The money had started to roll in as well. In just a year we had racked up approximately $50 million in salary and endorsement deals, and I was repaid all the money I had advanced against Vince's earnings.

It rankled me a little when Michelle called during that first season and asked to use the corporate jet to take her mother and some friends to see Vince play in Toronto. The jet cost me $18,000 per month, and I never charged a cent of interest on all the loans I'd made. It seemed presumptuous of her to ask.

But it all seemed to work out when Michelle decided that since everything was going so great with Vince she didn't want us to sign any more basketball players. In return, she agreed to extend Vince's contract with us and pay additional fees. Vince signed a new twelve-year contract, agreeing to pay my agency a thirty percent commission on new endorsement deals. Vince signed this new contract even after the national press started negatively reporting that I was under investigation for paying players. I was happy with the way things were working out. I enjoyed Vince's company and he had a lot going for him. He was a big hit with sponsors and we had only begun to develop his potential.

So, a few months later, when I got Vince's panicked call from Oakland about his pregnant girlfriend Cyndi, the stakes couldn't have been higher. I met her at a downtown Toronto hotel. Instead of a grasping, angry twenty-year-old girl, I found a pleasant, friendly, agreeable young woman.

"First of all, I want to be fair and up front with you," I said. "Vince is a little shaken up about all this. He's not ready to be a father."

"I guess Vince should have thought about that ahead of time." I couldn't stifle a laugh and she surprised me by also laughing.

Cyndi sipped her Coke. "You know, I told Vince that I talked to my mother about this, but I didn't really. The only person I told was Vince and I haven't decided yet whether to have the baby or not."

Over the next couple of hours she told me how she met Vince and how they spent a lot of time together in the beginning. We talked about the pluses and minuses of having a baby at such a young age. Although I had Vince's okay to offer her $50,000 and a new car, she said nothing to hint that she had her hand out or some other hidden agenda, and I thought it would be an insult to bring it up.

"I'm just upset with Vince because of the way he treated me. I mean, we had some fun together and I thought we had a good thing going. Then, just like that he gets in my panties and he stops calling me, I never figured Vince to be a dog like that."

Her story was a broken record to my ears. If the girl hadn't preyed on the famous athlete for some ulterior motive, then the athlete—trained and groomed to compete to win—had used the girl to satisfy his need to conquer, pillage, and move on. Or both. Like the game, the dating habits of so many professional athletes is driven by the thrill of the hunt. Once the quarry has been caught, they lose interest and the hunt begins again.

We parted after a long dinner, me for my hotel room and Cyndi to her apartment in Toronto. We agreed to meet the next day. I called Vince to let him know that she seemed like a reasonable person whose feelings had been hurt, and didn't seem inclined to go public. But he would have to deal with her straight up with an apology and a commitment to support her if she chose to have the child. How many times had I given that lecture. When I met the girl the following day, she said she had decided she wasn't ready to be a mother and would have an abortion. I was relieved, but still a bit wary. "Are you sure there isn't something you need? All you have to do is ask."

"I'm okay," she said. "But I think Vince ought to at least drive me to the clinic and then let me recuperate that night at his place. I can't tell my family about this, and I don't want to be alone in case of complications." I thought her request was reasonable, even generous. I called Vince to deliver the good news.

"Sure, Tank! I'll drop her off. No problem. Then I'll come pick her up after practice."

"You ain't gettin' it, Vince," I said. "It took two to tango, here. You've got to do this her way. You've got to give this girl some dignity and respect. After all, she's not having the baby and she isn't asking for anything. She wouldn't even take money for the abortion because in Canada abortions are free. All she wants is for you to take her to the clinic, stay there 'til she's done, and then let her spend the night in your place where she can rest up in private. No $50,000. No car. Just a little respect."

The procedure was scheduled on a day and at a time when Vince was supposed to be at practice with the Raptors. I called Coach Carter to let him know Vince had a pressing personal matter and might be late or even miss the session altogether. When one of a head coach's million-dollar super stars misses a practice for personal reasons, he wants to know if there's something he needs to know.

"What's this about, Tank?" Carter asked. "Is he all right? Do I have a problem?"

"Vince is fine, Butch. It isn't about him, but it is that important or I wouldn't be calling you. Everything's just fine, but he has to take care of some personal business and that's the only time he can do it."

"All right, but I have your word that if there's something up, you'll let me know, right?"

I assured Coach Carter that I would hold nothing back that might effect Vince's performance or the team. To avoid any unnecessary gossip that might be caused by the conspicuous absence of one of his key players at practice, Coach Carter canceled the practice session.

Vince performed his duty, picking the girl up, waiting for her at the clinic, taking her to his apartment for the night, and taking her home the next day. I was in Chicago for a Bears-Packers match when Vince called, giddy with relief.

"It all went off without a hitch. Thanks, man. I was really sweatin' it for awhile."

"Vince, I have to be honest with you. I know you didn't want me to tell your mom, but now that everything came out all right, I'm going to have to come clean with her."

Vince was shocked. "Why? Nobody got hurt. Why does she have to know? Man, ain't it embarrassin' enough without my mom gettin' involved?"

"I'm telling her because if I don't and she finds out some other way, she's gonna come down on both of us like a ton of bricks, and you know it. Better she hears it from me than you, and better she hears it from me than from anyone else. Your girlfriend treated you a lot better than she could have, Vince. A lesser person would have had a field day shakin' you down for some serious cash. But there's no guarantee this all won't come out sometime in the future, and it usually does.

"Now if you want, you can tell her, or I can. But one way or the other, she's got to know."

Vince chickened out, as I knew he would. Expecting her to blow up, I told Michelle the whole story. But she was so relieved that Vince's squeaky clean facade had been maintained, and that it hadn't cost anything, that she rolled with the punch.

"Just promise me this," she said. "Don't keep anything else from me in the future, okay?'

"Okay. But let's make sure there's nothing else to tell."

I called Cyndi a few times in the weeks that followed, to make sure she was okay, to see if she needed anything, and to make sure she wasn't having second thoughts about keeping the incident private. To my knowledge Vince never spoke with her again.

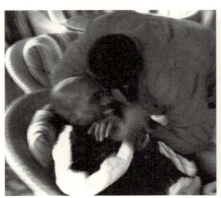

*Michelle, Vince and
Harry Robinson,
1998.*

*Vince and Raptors
head coach, Butch
Carter the day after
the NBA Draft, 1998.*

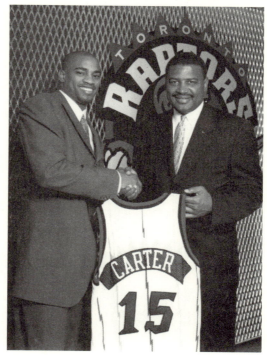

Opposite page:
*(Left) Me and Vince
having fun.*

*(Right) Vince and his
ex-wife, Ellen, before
their marriage.*

Lou Dobbs and me at the Rivery Ranch, Linton, North Dakota.

Me on my horse, Shadow, 1998.

Chapter 22

A RIDING TIDE OF TROUBLE

I T WAS ABSURD enough that I'd had to drop everything I was working on—player contracts, recruiting, the travel business, and all the rest—to fly off to Toronto to clean up after Vince. But the incident occurred in what had been a year of multiple crises, with more to come.

The first ripple of trouble came in early December, 1998, when Jim Franklin called me with urgency in his voice, "Tank, listen up real quick. Some DEA agents just visited Linda asking about John Bryant and they're on their way to talk to you."

"What about?"

"It's about some drug business with Dean Parker up in Detroit, but mainly they are tracking down leads because of the hotel deal we did with Bryant."

The DEA agents knew Linda was related to John Bryant in some way, but they didn't yet know she had been married to John's father. In there investigation they had traced the ownership of the hotel property to the corporation in South Carolina that Jim Franklin set up for us to use for the ownership.

Franklin told me the agents ask Linda if she knew Dean Parker and she lied that she never met him. The last thing we wanted was for the DEA to find out that we had taken money from Parker to invest in cash 4 titles.

"If they ask you, you don't know these guys. Remember, all we did was count the money and pass it on."

In the short time I had between the phone call from Franklin and the arrival of the DEA agents, I tried to remember if there was any connection with Bryant that would trip me up. The only thing I could think of was the trip to the Caymans and to Rio, but I didn't see how the DEA could know anything about that.

My principal concern was not that I'd done anything illegal. I was sure I hadn't. But just as it was important to protect the reputations of my players, I had my own reputation to guard, and especially now that I was lining up players for the 1999 NFL Draft in a big way. The worst thing that could happen to me would be for the press to report that Tank Black had been subpoenaed to testify about his association with a drug lord.

So I lied to the DEA without thinking on Franklin's advice. I said I didn't know Bryant, although I knew he had been a relative of Linda's. And I said I had no business dealings with him, which was also a lie because my company had taken over the hotel he had pitched to me in Detroit. There was even a paper trail leading from Bryant to a corporation I owned.

The lying was stupid, but we didn't realize just how stupid because the Detroit Free Press had published a story nearly two months earlier reporting that Bryant was in jail, accused by the U.S. Attorney's Office of running a cocaine ring of "breathtaking" proportions "stretching from California to Michigan." Had I known about the story, I might have handled myself differently, and I certainly would have been more likely to lawyer up from day one. Bryant had gone on that side trip to Rio during a visit to our off-shore bankers in the Cayman Islands. And six months earlier, we'd flown his partner Dean Parker and his family to Jamaica on the Challenger.

The Free Press had reported that three of the people with whom Bryant was accused of conspiring had disappeared—after Bryant threatened them. "The capture [of a fourth suspect] jolted a hearing already stitched together with testimony of Bryant's travels to the Caribbean and Brazil, carloads of cocaine, a .357 Magnum laser-sighted revolver and electronic bugging detectors."

I had unwittingly exposed myself to a world of high-level drug trafficking schemes masquerading as real estate investments through individuals I hardly knew anything about. I had earned a sizable commission on their purchases of Cash 4 Titles notes. I had helped Dean leave the country. And witnesses in a major Federal case involving hard drugs and large-caliber weapons were disappearing.

I had deluded myself into thinking I could lie to the DEA agents because I wasn't dealing drugs and I wasn't responsible for knowing where Bryant's and Parker's cash came from. I was a fool to listen to Franklin's advice, but I rationalized that he was a lawyer and knew what he was talking about.

What I would learn later and painfully is that a person can commit all kinds of crimes and still have a chance to beat the rap if there's enough doubt to convince a jury, but it's very difficult to beat a perjury charge. As Martha Stewart discovered in her insider trading case, you can be innocent of a crime, but land in jail for lying about it.

In any case, I had little time to ponder the implications for me of Bryant's problems because business was booming with a thousand details requiring my attention. We were expanding on our success with University of Florida players and Alfred Twitty, the recruiter who was helping me sign up college stars, had brought me another superstar—University of Florida Gators, linebacker Jevon Kearse, from Fort Myers.

Jevon was a big catch, and a kid with an improbable and compelling personal story, another black athlete who had overcome incredible odds. His father was a thug who had been murdered just before Jevon was born. His grandfather was shot to death in front of the family house when Jevon was an infant. A cousin was killed later the same year, in the process of committing an assault. Another cousin died in prison while serving time for attempted murder.

In spite of the violent, impoverished family environment; in spite of growing up during the worst years of the crack epidemic; in spite of a stutter; Jevon had managed to rise above it all. From his junior high school years he was an outstanding scholar and a gifted athlete.

By the time he graduated high school he'd been named a *USA Today* All-American and was on his way to earning his nickname, "The Freak," for his big size, long reach, amazing speed, and incredible record as a tackler. He graduated with a 3.6 Grade Point Average and was inducted into the National Honor Society. He was, in short, my kind of player.

His freshman season as a Gator he was such a success he was named to the All-SEC Freshman team. The family legacy continued to dog him, though. He himself was arrested and charged with stealing a car, but the charges were dropped when the police discovered they had the wrong person. And his younger brother, Jermaine, was murdered in a drive-by-shooting after Jevon's first season with the Gators.

By his junior year he had racked up such a shelf-full of records, honors, and awards that he decided to skip his final college season. He told a reporter that he had accomplished four goals he'd set for himself: "To become a better person, to win a national championship, to get an education and finally to have a chance to play in the NFL."

There was no doubt he would have that chance, so I had no qualms about helping him buy his dream car, a Mercedes-Benz S600V-12, the moment he became eligible for the draft. His season would officially end and his eligibility began after January 2, 1999, when the Gators would play Syracuse in the Orange Bowl.

I made arrangements to buy the car from a dealership in Atlanta where the salesman said he wanted to book the sale in

December to boost his commissions for the month. I wired the money—$140,000—on New Year's Eve with the understanding that the car belonged to me until Jevon could take possession of it after the Orange Bowl and thus preserve his draft eligibility.

The Gators handily defeated Syracuse 31–10. Two days later, Jevon flew to Columbia to sign as a client, and then to visit my bank where I co-signed a loan for him so he could pay me back the $140,000. Although the draft was a few months off, I had already been identified as the leading agent going in. A sports business magazine reported in mid-January that I'd signed twelve new players, five from the University of Florida. Eight of the twelve were expected to be picked in the top two rounds. My main competition was Tom Condon with IMG, the huge sports and talent agency, and even he was eating my dust. I got to know Tom back when I was selling disability insurance with Kocian, Dutt and Black. I have always had great respect for him.

It's one week before the 1999 NFL draft and I realize I could have possible the best draft I have ever had. I had represented over 30 number on picks in the NFL in contracts and management combined but no one agent had ever had over 4 number one picks in the same draft. The competition among sports agents for the NFL's top players is tremendous. Certain agents dominate certain positions. It was a known fact that wide receivers, running backs, defensive backs and linebackers were especially attracted to me and my company. That mainly came from the fact that among my first clients early on were Sterling Sharpe, Barry Sanders, Terry Allen, Carl Banks, Andre Rison and Donnell Woolford.

I had signed what I considered to be six premium college football players that all had a legitimate chance to be picked in the first round of the 1999 draft. Three of these players I was certain would go in the first round, they were, Jevon Kearse, Troy Edwards and Antuan Edwards. Then I had three that had a very good chance and they were Reggie Mcgrew, Al Wilson and Kevin Faulk. Mcgrew was a defensive lineman which would put a premium on his draft spot because good defensive lineman, are rare. I thought personally that Al Wilson was one of the better performance defenders in the country. He was a little on the short side for a middle linebacker but his proving ground was in the fierce and rugged Southeastern Conference not to mention that Al played college ball at the University of Tennessee and had just won himself a National Championship. Lastly Kevin Faulk was a former *USA Today* All-American H.S. quarterback from Carencro, Louisiana. He was now an All-American running back with multiple skills from Louisiana State University.

My experience with the NFL draft over the years had taught me that anything is possible. The truth is that any agent having even one number one pick is a great accomplishment when you take into account the number of registered agents and the fact that there is only 31 in this draft and today 32 first round picks.

Our top recruiters were Alfred Twitty in Florida and North Carolina, Randall "Banks" Menard in Louisiana, Gary Parker in North Carolina and Oliver Lucas in Colorado and California. We had all put hundreds of hours into signing the group of players for this years draft. Other agents were complaining that I was buying players and I would someday be criminally charged with buying players (charges that would eventually be dropped) but we never paid players to sign with us, NEVER! It is true that we loaned a few players monies while they still were in college with the agreement that those players would pay those loans back whether they signed with me or not. I acknowledge that practice was against NCAA rules for the players and was in a gray area for me especially under the state of Florida athlete agent statutes.

One fact that will always be true, almost all agents give and loan players things of value because that is the nature of the business. Any top agent who claims to never have given a player or loaned a player something is simply not being honest. College football players have needs and they are going to let you know what those needs are. They are usually small things and don't require a lot of money, maybe a couple of hundred dollars every now and then. Another fact about players is that a top player will not sign with an agent because that agent gave him a few hundred and even a few thousand dollars. The top players understand their value very well and they are going to make sure they get an agent they know has the experience and knowledge to help them be in the best possible draft position and get them the best possible contract after they are drafted.

It was finally the morning of the draft and I called each player we had signed to wish them luck and give them the latest scoop on what I had heard from coaches, general managers and the press. I reminded each player to remember that regardless of their draft pick position, being drafted into the NFL is a great accomplishment and even more so getting drafted on the first day which normally encompasses the first three rounds. All of our signees were fairly certain first day picks.

I had spoken at length with Len Pasquarelli with the *Atlanta Journal Constitution* and we traded what we thought of the first round picks. I had always had a great deal of respect and trust for Len and I enjoyed talking with him. He just always did exactly what he said he would do and would speak up for what he believed in.

The draft started that Saturday morning at 12 noon. Commissioner Paul Tagliabue had called 12 names before he called wide receiver Troy Edwards of Louisiana Tech to the Pittsburgh Steelers as the 13th pick. I was disappointed that Jevon Kearse had not been a top ten pick. I thought he was talented enough for a top five pick but many considered him to be a tweener, a player between defensive end and outside linebacker. I had watched him now for three years and I could see him wrecking serious havoc on NFL offensive schemes. I knew the best shot at going in the top ten for Kearse would be Detroit at #9. They took Chris Claiborne, an outside linebacker from Southern California. No disrespect to Claiborne who has been a good player but this would be another blunder by the Lions as Kearse would have been a steal for them at the ninth pick. At the 16th pick the Tennessee Titans would select Jevon Kearse. I spoke to Floyd Reese their General Manager and Jim Washburn, their defensive line coach who I had coached with at South Carolina. It was as if they had just won the lottery. They could not believe Kearse was there at the 16th pick. I was right and so was Floyd Reese. Kearse led the league in sacks his rookie year and made the pro bowl as a starter leading Tennessee to their first Super Bowl appearance. Eight picks later Paul Tagliabue would call Reggie Mcgrew, defensive tackle from Florida as the San Francisco Forty-Niners pick at number 24. The next pick I was fairly certain would be another one of my clients. The Green Bay Packers had the 25th pick, when Antuan Edwards ran on Clemson University's campus in March. Ray Rhodes the former head coach of the Philadelphia Eagles was the defensive coordinator of the Packers. Ray pulled me aside and told me that he did not know if Antuan would be there when they picked at 25 but if he was he would be a Green Bay Packer. Ray was a friend that I trusted completely so when Tagliabue approached with the 25th pick I knew Antuan Edwards name was on it. Tagliabue's words seemed like De Ja Vue when he said "with the 25th pick the Green Bay Packers select Antuan Edwards free safety from Clemson University".

I had four number one draft picks which tied the all time NFL agent record and I had two players who had a good shot at being one of the remaining six picks that were left in the first round. Al Wilson and Kevin Faulk both had good shots. The six remaining teams appeared to have defensive needs more than offensive. This gave Al the advantage. The picks started coming off the board and no Al Wilson or Kevin Faulk.

Then with the 31st and final pick of the first round my phone rung. It was the general manager of the Denver Broncos John Beake. He said the Bronco's wanted to select Al Wilson with their pick but wanted me to agree to at least a five year deal in duration.

I told them I wanted to speak with Al first which I did call him on his cell phone while keeping the Broncos on the other line.

Al and I discussed it and I told him there was indeed a big difference in the last pick of the first round and the first pick of the second round. I told him I would get him an excellent deal in the 31st spot. He agreed to do a five year deal. I told Denver we would do a five year deal but not a six. All of these conversations took place while Denver was on the clock and Tagliabue finally approached the podium and said "with the 31st and final pick of the first round the Denver Bronco's select Al Wilson, Linebacker from the University of Tennessee".

At that moment I smiled. I could only imagine Al, his mom and their family celebrating in Jackson, Tennessee. Then I realized that with that pick history had been made. No NFL agent had ever had more than four players selected in the first round of the NFL draft until April of 1999 when William "Tank" Black had five.

I would have three players drafted in the second round and one of them would be running back Kevin Faulk to the New England Patriots.

An interesting story about Kevin is when he was in college he had pretty much decided he was going to sign with me. His best friend was Randall "Banks" Menard who worked for me. In the process Kevin started hanging out with Master P and Mystikal and Master P's people. Banks said he would go over there and listen to freshly cut CD's that were not on the market yet and smoke marijuana with them. Banks wanted me to come down and have a good talk with Kevin about what he was doing and what he needed.

I flew into Baton Rouge and Banks picked me up at the airport in Kevin's truck. The Truck reeked with the smell of marijuana and Kevin's eyes were beet red from smoking that purple weed. I did not say anything in the truck but greeted Banks and Kevin. He was playing Master P's music so loud it would have been useless to talk. When we got to Kevin's apartment I told Kevin " listen you are smoking marijuana and you are high as a kite" it is okay for some musician to smoke this crap because they are not going to earn their living with their body and they are not going to be tested for drugs. You are going to throw your career down the drain before it even begins. It is okay for you to hang out with Master P and Mystikal but you cannot smoke pot with them and Master P cannot represent you because he does not know the first thing about the salary cap or present day values or unlikely to be earned incentives and how they benefit players.

I believe Kevin loved smoking marijuana and it is my guess that he has been smoking marijuana since high school and he is going to smoke marijuana long after his career is over. I did make him realize that night however that the time to smoke marijuana was not at that time for sure and he needed an experienced sports agent to represent him. Banks felt a lot better after I had that talk with Kevin that night and things went very smooth after that.

My company, Professional Management Inc, (PMI) had branched out into every aspect of our players' business lives. We had more than a dozen or so staff people and several subsidiaries, including a production company to create material for radio and television linking players with corporate sponsors. We adopted a motto: "It's up to you to become MVP. It's up to us to make sure everybody knows."

PMI co-sponsored with Wachovia Bank a celebrity golf event that spring to benefit the local chapter of the American Red Cross. The program included photos and bios of three dozen of our players, many of them well-known, outstanding athletes. PMI had become one of the leading player agencies in football, the leading agency at "powerhouse" University of Florida, a major new player in the NBA, and a prosperous local business in South Carolina with a reputation for generosity and a steady stream of

celebrity athletes to dress up the local restaurants and golf courses. I had become one of the most successful and recognized black
business people in the country.

And then all hell broke loose.

Me and Rev. Jesse Jackson at PMI Celebrity Golf tournament, 1996.

Family and clients at my surprise birthday party, March, 1993.

Attorney Robert O. Bragdon, my lifelong friend, never forgot about me and came to my rescue. He's the main reason I won the Vince Carter case.

Chapter 23

THE DAM BURSTS

A T THE BEGINNING of March, *The Wall Street Journal* published a major front page expose of the car-title loan industry, featuring Cash 4 Titles and quoting Richard Homa, the president. The headline was bad enough—"License to Owe: Title-Loan Firms Offer Car Owners a Solution That Often Backfires"—but the criticism was brutal. "Legalized extortion," was how one consumer advocate described it. Some states had been trying to shut down some of the companies.

There was nothing in the article that suggested Cash 4 Titles or any of the other companies were doing anything illegal. But the predatory nature of the business was now out in the open for all to see, including my players who, along with me and my family, had a total of about $18 million on the line.

Meanwhile, the investigation into John Bryant's drug dealing had produced a subpoena requiring me to appear before a federal grand jury in Detroit. On Franklin's advice, I lied to the grand jury about knowing Bryant, just as I had lied to the DEA when they visited my office. It was the biggest and dumbest mistake I would ever make, and the one that would cost me the most.

There was trouble brewing in Florida, too. In February I was notified by the NFL Players Association of allegations that I had been improperly recruiting players at the University of Florida.

The union claimed I was using unregistered agents to contact players. If true, I was breaking a Florida state law that carried criminal sanctions. It was a crock because under the union's rules, as long as I was registered as an agent, anyone who worked for me could talk to players about my becoming their agent. I got a call from a reporter at *The State* newspaper about the investigation and the first mention of it appeared February 13, 1999. I denied that I'd done anything wrong but it was an embarrassing development at best, and at worst threatened to undermine my relationships with my newly signed players. There was no doubt in my mind that the Players Association had leaked the story and that Berthelsen the unions chief counsel with whom I had locked horns over Sterling Sharpe's claim against the Packers, was behind it in some fashion.

I was equally certain that Brantley Evans, the heavy set kid that showed up to my house years earlier wanting to work for me, and who I had been mentoring and grooming during the years with the idea that he would one day take over my business, was the source of my problems. Bill Bradshaw, my original business partner, had tried to persuade me not to hire Brantley and I had learned that he had been a better judge of Brantley's character than I was.

Brantley's betrayal surfaced the summer of 1998. I was flying a large group of our players out to North Dakota to Hal Rosenbluth's retreat called the Rivery. We were taking these NFL players out to give the kids out there a free football camp coached by the pros. I was to take a group out with me on one flight and Brantley was to take a group out with him and we were to connect at mid day on a flight with other clients of ours coming from different cities connecting in Minneapolis and on into North Dakota. I caught the early flight and everyone was on that flight except Duce Staley. I was calling him but he wasn't answering his phone.

I called Brantley to see if he knew where Duce was and Brantley did not answer his phone. When we got to Atlanta and waited for Brantley to bring the other players I got a call from Lisa Adams our director of banking and finance at my PMI office. She said that Brantley had brought in his resignation and had offered her a job to come work with him and Ricky Leftt, Brantley's brother in law who was a local attorney.

Brantley and Ricky had been secretly forming a sports management company named Synergy Sports over the past few weeks while Brantley was still working for me.

This explained why Natrone Means, Thomas Smith, Duce Staley, Jamain Stephens, Raleigh Roundtree and a few others did not make there flights on the trip to North Dakota. Brantley had planned this coo to take over as many of my clients as possible.

Ironically, I had plans to turn the operations of PMI over to Brantley and make him CEO, but I felt he needed about another year of grooming before he was ready, and here he was stabbing me in my back.

Brantley had come to my house in an old beat up Datsun 280 Z. He had no job and no money. I took Brantley under my wing and treated him like family. I helped him get his first Mercedes, his home in Columbia and I taught him the agent business and recruiting secrets I had learned from years of recruiting.

On the plane to North Dakota Ike Hilliard and Reidel Anthony both told me that Brantley had called them to try to get them to fire me and hire him. Brantley was still very young about 27. I believe he had listened to Ricky Leftt tell him he can do this on his own and he did not need me. Brantley started having problems when me and Alfred Twitty started getting really close. He was jealous of Tweet and the high profile clients Tweet was signing. It was ridiculous because he brought Tweet to PMI.

Brantley's favorite book was about Sammy "the Bull" Gravano and how he ratted on John Gotti. Brantley would later go to the

NFLPA and make a deal with the NFLPA and tell them all sorts of things about me and our business, some true (which I never had a problem with anyone telling the truth no matter what it was).

The problem is the NFLPA would give Brantley immunity on anything wrong he did while he worked with me and PMI. Brantley told them lies about things that never happened. He had become the NFLPA"s confidential witness. He had plenty of motives, because he wanted to be me. Brantley Evans wanted to be Tank Black. He wanted to be a sports super agent and he thought he could be if he could take me down.

He would become the leader of a group of agents and NFLPA people who wanted to bring me down. Brantley would enjoy short lived success as an agent. Natrone Means, Thomas Smith, Duce Staley, Raleigh Roundtree and some other lesser known players fired me and hired Brantley. Brantley had put our players in the middle and ask the ones he had a hand in recruiting to go with him. They did not want to chose, but were pressured to do so.

I did not like being fired by players who did not have any problems with me or PMI and because they had been influenced by someone I had treated like a son. The player I hated losing the most was Thomas Smith. I liked Thomas from the very beginning. He was just a great guy with excellent character. I would continue to check in on Thomas ever so often.

The problem for Brantley was that most of those players owed me my contract fees for at least three years. Then, when my friend Ray Rhodes, Head Coach of the Philadelphia Eagles heard that Duce Staley had fired me and hired Brantley he called Duce in and told him he needed to go back and rehire Tank Black because he is a great agent and you do not need to be changing agents at this time. Duce did what Ray Rhodes said. He rehired me and I finished his contract. Duce told Brantley what Coach Rhodes had told him and Brantley was furious.

Ultimately, Brantley ended up out of the agent business. He did not know all of the things it took to build a business structure and he did not have the resources structurally, mentally or financially.

The worrisome thing was that I had been doing something else that was indisputably illegal, although virtually all agents did it—loaning college players cash or arranging other benefits through recruiters like Twitty. You couldn't compete as an agent unless you got in with the players, and the players knew they could get money from a lot of different agents. The system was rotten, but I often felt that I was making a little easier the life of a college student, many of whom came from homes with meager resources.

Now some of my Gators players were being interrogated by the University of Florida police department about the money they had received. The investigators were also looking into the Mercedes-Benz I had pre-purchased for Jevon Kearse. This transaction was completely legit. But the word was out and began to spread in the professional football world. The whale was wounded and the sharks began to assemble.

In an effort to counteract what felt like a witch hunt, I asked Rev. Jesse Jackson for help. We'd been friends for several years. He wrote a letter on my behalf to Gene Upshaw, the Players Association's executive director, appealing to him to resolve the allegations "without further delay so that [Tank] can put to rest the concerns of his clients." It was clearly a brother-to-brother message.

"The life of black sports agents has been difficult enough without the sword of Damocles dangling over their heads," he wrote. "Tank has enjoyed unparalleled success rarely enjoyed by black agents, but there has never been any indication that he has broken any rules."

Upshaw wrote back a week later, saying only, "I can assure you that due process will be followed and a speedy resolution to this matter will take place." But Upshaw, who with Berthelsen had held me responsible for failing to steer Sterling Sharpe away from hiring Grady Irvin to handle his dispute with the Packers, showed no sign he was interested in speeding up anything or due process.

Things went from bad to worse when further news of the investigation appeared in the press in the week leading up to the NFL Draft in mid-April. The timing was devastating. I found myself arguing in the media with Berthelsen over whether or not my Gators players had given statements confirming they had received money from me through Alfred Twitty. I made one mistake after another, loudly proclaiming my innocence when I probably should have kept my mouth shut. Little did I realize that I was building my own coffin.

By the beginning of May, just three weeks after my triumph at the NFL Draft, the victory had gone up in smoke. My new players—Jevon Kearse, Johnny Rutledge, Mike Peterson, and Reggie McGrew—all fired me. Kearse, Rutledge, and McGrew had already made verbal agreements to go with a new agent. If I hadn't been under such scrutiny, a move like that would have been outrageous, but I had become radioactive. I managed to keep Vince Carter on board by assuring Michelle that I would survive the onslaught. In any event, it wasn't the NBA Players Association that was after me. But I rapidly discovered that my troubles were just beginning.

On May 19, 1999 the NFLPA filed a five-page complaint against me, charging improper recruiting and representation and threatening me with a lifetime ban. Jesse Jackson persuaded the Florida chapter of the NAACP to investigate possible racial bias and I filed a defamation-of-character lawsuit against the union.

Then, just two days after the union filed its complaint, detectives from the University of Florida police department showed up at my office with a criminal warrant issued by a South Carolina judge giving them permission to search my office and seize my records. I was dumbfounded. Although I was no lawyer, I knew it was bizarre that some campus cops from another state could just waltz into my business and turn it upside down looking for evidence that I had violated the Florida sports agent law. I was legitimately licensed in the State of Florida as a sports agent, but the warrant was based on the false allegation that I wasn't, a crime carrying a five-year prison sentence.

The University police spent an entire day rooting through every scrap of paper in my place. I begged them to tell me what they wanted so I could just give it to them and leave the rest of my business unmolested. "You don't have to tear the whole place up! For God's sake, I have players all over the country that have nothing to do with Florida. I'll be happy to give you whatever you want if you'll just let me."

But my pleas fell on deaf ears.

By the time they were done emptying my filing cabinets and desk drawers, unplugging and packing up computers and other electronic records, there were eighty-five boxes stacked up at the door—my entire life's work. Then they loaded them into a truck and drove off, leaving my office looking like a bomb had gone off. Photos of my players, plaques, and other memorabilia that had been on the walls were scattered on the floor.

It felt like I had been robbed, or mugged. I went home in a state of shock and disbelief and sat up all night, knowing something was terribly wrong but not understanding what was really going on. It was a nightmare I couldn't have imagined.

The unbelievable was followed by the incomprehensible. I discovered that the University of Florida police had shipped everything they seized to Richard Berthlesen at the NFL Players Association in Washington. A state agency from Florida had obtained a criminal search warrant in another state on false pretenses, seized all my business records, and then turned them over to a private organization that was determined to destroy me.

I sued and ended up winning a hollow victory some months later when a South Carolina judge ruled that the University of Florida police were wrong, and ordered my records returned to me, and ruled that that the search warrant was based on misleading, untruthful, and incorrect information. But by then my business was reeling from defections, huge legal fees, and the distraction of my very public feud with the union. I accepted that I might lose my agent certification. The Players Association held all the cards and intended to play them. I hoped that I would be able to keep enough credibility to continue to manage players and negotiate endorsement deals. I didn't need a license to manage, and there was more money in it anyway.

But as the stream of bad press turned into a torrent, fewer and fewer people were willing to stick their necks out for me. Michelle, Vince's mother was one. Reidel Anthony and Fred Taylor were quoted in the press saying they felt that I was family to them. Gene Burrough, an agent based in Jacksonville, Florida, told a reporter, "I hate to see that Tank Black is the only one being picked on. What he's being accused of is being done by a number of agents."

It would be hard to imagine a month worse than May of 1999. My players were jumping ship or being poached by competitors, the union was trying to put me out of business, the University of Florida had illegally swiped all my business records and turned them over to my enemies, and I had clumsily lied my way through a grand jury interrogation about my relationship with a dangerous cocaine kingpin.

In July, as part of a mutual settlement the NFL Players Association revoked my certification as an agent for three years. It was the stiffest penalty ever meted out to a football agent. I was pursuing my lawsuit against the union for spreading malicious rumors and damaging my business. Nevertheless, I decided to get out of the way of my players' affairs. There was no way I could run the business and fight these enormous battles.

Also that summer, rumors had begun to circulate that there was something fishy going on with Cash 4 Titles—the Securities and Exchange Commission was snooping around asking questions. I decided it was time to lighten the exposure of my players and began asking for their money back from those high-yielding promissory notes. In spite of the understanding I had with Mike Gause, that those investments could be repatriated on a day's notice, I became concerned when I learned he'd been complaining that we were using the investment "like a bank." The company was starting to impose restrictions on how much could be withdrawn at any one time, and offering dubious excuses for delays.

By October I had managed to badger Gause's people into paying back about half the money our clients had invested. The other half of the players funds were to get returned within the week I was told. Then one morning I was in my car driving home from Atlanta, I got a call from Linda Wilson, who was waiting on a flight at Detroit Airport. She was as grim as I'd ever heard her.

"Tank, have you heard about Mike Gause?"

My heart began to race. "What about him?"

"It's in *The Wall Street Journal* today and it ain't good. He's been arrested for money laundering and running a Ponzi scheme. The article says there's nothing left in Cash for Titles."

"What the hell's a Ponzi scheme?"

Reidel Anthony, wide receiver Tampa Bay on horse at the Rivery Ranch, 1997.

LAW

SEC Sues Sports Agency for Defrauding Pro-Athlete Clients With 'Ponzi' Scheme

By HUMBERTO SANCHEZ
Dow Jones Newswires

The Securities and Exchange Commission said it is suing prominent sports agent William H. "Tank" Black, his business partner, his Columbia, S.C., sports-management company and an affiliate for allegedly defrauding about two dozen of the agency's clients.

Mr. Black, 42 years old, founded Professional Management Inc. in 1988 and is the firm's chairman and chief executive. PMI represents professional athletes in the National Football League and the National Basketball Association in contract negotiations with their respective teams. PMI's clientele has included NFL players Fred Taylor, Duce Staley and Terry Allen as well as budding NBA superstar Vince Carter of the Toronto Raptors.

Mr. Black's business partner, James A. Franklin Jr., 32, general counsel for PMI as well as executive vice president and chief operating officer of the affiliate named in the suit, Professional Management Consulting Inc., was also named in the SEC's suit filed in a federal court in Tampa, Fla.

PMC is co-owned by Mr. Black and Mr. Franklin and purportedly was established to provide legal and business-consulting services to PMI clients, the SEC said.

"The allegations contained in the SEC's complaint are false and do not reflect actual events. We will respond vigorously with the facts at the appropriate time," said a spokesman speaking on behalf of Mr. Black, Mr. Franklin, PMI and PMC.

According to the SEC's complaint, Mr. Black and Mr. Franklin defrauded about two dozen of PMI's clients in three schemes, starting in early 1996 and continuing through the present, which together reaped about $5 million in profit.

In the first scheme, the SEC alleges Mr. Black obtained free stock from BAOA Inc. by falsely promising that his clients would provide promotional services to the company. Mr. Black then advised his clients to invest in BAOA, an acronym for Black Americans of Achievement, and sold his clients stock he had received in their names for free, misappropriating the proceeds, the SEC said. According to the SEC Mr. Black was named president of BAOA in 1995 and a director in 1996.

Atlanta-based BAOA was not charged with any wrongdoing in the suit.

In the second scheme, Mr. Black and Mr. Franklin defrauded PMI clients by encouraging them to invest millions of dollars in a purported program to fund a car-title loan business that was, in fact, an offshore "Ponzi" scheme, the SEC alleges. A Ponzi scheme is a fraudulent investment technique wherein money from later investors is used to pay off original investors in an effort to attract more funds.

The SEC contends that Mr. Black and Mr. Franklin conducted no due diligence into the safety of the underlying investment or the soundness of the business and that the recommendations were instead motivated by Mr. Black's and Franklin's desire to access clients funds and to skim a substantial part of their clients monthly investment returns.

In the third scheme, the SEC alleges that Mr. Black and Mr. Franklin misappropriated more clients' funds through companies in the Cayman Islands that they controlled.

The SEC has obtained a temporary restraining order freezing the assets of the defendants and relief defendant Silverline Development Corp. LLC. Silverline, a South Carolina entity controlled by Messers. Black and Franklin, was unjustly enriched when it received the proceeds of certain PMI client investments and diverted or misappropriated those funds, the SEC said.

The order also prevents the defendants from exercising control over their clients' accounts and directs the defendants to account for and repatriate all assets held offshore. Additionally, the SEC is seeking repayment of alleged ill-gotten profits and civil penalties.

Article that appeared in The Wall Street Journal, February 28, 2000. The Federal Court would later clear me and my companies of all the allegations in this article.

Used with permission of *The Wall Street Journal*, copyright 2000.

Chapter 24

A LAST HAIL MARY

FOR SEVERAL YEARS leading up to the fall of 1999 I'd toyed with the idea of selling my business and starting something new that might be less stressful. Now, selling was my only hope of salvaging the money my players had invested in Cash 4 Titles, and I could sense that the window of opportunity would not remain open long.

I pulled off the highway after getting Linda's call from Detroit and bought a copy of the *The Wall Street Journal* at a convenience store. Then I sat in my car and read news that was as bad as it could possibly be: "Stock Promoter Gause Faces Charges Of Securities Fraud, Money Laundering." Mike Gause had been arrested at his $7 million waterfront mansion in Fort Lauderdale. Dick Homa either was or soon would be behind bars. Both were charged with running a con game in which "virtually all" of some $300 million they raised had been "dissipated."

They'd started their scheme in 1997, right about the time I hired Jim Franklin as my in-house counsel and he pushed the Cash 4 Titles notes as a good investment for our players and a money-maker for us. My blood ran cold when I read that federal prosecutors had a "CW"—a confidential witness—who had participated in the con, had been at meetings in the Cayman Islands, and had even recorded phone calls with Gause. The way the story was worded, it was clear the government had flipped an insider, and my guess was Homa. Whoever it was had exposed a massive fraud in which they had been juggling new investors' money to pay old investors' interest and meet redemption calls like mine.

It had all been a shell game and I had allowed myself to get sucked into it, right up to my neck. How could I have been so stupid? And how was it that neither Jim Franklin nor anyone else smelled a rat? It felt like the floor had dropped out from under me.

The Securities and Exchange Commission had seized all the assets they could find and it looked like my players funds were frozen at the tune of around $9 million.

I had more than a million of my own money tied up in Cash 4 Titles, but I had made money in the form of commissions on the interest payments being made to my players. They had trusted me to watch their backs and I failed. My first instinct was to find a way to make them whole. I could stand any amount of humiliation or punishment if I knew that I had at least accomplished that goal.

The only option was to sell what I could as fast as I could, before the rising tide of legal problems swept away what was left. If I could hold onto Vince as a management client there would be some legitimate, untainted cash revenue to keep us afloat.

Sitting in the parking lot of the convenience store gas station off Interstate 20 between Atlanta and Columbia, I made a mental inventory of the implications. It was only a matter of time before I got a visit from the SEC. The corporate jet, the trips to the Caymans, the fees my company had earned on my players' investments, and the bags of cash I had handled for two now-notorious drug lords—every direction I turned there was grave danger. Gause had orchestrated a massive fraud involving offshore bank accounts and shell corporations. I made a mental list of competing agents and others who might want to buy my company and let me continue to work as a rain-maker. Butch Carter, head coach of the Toronto Raptors, had told me that Percy Miller, the rap singer known as Master P, was trying out for the team and had talked about buying a sports management company. Percy was in the top ten of the highest paid entertainers in the country (about $56 million in 1998) and had been branching out into related businesses.

I called Butch and within an hour he had arranged a meeting with Master P's financial people the next day in Los Angeles. Next I called Jim Franklin.

"You heard the news?"

"Yeah, I read the story. It's a mess."

"Well, we're goin' to sell the company and you and I are goin' to LA tonight to see some people about buying it. I'm on my way to pick you up and then we're going to drive to Charlotte for a flight to California. I'll be there in about two hours. Be ready. We've got to move fast."

Based on the players we still had under contract and the expected future cash flow from commissions we'd expect to earn on endorsement deals, I calculated the business was worth about $100 million. With all the legal baggage weighing us down, $40 million seemed like a price that would trigger a quick sale.

Some of that I expected to take in stock, but my goal was to come away netting about $15 million in cash—enough to pay back all the players for their Cash 4 Titles losses, and pay the enormous legal fees I was incurring. To protect my investment and give me some income, I hoped to negotiate a sale with a multi-year consulting agreement.

We left California with strong interest but no agreement, other than to meet again a week later in Toronto. The pressure was on, from all sides. When we got back to Columbia I began to scrape together every nickel of spare cash and dole it out to some of my hardest hit players, those I knew needed the money to live on. I managed to pay back several hundred thousand dollars.

The next wave of bad news came at the end of October when the University of Florida police filed formal charges against me and my recruiter, Alfred Twitty, charging me with "unlicensed agent activity." There were three counts and the penalties for each were five years in prison and a $5,000 fine. Every time my phone rang I dreaded answering it.

Vince's mother and I had been speaking numerous times a day throughout my troubles, which began just as we were concluding the new contract with Vince that effectively barred us from taking on any other NBA players. I made a point of telling her everything that was going on, and everything she might hear or read about. I treated her like a business partner, which in a practical sense she was as the CEO and CFO of Vince's affairs, almost all of which was handled by my company.

I had to tell Michelle and Harry, who had become friends, sordid details of the allegations against me and reassure them that I wouldn't let any of it interfere with Vince's career, those were often tough phone calls.

Although there was no risk in all this to Vince or his continuing success, it was embarrassing to talk about the things I was being accused of with people I regarded as the next best thing to family. Although I disapproved of Michelle's obsession with money and her need to dominate Vince, her hard edges were softened by her husband Harry and we enjoyed the times we spent together. They and Vince had been guests in my home on numerous occasions, and they trusted me.

In that same spirit, I didn't think twice about dropping everything to fly to Toronto and spend a day comforting the young woman Vince had gotten pregnant, to make sure his reputation remained unstained and his income unaffected. With all the bad news around me, I assumed Michelle was getting advice to cut her ties with me. Anyone looking at it from the outside would have understood.

But that would be a complicated choice for her. We were in the heat of promising negotiations with several big sponsors including Ford of Canada, Microsoft, Gatorade, Spalding, Skybox trading cards, and Kellogg's. I had earned my keep by defusing a potential public relations disaster. In spite of my public relations woes, Michelle still needed me.

The winter months of 1999–2000 the Cash 4 Titles scandal reached critical mass. Jimmy Roof and Bob Ellenburg, the two local businessmen who were working with Cash 4 Titles on commission and who I'd spent a fair amount of time with, had been named as defendants along with Gause and Homa. They claimed they were victims, not perpetrators, and I suspect they, like me, had rationalized away their suspicions about a financing scheme that accepted boxes full of cash and appeared to be making a lot of money for everyone. Gause and Homa lived like pharaohs, and all along the way everyone was getting a cut—Roof and Ellenburg got theirs, I got mine, Mayor Clarence Anthony got his and the players got theirs.

In the case of Reidel Anthony, Reidel's father, Mayor Clarence Anthony, had been getting a commission on his son's investment in Cash 4 Titles along with the other Gators player's investments, commissions he never disclosed to Reidel. Everyone had their hand in the Cash 4 Titles cookie jar.

There was ample evidence that I knew nothing about the Gause and Homa Ponzi scheme. If I'd known I wouldn't have put my player's money in, let alone my own money. There was also proof in the form of excerpts from secretly taped telephone conversations included in Gause's indictment. In the excerpts, Gause complains to Homa about me asking for my players' money back, and the two of them concoct a story to explain why they couldn't give it all back.

But Gause's indictment also contained a disturbing reference to the investigation by the University of Florida police into my player payments and mention of the FBI. The isolated fires I had been fighting were beginning to merge into one giant fire storm. The press was already reporting stories about the famous players and other sports figures who had lost money in Cash 4 Titles, and

I was starting to get the blame. Plus there was the nagging fear in the back of my mind about the secret connection between Parker and Bryant, their drug cash, and Cash 4 Titles.

That Christmas, 1999, I did my best to insulate my family life from the incredible stress of my business life, but it was hard to keep up the appearance that everything was all right when just about everything seemed to be going wrong.

Fred Taylor, one of my favorite players of all time.

PMI complete staff portrait, 1993.

Chapter 25

UNSPECIFIED UNLAWFUL ACTIVITIES

THE BEGINNING of the end came in February 2000, right after the NBA All-Star Weekend in Oakland, California. Vince Carter won that year's Slam-Dunk Contest. I was there with Michelle and Harry the weekend of February 12 and 13. It was a huge deal, the Super Bowl of basketball, and it cemented Vince's national reputation as one of the greatest players the game had ever seen. He had become a regular on sports programs featuring clips of his amazing stunts. Vince would go down as possibly the greatest dunker basketball has ever seen.

His performance helped fast-track some of the endorsement deals we were working on, including one with Fleer Skybox, a sports card producer and distributor. I met in Oakland with the head of Fleer, Roger Grass and we ended up negotiating a five-year, $7.5 million deal with incentives, including almost $2 million up front the day Vince signed.

The next week after the trip to Oakland Jim Franklin and I had to fly to Detroit to give hand writing samples for the grand jury investigation of Bryant and Parker. This was a command performance in response to a subpoena so we couldn't refuse. The purpose was unclear, but the request was unnerving. I had flown up one evening and came back the next but Franklin flew up one evening after I did and stayed a couple of days which struck me as strange. "Just some other business I had to take care of," he muttered, avoiding my eyes. This unexpected change of his plans threw me. Why would he stay in Detroit when he had no apparent business there. Something was up, but I decided not to press the issue. I had a full plate as it was.

Attorney Peter George, called me with the news that the Securities and Exchange Commission had filed a civil suit charging Jim Franklin and I with defrauding my players of some $5 million through Cash 4 Titles. The SEC had obtained a court order freezing all the company's assets and prohibiting me from having any control over my clients' funds. They had thrown in everything they could think of related to investment activity governed by the SEC, including the Black Americans of Achievement penny stock on which none of my players had lost a cent. They made it sound like some grand scheme.

A few days after the Detroit trip, I arrived at my office in Columbia one morning to discover that during the night Jim Franklin's office had been stripped of every scrap of evidence he had ever worked there. The only thing left was trash and picture hooks. He just disappeared. It left me with a sick feeling in my stomach. He was either a fugitive or a cooperating witness. Either way, it was a bad sign.

But the worst news was that on the same day the U.S. Attorney's office in Gainesville—home of the Gators—had gotten a grand jury to indict me, Lisa Adams, Linda Wilson, Jim Franklin, and Alfred Twitty on multiple fraud charges, obstruction of justice, and money laundering of cash from "unspecified unlawful activities. Peter George faxed me the indictment, which had been issued from Gainesville but had not yet been unsealed.

It was a horror story, portraying us as having orchestrated a massive fraud that had as its goal the recruitment of college players so we could steal their money and hide it in the Cayman Islands. It mentioned half a dozen players who'd lost money in Cash 4 Titles and it mentioned cash we had paid to college players by wiring it to Twitty through Western Union. It was maddening to see how the government could weave together a bunch of half-truths into a total lie, and then have it essentially certified by releasing it for publication in *The Wall Street Journal.* For most of America, if we read it and the government says it we believe it regardless of the lack of proof or evidence. That is a sad truth of most American citizens.

Any hope I still had of selling the business was dashed. The initial interest from Percy Miller/Master P had cooled since the fall, no doubt when his business advisers started picking up gossip about the Florida investigation.

The only assets I had left were Vince's contracts, and the commissions I was owed on contracts I had previously negotiated for other players. I was owed many millions that I would need, to defend myself in court. Although I was effectively out of business, I still would have cash coming in.

Reading the indictment was the second worst experience of my life, after the death of my grandmother. The only consolation was that she didn't have to live through the nightmare with me. In fact, there were so many specific details about the inner workings of my business that I concluded there was only one way the government could have gotten them—from Jim Franklin. He had been a trusted legal source and business partner for more than two years, he had advised me to perjure myself about Bryant and Parker, and he had been responsible for ensnaring me in the Cash 4 Titles scam. That extra day he spent in Detroit now started to make sense—he'd become a government witness.

The indictment revealed why. I learned for the first time that while Franklin was working for me and earning a salary of $120,000 plus commissions, he was getting secret kickbacks from Roof and Ellenburg. He had been making up phony invoices for legal and consulting services that he submitted to the Cash 4 Titles guys who had been paying him $6,000 a month to steer our players' money into their promissory notes. In all, Franklin had collected $90,000 from Roof and Ellenburg.

I had managed to surround myself with people of evil intentions. I intended to fight all of it, and because I'd never been in trouble before, I naively believed that I could prove I was innocent of any wrong-doing beyond the practices common among sports agents who woo college athletes by paying their rent or putting some cash in their pockets.

I hadn't stolen anything from anybody, but I hadn't yet grasped the seriousness of having obstructed a federal investigation. I barely had time to process all of this, because the next day I was scheduled to fly to Toronto to meet with Michelle and sign the Fleer deal with Vince.

My attorney had made arrangements for me to surrender in Gainesville the following Monday when the indictment would be unsealed and I'd have a bail hearing. I called Michelle the night before we were to meet in Toronto to warn her about the news of the SEC civil case, and to assure her that if things got bad enough, I'd hand Vince off to someone else so he wouldn't be tarred with my brush.

She'd already heard from reporters in Toronto calling her for comment. She told the *Toronto Sun*, "Some person or persons want to run [Tank] out of business, and I think this is their way of doing that. We are sticking by Tank Black." Vince told the *Toronto Globe and Mail*, "He didn't do anything to me. I'm not worried and I'm sticking behind him, plain and simple."

The business meeting with Fleer was awkward for me. I was preoccupied with what lay ahead yet I managed to stay focused enough to close the deal without any glitches. We got the paperwork signed and I returned to Columbia to prepare for the drive to Gainesville, where I was to surrender for booking and find out what kind of bail I'd need.

There was some solace in knowing I had a payment coming from the $2 million Fleer signing payment. My share was about $600,000 and I was going to need it. As we wrapped up the Fleer deal in Toronto, Michelle had announced that instead of having the check sent to my office as they always had been in the past, she wanted the check sent directly to her. Under the circumstances, I didn't question her decision. With the federal courts freezing my assets, she had every reason to be cautious. But she promised she would send me my commission as soon as the check cleared.

On Monday, February 28, I met my attorney at the federal courthouse in Gainesville to face the Florida criminal charges. I had no idea what to expect but I thought the hearing would be over in a few minutes. I had never been arrested in my life, I was a long-standing member of my community, a philanthropist, owner of real estate, a father and husband, and in my mind obviously no flight risk. I had just returned from being out of the country to face these charges in Gainesville.

But the Justice Department had no intention of making it easy for me. I was the person at the intersection of two heinous conspiracies, one of which involved a desperate fugitive—Dean Parker. The bail hearing dragged on over nine hours and the government hammered away at my unknown connections to the cocaine ring and the laundering of their cash. They did everything they could to portray me as a callous crook, who should be locked up without bail.

It was bizarre sitting there and listening to the way my life was being described. I was still in denial about my culpability. I still harbored the fantasy that those garbage bags full of cash were not my problem if I didn't know where the money came from. I continued to believe that because I didn't actually steal any money from anyone I would ultimately prevail.

After almost ten exhausting hours, the judge set my bond at $1 million, which meant I only had to come up with $100,000 in cash. But I was now officially under the jurisdiction of the federal Probation Department. I would have to wear an ankle bracelet and my every move had to be approved in advance. I was represented at this time by Attorney Peter George, of Tampa Florida.

Peter George is an excellent attorney with excellent character.

I drove from the bond hearing in Gainesville to Daytona Beach to meet with Michelle. I wanted to know if she was okay and had not been swayed by all of the negative press. She assured me that she was okay, and Vince would stick with me. But her body language betrayed her real intentions.

I returned home to Columbia to find a fax from Michelle announcing that my services were no longer required. She was firing me. I shouldn't have been surprised, but I was stunned that a week after telling the Toronto papers that she would stick by me, and hours after she told me so to my face, she cut me off without the courtesy of a phone call. I tried to reach her by phone but she wasn't taking my calls. The big check I was due never arrived.

After days of trying, I finally got her on the line.

"Well, I'm sorry about all this." she said. "But our attorneys advised us that we should terminate our relationship with you. You said yourself that if things got bad enough you'd let Vince go to somebody else. Well, things look about as bad as they can be, so that's what we had to do."

"I can understand all that," I said, "but you could have called and let me know instead of just sending me a fax. And what about the commission you owe me on the Fleer deal?"

She hemmed and hawed until I badgered her into confessing that "our attorneys" advised her not to pay me anything "until we can do a full accounting."

I was livid. "Michelle, there ain't no accounting to do. When you get paid, that's when you pay me what you owe me. You promised! How can you do this to me just when I need it the most, I earned it!"

She wouldn't budge and I hung up the phone feeling like a friend had just died. It was emotionally devastating. I could survive on the money I was getting from other contracts that were still yielding revenue, but I felt betrayed by this person with whom I had had more conversations than any other single person of all our clients. I looked at Michelle as a very close friend. It was the last time we would speak, although I would end up with the last word. Michelle showed more of her true colors when, soon after, she divorced Harry Robinson and cut him off from Vince both as a step father and financially. It is sad that Vince would make so many millions of dollars and not do much of anything for Harry who had been there for him and Michelle. Including what Harry said was a serious income tax fraud case Michelle faced in the mid 1990s'. He said Michelle had cheated on her taxes and he had to borrow money from his mother to help her settle the case. Harry said he lost his house helping Michelle through that tough time. Harry Robinson is a good man and deserved a better fate from Vince and Michelle.

The next few months were relatively quiet as the initial frenzy of news coverage died down and I occupied myself with the business of preparing to fight the SEC and the Justice Department. My career as a sports agent was over, but I thought I'd come out all right once all the facts became known and I had a chance to tell my story to a judge and jury.

But before I could, *Sports Illustrated* ran a long feature article entitled "Web of Deceit," with a grotesque illustration of my grinning face on the body of a spider in a web with pictures of some of my former clients, including Vince, Fred Taylor, and Jevon Kearse. The article was full of inaccuracies, and one-sided, (they never contacted me for my side of the story) and painful to read. I stole no money from players, as a Federal Court would later rule, but that's what the government alleged and that's the way the magazine presented it.

Coupled with the Dean Parker business, the dispute with the NFL players association, and all of the rest, it was a total demonization that hurt all the more because of all of the good I had done in my life and career. I was no saint. I had cut corners and I had rationalized some of my behavior, but I had never intentionally hurt anyone and some of my players thought I had which really broke my heart. I was forbidden by the courts to speak to my clients to explain what really happened, therefore, they only got the government's side of the story and silence from me.

Fred Taylor's cash for titles investment of $3,000,000 was frozen, was quoted as saying he was very upset. "A *go-grab-a-gun* type of upset."

In early May the lawsuits started to arrive. Players like Fred Taylor sued me to recover the money they'd lost in Cash 4 Titles. I would be cleared by the Federal Civil Court of any and all fraud involving Cash 4 Titles and my player clients and those lawsuits would go away.

" To Fred Taylor and my other clients that had funds frozen in Cash for Titles. I am sorry for recommending this investment. I invested also in it. I received commissions from it. I never knew or thought is was a fraudulent investment and the Federal Court ultimately cleared me and my companies. Unfortunately I had already been sent to prison and lost my companies.

Michelle was quoted as saying, "Tank is a very nice person. But somewhere along the line he lost sight of the right way to do things and started looking only at the bottom line. Vince was a victim, and I can't forgive Tank for that."

A former business associate said, "I think Tank's in denial as to what he's really facing. He thinks that somehow he's going to work through this and get back to where he was."

The article reported that the grand jury in Detroit was considering whether to indict me for laundering drug money. And there was a picture of Dean Parker, along with the allegation that I had helped him flee the country. I figured Dean was long gone, hiding out in Brazil or some other exotic locale and that I would never see him again. That's what I hoped.

But one day shortly after the article appeared Linda phoned me on a Friday evening from Detroit where she was visiting relatives and said she had a message for me, conveyed through a relative. "You're gonna have a visitor tomorrow from someone you're not going to be happy to see." She sounded shaky. My heart sank.

"You mean Dean?"

"Yeah."

"Here? In Columbia? What the hell?" My stomach fluttered.

"He's gonna page you at 11 o'clock Saturday morning. He wants his money.

Tomorrow"! How'm I gonna get my hands on that kind of money on a Saturday morning? I can't do that. He's got to give me more time Linda!

She sighed. "I don't know how to tell you this, Tank, but Dean said he needed the money tomorrow and he sounded desperate." My wife and children! Should I send them out of town? Was Dean watching me right now? Did he really expect me to suddenly produce hundreds of thousands against the money he had in Cash 4 Titles? I told Linda to send a message back that I needed until noon. Then I drove to the office and got a few thousand dollars from the petty cash safe and some emergency money I kept at home.

All I managed to scrape up was $9,000 by the time my pager went off at noon the next day. I drove to a pay phone and dialed the number. Dean answered.

"You got my money, Tank?"

"Dean, it's the weekend. I did the best I could but all I got was $9,000 and that ain't goin' to take you very far. You've got kids to think about. You've got your wife and kids. Don't you think it'd be better to turn yourself in?"

He was having none of it, and I was terrified I was being followed. So I arranged to leave the money in an envelope in a public place where he could pick it up later. I lived in fear the next several days, jumpy and wondering if he would suddenly show up one day. But I never saw him again.

I kept my nose clean, met all my court obligations to report in to the Probation Department and my lawyer told the U.S.

Attorneys office in Detroit that if they decided to indict me, I would agree to turn myself in. I expected I would have to face the music up there one way or another.

But on July 5, 2000, as I drove down Two Notch Road in Columbia on my way to the office, I was pulled over, handcuffed and arrested on a warrant out of Detroit for obstruction of justice and money laundering. I couldn't figure out why until later when my lawyer explained to me that the Michigan office wanted to grab me and stick me in jail in Detroit before the Florida case went to trial. In a turf battle between two U.S. Attorneys, Detroit had won.

It would be seven and a half years before I would regain my freedom.

The Orlando Sentinel archive

TEACHER, 36, ACCUSED OF CHEATING ON TAX RETURNS

Published: Wednesday, December 19, 1990
Section: LOCAL & STATE
Page: D3

A Daytona Beach school teacher was charged Tuesday with 12 counts of submitting false information to Internal Revenue Service agents during a tax audit.

Michelle Carter Robinson, 36, of Ormond Beach, was charged in a complaint filed by the U.S. Attorney's Office in Orlando. She was charged with the misdemeanor charges after IRS investigators determined that she altered and inflated the dollar amount on checks given to local charities or businesses. She is accused of inflating the charges by nearly $3,000 in 1986 and 1987.

Robinson, a teacher at Campbell Middle School, faces 12 years in prison and $1.2 million in fines. She will be summoned to appear before a U.S. Magistrate in Orlando over the next few weeks.

Article that appeared in The Orlando Sentinel, *December 19, 1990.*

Used with permission of the *Orlando Sentinel*, copyright 1990.

Epilogue
ANSWERED PRAYERS

O NE OF THE ODDEST experiences of my life has to be the day I was in an activity room in Milan Federal Prison near Detroit when one of the other inmates shouted, "Hey, that's him! It's Tank!"

I looked up and several of the men were staring at me and pointing at the television set mounted on the wall. I hadn't been paying attention to the show. It was "America's Most Wanted" and sure enough, there I was on the screen, in the prison visiting room being interviewed about Dean Parker.

It was Saturday night, June 16, 2001, just two days after I'd been to court to be sentenced to 82 months after entering a brokered guilty plea. Under threat by the judge, Lawrence P. Zatkoff, of an even harsher sentence had I gone to trial and lost, I pleaded guilty with a legal gun to my head to helping John Bryant and Dean Parker launder dirty cash.

It would have been absurd if my life hadn't been on the line. I had to say I was laundering dirty cash even though the government acknowledged that I had no idea it was dirty.

By the time I was sentenced, I'd already been in prison in Michigan almost a year, since my arrest on Two Notch Rd. in Columbia the summer before. Linda Wilson was in jail in Michigan, too. We had both waived extradition from South Carolina because we wanted to get on with whatever lay ahead. There was nothing left behind us. The business and all of our records and equipment and assets had been seized and frozen.

The sentencing had been a horrible experience. My wife, who was dealing with health issues, was there along with other family and friends. I felt such guilt for all of them having to suffer through it with me. Judge Zatkoff was sarcastic and dismissive. My lawyer noted that I had channeled my energies into being a model prisoner, to tutoring and mentoring other inmates. Judge Zatkoff mocked a character testimonial submitted by a fellow inmate by saying "It takes [a liar] to know one."

My attorney Jim Thomas did a great job of making a case for leniency but the judge insisted on giving me more time than the 78 months the U.S. Attorney's office had agreed would be the recommended upper limit. The U.S Attorney recommended the lower guideline which was 57 months. Instead Judge Zatkoff gave me 82 months, not because of my role in Michigan but rather because he had been told by the Securities and Exchange Commission that I had stolen huge sums of money from my athlete clients. It just didn't make sense. Two of the drug dealers on my case had already been sentenced and they got 36 months and 48 months respectively. I didn't know the first thing about drugs and I got double what the drug dealers got.

I was learning the hard way that lying to the DEA and the grand jury had been fatal mistakes. In fact, one of the investigators involved in my case had said to me at one point that if I had told the truth about Parker and Bryant from the start, I probably wouldn't have served a day in jail. Instead I might have been treated as a cooperative witness in a major drug case. I had cooked my own goose.

John Bryant had already pleaded guilty in the cocaine conspiracy with Parker and was off somewhere else doing his time. Linda who had also followed Jim Franklin's advice to lie to the government and the grand jury, had been sentenced to prison as well, and would end up serving five years she didn't deserve.

Jim Franklin, who I had trusted and whose advice I had followed without knowing he was betraying me and protecting himself, was also in prison after pleading guilty to a federal money-laundering charge and drawing a 32-month sentence on that charge. Jim Franklin would serve the least amount of time in our case mainly because he cut a deal to become a witness for the prosecution and was willing to say whatever the government needed him to say to get out of prison. He would serve about three years total and he was eventually disbarred.

I blame myself for my own misbehavior and poor judgment, but I hold Jim Franklin responsible for his pivotal role in destroying so many lives and so much wealth with such impunity. He abused his position as a lawyer by giving bad and tainted advice, vouched for the Cash 4 Titles people which led me to recommend the investment, all the while he was getting secret payments from Jimmy Roof and Bob Ellenburg and helping them run their Ponzi scheme.

The one person remaining to be brought to justice was Dean Parker, which is why America's Most Wanted producer Tom Morris wanted to interview me. Dean was still on the run and the government badly wanted to get him behind bars. I didn't have a lot to offer since I'd only met him a couple of times. But America's Most Wanted had told the government they would only run another show featuring Parker if I would interview for the show.

Three months later, somebody who'd seen the show recognized Kim Parker in California and within a week Dean Parker was dead after a crazy series of events. It began with the arrest of his wife Kim, Dean showing up in St. Louis and getting wounded in a shoot-out at a night club, ending up in a hospital under an assumed name, escaping in his hospital gown, and ending up across the Mississippi in East St. Louis with a .45-caliber pistol and a female hostage reading to him from the Bible as he blew his brains out. Ultimately my sentence in Michigan was reduced to 48 months for my cooperation with America's Most Wanted.

The Michigan case was bad enough but worse was the fact that the U.S. Attorney's office in Gainesville, Florida was determined to convict me of defrauding my players because of their losses in the Cash 4 Titles investment. I was accused of "stealing" some $14 million, which was a complete falsehood. I was guilty of bad judgment by not investigating Cash 4 Titles more carefully, but Jim Franklin and Randy Thurman had both given their blessing to the deals, so I thought I had done adequate due diligence. Instead, I had unintentionally steered my players and myself into a ponzi scheme.

My criminal Judge in the Gainesville case was Stephen P. Mickle, the first black law graduate of the University of Florida. He came to trial with a Florida Gators watch on that was visible to the jury. My case involved Florida Gators football stars and on top of that my attorney Jon Uman, told me Judge Mickle had recently been arrested for driving while intoxicated. Jon said that somehow it had gotten swept under the rug and disappeared. When you put all of these pieces together it didn't take a rocket scientist to figure out that I was in serious trouble.

This was a case I felt I had to fight, so I was transferred from Michigan to Alachua County Jail in Gainesville so I could attend my trial and help my lawyers. The government came at me from every possible angle, even subpoenaeing Jevon Kearse and Johnny Rutledge to testify that they had gotten money from me before they were eligible for the NFL Draft. They brought in women I had known to give unflattering personal testimony.

They also brought in my nemesis Richard Berthlesen the general counsel of the NFLPA. Berthlesen would commit perjury while under oath by saying that the NFLPA never granted Brantley Evans immunity regarding statements he gave against me. Berthlesen knew this was an outright lie. The NFLPA granted Brantley Evans immunity on March 31, 1999 regarding anything associated with me and my company. The same person who tried to steal my clients and had secretly started another sports management company while working for me was given a license to lie about anything to bring me down.

At the end of the day Brantley Evans jealousy and greed is greatly responsible for bringing down me and PMI and in the end pushed Brantley out of the agent business. If only I had listened to Bill Bradshaw I would have avoided Brantley and his willingness to lie about things I had done and turn his back on the one person who had helped him achieve so much at such a young age. He had cut off the hand that fed him.

I had a Securities and Exchange Commission civil suit outstanding that charged that I was acting as an unregistered investment adviser, and the U.S. Attorney in Florida introduced those allegations along with the Black Americans of Achievement stock deal as further evidence of the "massive" fraud I supposedly conducted. The Securities and Exchange Commission failed to mention a very important fact to the court,I had returned all of the monies to the players who invested in Black Americans of Achievement as promised. Once the Court realized that fact they knew there was no fraud concerning that investment.

Linda was on trial with me in that case also, and we thought we had a great chance of winning because there was no evidence that I took money or defrauded anyone. Jim Franklin testified against me as a government witness and even he admitted in court that I never knew anything about Cash 4 Titles being a fraud.

The case went on for two weeks and when the jury came back with their verdict, five were crying—four women and one man.

I whispered to my attorney, "Why are they crying? What's going on?"

"You're guilty," he said.

"How do you know?"

"Well, they're sending you to federal prison, and they don't agree with it."

Sure enough, they convicted me of obstruction of justice, mail fraud, wire fraud, and defrauding the government. They didn't find me guilty of taking money from players but that didn't stop the media from reporting it that way: "Sports agent Tank Black convicted of defrauding NFL players."

It was a devastating result either way that got worse when it came time for sentencing. I expected a stiff sentence but my attorneys told me that since I already had a stiff sentence from Detroit, it was customary for sentences in related cases to be served concurrent, meaning it would not be added to the time I was already serving.

Instead, the judge gave me the maximum five years with a consecutive sentence, this meant that my Florida sentence would not start until I was finished serving my Michigan sentence. They don't give most murderers a consecutive sentence. I couldn't seem to catch a single break.

Meanwhile, I was owed millions by players whose contracts I had negotiated but refused to pay me, knowing I was in prison and there was little I could do about collecting. Chief among them was Vince Carter or, more accurately, his mother. By my reckoning, I was owed nearly $10 million in commissions.

It's just about impossible for a prison inmate to get a civil suit going and the statute of limitations was running out when a childhood friend came to the rescue.

Robert Bragdon was a football and track star when I was in high school in Greeneville. He'd gone on to law school and opened a practice in Murfreesboro, Tennessee. He'd read about my troubles and wrote to me, offering solace and support.

By this time I had been transferred to a federal prison in North Carolina, so one day Robert and his partner Rob Gritton drove over from Tennessee to visit me. I explained my predicament and they agreed to help with my cases, especially against Vince. There were others, but Vince was the big one and when the case got filed, Robert reported back to me with amazement, "You wouldn't believe these guys working for Vince. They got some good ol' boy lawyers from Columbia and they wanted to know, 'How come y'all are filin' this frivilous lawsuit?'"

He said in every case where a player owed me money, the answer was, "We're not paying because he's in jail." Robert called it the good-versus-evil defense. He managed to collect owed commissions from several of the players who fired me right after my last, record-breaking NFL Draft, including Troy Edwards, Al Wilson, Kevin Faulk, and Antuan Edwards.

Among the ways I occupied myself in prison was in the prison law library studying the securities laws. The SEC civil case against me, filed in Tampa, had been ruled to be an instance of collateral estoppel, meaning that because I had been found guilty of virtually the same fraud in Gainesville based on the SEC's allegations, there was no need to decide the civil charges. I was automatically guilty without a trial, as long as there was some supporting evidence of fraud on my part from my trial transcripts.

I learned enough to file my own petitions and briefs with the court and after what seemed like an eternity and a lot of jockeying back and forth, four years later in prison, I had my first break. I won!

Judge Richard Lazzara ruled that there was never any evidence to support the allegations of fraud, stealing or misappropriation of funds regarding my athlete clients. Judge Lazzara studied the trial transcripts and realized that there was not any evidence at my fraud trial to support my fraud conviction.

The Wall Street Journal wrote a devastating story regarding the allegations of fraud against me and my companies on February 28, 2000. Me and my companies were exonerated of all of the terrible allegations in that article that was reproduced all over the United States, Canada, Mexico and Europe.

Not only was I personally exonerated of the fraud charges but all charges against my companies PMI, PMC and Silverline Development were dismissed. It was a major but silent victory that was never reported in the press.

What I had done was recommend an investment that I thought was a good, legitimate investment and it turned out that the owners were stealing the money and using it for their own personal gain. When I was charged with conspiring with these people it was such a joke. I had invested millions. The unfortunate fact is that the government knew I had nothing to do with the Cash for Titles fraud and made the decision to indict me anyway.

What very few people ever knew is that the government had FBI transcripts of taped conversations between Dick Homa and Mike Gause, the cash for titles crooks. I had called and voiced my overwhelming displeasure at how long it was taking them to return the players their monies invested with them.

These FBI transcripts of the taped conversations between them prove without a doubt that I was not a part of the cash for titles fraud. In these conversations Gause tells Homa "I need to take at least $10 million, and give it back to Tank Black, I think that is a priority. Tank's got this thing all stirred up, he's accused us of having a ponzi scheme."

I had already gotten the funds back for the majority of players invested which included Reidel Anthony, Jacquez Green, Johnny Mcwilliams, Deon Figures, Duce Staley, Jamain Stephens, Eric Bieniemy, Harold Green and Rae Carruth. These funds returned totaled $3,276,000 and all of these players not only got their investments back in full but all of these players made substantial interest income on their investment.

Jacquez Green committed unrefutable fraud when he got his investment returned to him and then filed paperwork with the government receivership claiming he had not gotten his investment returned. This was a $480,000 fraud that caused other players to get less back from the government. I told FBI agent Jeff Thornburg about this fraud and he just laughed about it.

The really sad part of this situation is that Gause was going to send the $10 million on that Monday after the weekend and on that Friday evening the Securities and Exchange Commission froze all of cash for titles assets and my chance to get the players all of their investments back was forever lost. This $10 million would have returned all of the remaining players funds, Fred Taylor, Terry Allen, Robert Brooks, Germane Crowell, Ike Hilliard, Vince Carter, Kenny Bynum, Gerald Dixon and Roosevelt Blackmon.

They had chosen me to be the person to pay the piper for the players losses whether it was true or not.

I wanted to be able to speak with Fred Taylor, Robert Brooks, Terry Allen, Ike Hilliard and others to explain what really happened. Unfortunately the Judge forbid me from speaking to my player clients. "Why would they do that? I have business with these clients".

For those players who had funds frozen in cash for titles and had to wait to get their funds from Stenger and Stenger and still did not receive 100% of the money back, I am so sorry I recommended this investment.

I pray that each of you will check the Federal Court ruling to confirm that I was never involved in this scheme or any scheme to harm my player clients. I gave hundreds of thousands of dollars to my player clients when the cash for titles funds became frozen. I tried to sell PMI to get the money to protect my player clients. I pray that all of you can forgive me for unintentionally steering you in the wrong direction. This mistake has cost me dearly.

I lost my freedom. I lost legitimate multimillion dollar businesses. I was detached from my children and my family. I have a son, Matthew Donovan Hampton, who was four years old when I was arrested. I have only seen him one time since the day I was arrested over nine years ago. I pray that reading this book will explain my absence in his life and allow him to forgive me for not being there for him. I have always loved Matthew and a day never passes without me praying for him.

The main public event took place in the fall of 2004 when my case against Vince came to trial in Columbia.

It was the first time we'd seen each other—Vince, Michelle, and myself. Vince gave me a friendly glance and grin, but Michelle avoided looking my way. It was a packed courtroom, full of reporters.

Robert Bragdon, Dawes Cooke and Robert Gritton my attorneys were worried about the judge because of some rulings she'd made that seemed to suggest she had a bias against our case. Furthermore, Harry Robinson, Michelle's ex-husband, was going to testify for our side until Michelle's lawyers warned him not to and he got cold feet. Finally, the judge, Margaret Seymour, a black female was overly friendly with Michelle when she took the stand.

But we were prepared and we caught Michelle in some bold, on-the-record whoppers that completely undermined her claim that I wasn't owed the money. The jury awarded me the money I was due, about $5 million plus interest, a total victory. Vince had already left town but his attorneys and Michelle had such a look of shock on their faces that Robert Bragdon whispered in my ear, "Priceless."

No one gave me a chance at winning my case against Vince but the truth was on my side and my attorneys were clearly superior in the courtroom.

It was an emotional moment for me, especially when I got back to my cell. I got on my knees and said a prayer. God had blessed me in so many ways. I had been vindicated of ever taking anything from any players. News of my win against Vince was widely covered so I knew all those who had an interest would see it and have second thoughts about their judgments of me. It might not change their minds, but it would be a first step on my path to redeeming myself and restoring my reputation. This book is the second.

FILED

04 APR -9 AM 8: 02

_____ CT COURT
_____ CT OF FLORIDA
TAMPA, FLORIDA

UNITED STATES DISTRICT COURT
MIDDLE DISTRICT OF FLORIDA
TAMPA DIVISION

SECURITIES AND EXCHANGE
COMMISSION,

       Plaintiff,

v.   CASE NO: 8:00-cv-383-T-26TGW

WILLIAM H. BLACK,

       Defendant.

_____/

O R D E R

This cause comes before the Court on Defendant William H. Black's Pro Se

Motion to Reconsider and Set Aside Judgment for Disgorgement Amount with exhibits

(dkt. 116) and supporting declaration (dkt. 117) and Plaintiff SEC's response in

opposition thereto (dkt. 120).

On December 15, 2003, the Court granted final summary judgment in favor of

Plaintiff SEC and directed entry of final judgment against Defendant Black on all counts

of the Complaint and in the amount of $2,649,990.60, for disgorgement and prejudgment

interest. (dkts. 113 & 114) The Court did so on grounds of collateral estoppel because

the operative facts and fraud charged by the United States in Black's criminal case, where

Black's conviction was affirmed on appeal, and by the SEC in the instant case were

Federal Court Order clearing me of fraud regarding player clients.
It took four years to get this ruling. (Page 1 of 3.)

virtually identical. (dkt. 113) The cases were tied to two schemes by Black to defraud his clients, professional athletes, for his own personal gain. (dkt. 113)

Plaintiff now asks the Court to reconsider and set aside its judgment for disgorgement amount, arguing that he has refunded all of the players' funds invested in BAOA, that he did not gain anything and actually lost money due to his involvement in the BAOA investment, and he suggests that the maximum possible disgorgement amount related to BAOA should have been limited to $240,000.00. (dkt. 116) The SEC, on the other hand, requests that the Court maintain its prior findings regarding Black's illegal gains and order $2,616,464,08 as disgorgement, consisting of: (1) $1,022.400.00 in illegal gains from the BAOA scheme and prejudgment interest thereon in the amount of $740,012.92; and (2) $624,719 in illegal gains from the Cash 4 Titles scheme and prejudgment interest thereon in the amount of $229,332.16. (dkt. 120) Alternatively, the SEC suggests that should the Court credit Black for BAOA funds returned to his clients, the Court should order disgorgement in the amount of: (1) $240,000.00 in foregone interest from BAOA; and (2) $624,719.00 in illegal gains from Cash 4 Titles, plus prejudgment interest thereon in the amount of $229,332.16. (dkt. 120)

The initial burden of proof that disgorgement amounts are a reasonable approximation of illegal gains lies with the SEC and the burden must be proven by a preponderance of the evidence. See SEC v. Chemical Trust, 2000 WL 33231600, at *12 (S.D. Fla. 2000). This Court's further review of the SEC's evidence of Black's illegal

-2-

Federal Court Order. (Page 2 of 3.)

gains, as well as the instant motion and response, reveals that the SEC has not met its burden of proof in all instances. Black makes a compelling argument that he should indeed be credited for BAOA funds returned to his clients. He also makes a compelling argument that the Cash 4 Titles transactions were not the substance of illegal gains. (dkt.116, p. 4) The SEC fails to sufficiently counter Black's arguments. As such, the Court finds that the total disgorgement amount will be limited to the amount of foregone interest that has been proposed by both parties, or in other words, $ 240,000.00.

ACCORDINGLY, it is ORDERED AND ADJUDGED:

1. Defendant William H. Black's Pro Se Motion to Reconsider and Set Aside Judgment for Disgorgement Amount (dkt. 116) is granted.

2. The Clerk shall amend the final judgment entered in this case in favor of Plaintiff SEC and against Defendant Black to reflect a total judgment amount of $240,000.00.

3. Defendant Black's request for an evidentiary hearing is denied as moot.

DONE AND ORDERED at Tampa, Florida, on April 9, 2004.

RICHARD A. LAZZARA
UNITED STATES DISTRICT JUDGE

COPIES FURNISHED TO:
Counsel/Parties of Record

-3-

Federal Court Order. (Page 3 of 3.)

UNITED STATES DISTRICT COURT
FOR THE MIDDLE DISTRICT OF FLORIDA
TAMPA DIVISION

SECURITIES AND EXCHANGE   : No. 8:00-CV-383-T-26B
COMMISSION.   :
                                            :
              Plaintiff.   :
                                            :
-v.-   :
                                            :
WILLIAM H. BLACK. et al.,   :
                                            :
              Defendants,   :
                                            :
_____   :

[PROPOSED] ORDER

UPON DUE CONSIDERATION, it is ORDERED AND ADJUDGED that

Plaintiff SEC's Motion for Voluntary Dismissal of Corporate Defendants (Dkt. _169_) is

granted.

Pursuant to Fed.R.Civ.P 41(a)(2). the SEC's action against the corporate

defendants Professional Management, Inc., Professional Management Consulting.

Inc., and Silverline Development Corporation. LLC is dismissed.

DONE AND ORDERED at Tampa, Florida, on _November 26_. 2005.

_____
RICHARD A. LAZZARA
UNITED STATES DISTRICT JUDGE

Federal Court Order clearing my companies, PMI, PMC, and Silverline Development, of any wrong doing. Getting this order took five years.

GAUSE:	So we're, we're making a lot of progress.
CW-1:	Okay, good enough.
GAUSE:	Yeah, but it'll help if you send that, whatever it is, 3.2.
CW-1:	All right, I'll send it. That'll keep us even-Steven, because the, that, the, the, and yeah, I'll send the 3.2 up. Uh, I'll try to wire that out today or tomorrow.
GAUSE:	Okay, I felt like, I told Bob, I said, "All I'm doing is just robbing Peter to pay Paul. I'm just, you know, swapping funds (U/I) every single few weeks."
CW-1:	All right, well.
GAUSE:	One thing we have to do, and now I've spoken to Joe about it, it's just people treating this thing like a bank. And Tank's the same way. We've just gotta get a little more restrictive clauses in here about this return of principal to people just pulling money out at a whim.
CW-1:	Oh yeah, well, that.
GAUSE:	It's absolutely killing us.

It is my understanding that when GAUSE referred to "robbing Peter to pay Paul," he meant that he was using funds raised from new investors in the Cash 4 Titles Securities to pay principal and interest due to existing investors. I also understand that when GAUSE referred to "getting more restrictive clause's in here about this return of principal," he meant that the terms of the Cash 4 Titles Securities should be modified to limit investors' rights to seek redemption of securities.

46. GAUSE also discussed with CW-1 his use of new investors funds:

The FBI taped conversations proving I was never a part of any Ponzi scheme regarding Cash 4 Titles. Even knowing this, they charged me anyway. (Page 1 of 5).

GAUSE: Well, it's, it's been crazy
            because, that's what I was saying
            too. Like, you know, the first of
            the month. I mean, you're supposed
            to pay me. But I, it never has
            happened, so, I've had to, you
            know, just pay interest out of the
            money I raise.

CW-1:   Right (U/I).

GAUSE: So that's been absolutely crazy,
            huh.

It is my understanding that when GAUSE stated that he had "pa[id]
interest out of the money I raise," he meant that he had used
funds received from new investors in the scheme to pay interest
due to existing investors.

C.   The September 7, 1999 Telephone Call

        47. On September 7, 1999, CW-1 spoke by telephone with
GAUSE. The call was consensually recorded and monitored by the
FBI. I have listened to the tape recording and reviewed a draft
transcript of it.

        48. During the call, GAUSE discussed with CW-1 a
request that Robert Ellenburg had made for the return of
principal that Ellenburg had raised from investors. GAUSE
explained that the requested principal was not available to be
returned, stating, "Okay, you know we've got, we've got about $3
million in the account right now. So, I mean, I can cover the
1.1, but Bob asked me for 9.1 and so I said, 'Bob, uh, we don't
have it!'"

        49. GAUSE and CW-1 also discussed limiting the amount
of principal that would be returned to investors by arranging for
the creation of a promissory note between two Cayman Islands
entities, which note would contain a clause restricting
withdrawals of principal:

GAUSE: Let Inter, well, let Inter-
            Professionals do a note for this
            amount to Interworld Holdings.

CW-1:   Okay.

GAUSE: Abel can sign it. And then, in
            that note, you, we'll have in
            there, no more than 10%, you know,
            may be redeemed at, you know, any
            one month, or whatever.

17

The FBI taped conversations. (Page 2 of 5).

CW-1:	Alright, well, just have him do the note then.
GAUSE:	Yeah. I'll have Inter-professionals do the note. 302 million. 525. Something, 7.40 at seven and a half percent.
CW-1:	Okay.
GAUSE:	What will happen then, then Interworld will do a note to Jibo for what he has in it.
CW-1:	Okay.
GAUSE:	And then what Bob will say, "Well Tank, here's the problem. Jibo has a note with Interworld and it states in there that no more than 10% may be redeemed and ... in any one month.
CW-1:	Okay.
GAUSE:	And I can back it up. Say, well, Interworld, and the problem I have too is that, you know, that Interworld cannot get back more than 10%. So that'd, that'd help, hopefully, alleviate some of the problem in case, just in case, the University of Florida Police or FBI try to get crazy with us.

It is my understanding that GAUSE's references to "Inter-Professionals," "Interworld Holdings," and "Jibo" were to Cayman Islands entities used in connection with this scheme. I also understand that GAUSE's reference to the "University of Florida Police" and the FBI referred to an ongoing criminal investigation of one of GAUSE's associates.

D. The October 4, 1999 Telephone Call

50. On October 4, 1999, CW-1 spoke by telephone with GAUSE. The call was consensually recorded and monitored by the FBI, and I have listened to the tape recording.

51. During the call, GAUSE discussed with CW-1 his plan to use the proceeds from the sale of new securities to return principal to existing investors:

18

The FBI taped conversations. (Page 3 of 5).

GAUSE: Okay, well I need to take, I need
to take at least $10 million, and
give it back to Tank Black.

CW-1:   Okay.

GAUSE: I think that's a priority. (U/I)
was gonna send 40. Take 20 of that
and to send it to, uh, pay off the
bonds.

CW-1:   Okay.

GAUSE: And, uh, if there's any extra, I've
got a, we have a summons here we
have to answer. I gotta get an
attorney in California. I'd rather
not to have to deal with all that
stuff. It's about seven million
dollars, and I'd like to buy them
out. 'Cause they're causing me a
lotta grief now.

CW-1:   Okay.

    52.   During the call, the following exchange also
occurred:

CW-1:   You know, [my attorney's] asking me
questions on this thing, because
the paper flow shows that we're,
you know, just raising money to pay
off old money, and it's not getting
to Cash 4 Titles or anywhere else.
It's just, uh, goin' that way, and
so, you know, I'm real concerned
where we're at, what's gonna to
happen. Uh, 'cause Tank's got this   ←
thing all stirred up.

GAUSE: Well, I know, he's accused Everest   ←
of having a Ponzi scheme down here.

It is my understanding that "Everest" is a Cayman Islands entity
which GAUSE employs to conduct many of the monetary transfers at
issue in this scheme.

    53.   During the call, GAUSE and CW-1 also discussed the
status of interest payments due to investors:

The FBI taped conversations. (Page 4 of 5).

CW-1:   No, I was really asking, "Are we t
to date on interest, or how far
behind are we on that?"

GAUSE: Oh, I'm a little bit behind on sor
people. But they're okay. I've
got 'em convinced to roll over. bu
I can't keep doin' it month after
month.

CW-1:   No, I know.

It is my understanding that when GAUSE referred t
people to "roll over," he meant that he had indu
forego interest payments due to them.

54.   Based on my training and experience in the
investigation of so-called Ponzi schemes, it is my understanding
that perpetrators of such schemes frequently attempt promote
their schemes by deferring interest payments due to investors,
thus reducing the amount of capital that must be raised from new
investors for the scheme to continue.

Conclusion

55.   Based upon my training and experience in the
investigation of securities fraud, I believe that the
truthfulness of the statements made to investors in the Cash 4
Titles Securities regarding the use of the proceeds from the
sales of such securities would be material to the reasonable
investor in the Cash 4 Titles Securities.

WHEREFORE, deponent prays that a warrant be issued for
the arrest of the above-named individual and that he be arrested
and imprisoned or bailed as the case may be.

(signature)

FRANK B. GODBOLD III
SPECIAL AGENT
FEDERAL BUREAU OF INVESTIGATION

Sworn to before me this
12th day of October, 1999.   OCT 1 5 1999

(signature)

UNITED STATES MAGISTRATE JUDGE
SOUTHERN DISTRICT OF NEW YORK

20

THEODORE H. KATZ
UNITED STATES MAGISTRATE JUDGE
SOUTHERN DISTRICT OF NEW YORK

The FBI taped conversations. (Page 5 of 5).

```
 1   Q.    And Brantley Evans wasn't disciplined with regard to
 2   his relationship to Mr. Black at all.  Was he?
 3   A.    He was not.
 4   Q.    And to the best of your knowledge, was he granted
 5   immunity for his assistance and testimony with regard to
 6   those proceedings or other proceedings?
 7   A.    Not by us.  I mean, there was immunity, I believe,
 8   with regard to other matters that we weren't prosecuting.
 9   Q.    And, I mean -- just so I understand you correctly,
10   it's a violation of the rules of the NFLPA for him to become
11   president of a company that he is selling stock to his
12   players?
13   A.    No.  Not at all.
14   Q.    Oh, it's not?
15   A.    No.  You are talking about Mr. Black?
16   Q.    Yes, sir.
17   A.    No.  It's a violation of the rules to sell stock at an
18   inflated value to the players, and then take the money and
19   give it to the company, instead, and put it in your own
20   account.
21   Q.    Okay.  The inflated value.  Upon whose information did
22   you base your conclusion that there was an inflated value?
23   A.    You can find out the trading price for a stock at any
24   point in its history -- or, at least its recent history --
25   by going on line through a vehicle that the SEC, I believe,
```

National Football League Players Association General Council Richard Berthlesen lied under oath at my trial saying that Brantley Evans was not given immunity by the NFL Players Association.

NFL Players Association
2021 L Street, NW
Suite 600
Washington, DC 20036
202.463.2200
Fax 202.857.0380

PRIVATE AND CONFIDENTIAL

VIA FACSIMILE AND FEDERAL EXPRESS

DEFENDANT'S
EXHIBIT

CASE
NO. _____

EXHIBIT
NO. 302

March 31, 1999

Clarence Davis, Esq.
Nelson, Mullins, Riley &
    Scarborough, L.L.P
Keenan Building
Third Floor
1330 Lady Street
Columbia, SC 29201

Dear Mr. Davis:

This is to confirm on behalf of the NFLPA Disciplinary Committee and the NFLPA, that your client, Brantley Evans, will be given immunity from any and all violations of the NFLPA Regulations Governing Contract Advisors (Regulations), in return for his providing affidavit testimony and live testimony, if necessary, which provides evidence that William "Tank" Black violated the Regulations while Mr. Evans was working with Mr. Black. This grant of immunity will apply to the acts and conducts of Mr. Evans only when he was in the employ of Mr. Black and/or when he was associated with Mr. Black in representation of NFL players.

Sincerely,

Arthur McAfee
Staff Counsel

cc: NFLPA Disciplinary Committee

AJM:bab

A copy of Brantley Evans immunity agreement with the National Football League Players Association dated March 31, 1999 confirming that the NFL Players Association's General Council Richard Berthlesen committed perjury under oath.

Final Thought

Winning my last rounds in court were victories tinged with remorse: I could have avoided all the pain and loss and guilt by paying attention to my better instincts and simply telling the truth from the start. If I hadn't torpedoed myself, I would have been earning a living and I could have made my players whole.

Instead, by the time I was released from custody on May 16, 2007, I had served 2,875 days or 95 months, just shy of eight years. When I was arrested, Bill Clinton was president. When I was released, Barack Obama was about to be. When I was arrested, the U.S. had just normalized trade relations with China. When I was released, the U.S. had become financially dependent on China. The world had moved on while I stood still.

It's difficult to describe the prison experience in a way that truly conveys the feeling of being left behind, and the way time seems to decelerate. Some have likened it to standing on a railroad platform watching the rest of the world pull out of the station like a just-missed train disappearing down the track.

The world may have changed in those long years but the responsibility I felt about the losses my players had sustained never went away, nor the frustration at being denied the opportunity to explain to them what really happened. I had always thought of myself as a generous, loyal person and friend. I was the agent who stood by his players through thick and thin. I'd sat in Sterling Sharpe's hospital room for days waiting for him to recover from his neck surgery only to learn he'd never play football again. I had paid some of Rae Carruth's legal bills out of my own pocket when he was charged with conspiracy to murder his pregnant girlfriend.

So the greatest hurt I've had to learn to deal with is knowing that all the good I felt I'd done in my life was buried under an avalanche of one-sided negative publicity which drove away most of my friends. My head understands that those people were afraid of guilt by association or perhaps had something to hide or simply lacked courage. My heart aches to know that people I cared about and who trusted me might have been persuaded to believe what they'd read. It's my hope that by telling my story faithfully some of them will understand what really happened and see me in a new light.

God has brought me through an unbelievable storm, and for that, I will always be thankful. It would be an understatement to say that my experiences have taught me a great lesson.